HOW TO CLEAN
PRACTICALLY ANYTHING

Monte Florman was Technical Director of Consumers Union from 1971 to 1982, when he took early retirement. Now a Consumers Union consultant, Florman began his long CU career in 1948, two years after graduating from New York University with a degree in electrical engineering. Initially a test engineer in CU's Appliance Division, Florman headed the division from 1955 to 1965. He then served as CU's Associate Technical Director until 1971, when he was named Technical Director.

HOW TO CLEAN PRACTICALLY ANYTHING

The Editors of Consumer Reports Books
with Monte Florman

CONSUMERS UNION • MOUNT VERNON • NEW YORK

Library of Congress Cataloging-in-Publication Data
How to clean practically anything.
Includes index.
1. House cleaning. 2. Cleaning. I. Florman, Monte.
II. Consumer Reports Books.
TX324.H69   1986   648'.5   86-70831
ISBN 0-89043-088-8

No copyright is claimed for the United States Department of
Agriculture's "Home and Garden Bulletin No. 62."

First printing, March 1987

Manufactured in the United States of America

How to Clean Practically Anything is a Consumer Reports Book published by Consumers Union, the nonprofit organization that publishes *Consumer Reports*, the monthly magazine of test reports, product Ratings, and buying guidance. Established in 1936, Consumers Union is chartered under the Not-For-Profit Corporation Law of the State of New York.

The purposes of Consumers Union, as stated in its charter, are to provide consumers with information and counsel on consumer goods and services, to give information on all matters relating to the expenditure of the family income, and to initiate and to cooperate with individual and group efforts seeking to create and maintain decent living standards.

Consumers Union derives its income solely from the sale of *Consumer Reports* and other publications. In addition, expenses of occasional public service efforts may be met, in part, by nonrestrictive, noncommercial contributions, grants, and fees. Consumers Union accepts no advertising or product samples and is not beholden in any way to any commercial interest. Its Ratings and reports are solely for the use of the readers of its publications. Neither the Ratings nor the reports nor any Consumers Union publication, including this book, may be used in advertising or for any commercial purpose. Consumers Union will take steps open to it to prevent such uses of its material, its name, or the name of *Consumer Reports*.

Our thanks to the following Technical Department staff members for their review of the contents of this book:

Thomas Deutsch
A. Larry Seligson
David H. Tallman

Contents

Laundry

Metals

Miscellaneous

Personal care

Stains and Spots

How this book can help you

American consumers spend close to $10 billion a year on powders, creams, pastes, liquids, foams, aerosols, paper products, and other forms of disposable cleaning supplies. That's a great deal more than the amount spent just a few years ago. Several factors may account for this large expenditure on cleaning supplies, but the main reason seems to be the success of manufacturers' unrestrained promotions of an awesome diversity of products. Manufacturers and advertisers have convinced the public that they've formulated and packaged an individual product to "custom clean" almost anything. The marketers' multimedia selling efforts have been loud, clear, and very persistent. Supermarket shelves are piled high with every sort of antidote for every conceivable kind of soil or odor. Appliance sellers have made their contribution to this cluttered picture with expensive hardware: the long lines of vacuum cleaners, washing machines, air and water filters, and other items that fill department store aisles. One survey found five thousand brands of thirty-nine different types of disposable cleaning products—and did not include in its count appliances, considered nondisposable, and such accessories as wastebaskets and plastic bags.

If one is to believe the cleaning product manufacturers' multi-million-dollar advertising campaigns, housecleaning should be easier now than ever before. It's just a matter of buying the right product for a particular job. But following such reasoning can lead to a sizable outlay of money and surrendering valuable storage space to a possibly unnecessary arsenal of dirt-fighting products. *How to Clean Practically Anything* brings perspective to the marketplace by separating the good from the not-so-good products. It gives tips and tricks for making one cleaner do the work of several, outlines the right and wrong ways to use cleaners, and often describes how to make a cheap home brew that works as well or better than one from the store. And if you're dealing with an emergency or difficult stain, you can check Tips on How to Clean Practically Anything (page 224) or the Fabric Stain Index (page 214) for advice and procedures.

How to Clean Practically Anything is also intended to provide a reference source that will save time, money, and effort, and help you get better value for your dollars when buying and using cleaning appliances as well as accessories.

For more than fifty years, objective articles in *Consumer Reports* magazine have provided consumers with information on the best products and how to shop for and use them. These articles are based on the results of tests conducted by Consumers Union's engineers and the calm, reasoned judgment of its staff. Revised and updated, they are the basis for *How to Clean Practically Anything*. Consumers Union test results and brand-name Ratings are included, along with advice on how to use these products to the best advantage. Some of the material, notably the section on stain removal from fabrics, has been adapted from the United States Department of Agriculture's "Home and Garden Bulletin No. 62."

How to use this book

In addition to the general advice and information about what various products and appliances will and won't do, you'll find detailed test findings in the form of Ratings charts. The Ratings charts give specific information by brand name and include the date that the test results originally appeared in *Consumer Reports* magazinc. You should also read the introductory section that precedes each set of Ratings. That will inform you of the basis on which the Ratings order was decided and how best to use the product. Check-rated models (✓) are high in quality and appreciably superior to other products tested. Best Buy Ratings are given to products that rate high and are also relatively low-priced.

When products are listed in order of estimated overall quality, CU's technical staff judged the brand (or product type) listed first to be best, the next listed second best, and so on, in descending order. Note that in some cases products are listed alphabetically or in order of increasing price.

Model changes and prices

The formulations of disposable cleaning products tend to change quite frequently, often an effort by manufacturers to match competition or to stimulate sales by offering something new. It is probably a good idea to watch for sales, and to take advantage of specials as they occur in your neighborhood. You may sacrifice something in quality on occasion in favor of better price, but your relationship with that brand may well end the next time you shop for the item when another brand—perhaps of better quality—may be the one on sale.

It isn't possible to be flexible when purchasing nondisposable products, such as vacuum cleaners or dishwashers. Once you have made the purchase, you must live with it for a considerable time. With these "hard goods," the particular brand and model you choose from the Ratings chart in this guide may be out of stock when you try to buy it, or it may have been superseded by a later version. However, the general information provided will still be invaluable to you in making a choice.

Usually, disposable products prices are what was paid (or an average of what was paid) in the store by Consumers Union shoppers. These products do not ordinarily carry manufacturers' "list" prices. Therefore, the price you encounter is almost certain to be different from the price in the Rating—often drastically different. So it is to your advantage to comparison shop and be aware of sales and price wars.

The list price of most nondisposable items is difficult to define. Not only are discounts from list frequently available, but the list price itself is sometimes a fiction designed to enable the retailer to appear to be offering a bargain. Nevertheless, list prices do remain a rough guide that can be useful in comparing prices of competing models.

We hope *How to Clean Practically Anything* will steer you toward safe, practical, and inexpensive home cleaning products. Keep it in a handy place, thumb through it, and use it as a reference to cope with stubborn cleaning problems and to narrow down choices toward purchasing products that work for you. While no book can actually *do* the cleaning chores, we hope this book will prove itself a labor-, time-, and money-saving "device" in its own right.

Dishes

Dishwasher detergents

No dishwasher detergent is likely to satisfy you completely if your dishwasher isn't superior at washing dishes, glassware, and flatware. Dishwasher detergents are not all that different from one another, at least not within a given geographical region. Every load you wash is apt to produce some glassware and flatware that is spotted by drying water. But that doesn't necessarily mean the dishes are dirty; they are probably cleaner than hand-washed dishes.

If you are in the habit of washing full loads, water spots (and sometimes a greasy film or bits of food) are more likely to turn up, especially on spoons, bowls, and glasses, than if you do small loads. That's true even if you wash in soft water and use a rinse agent, as the dishwasher makers recommend.

Some detergents contain an ingredient that is supposed to prevent water spots. But the extra ingredient doesn't guarantee spot-free glasses.

Delicate china

The chemicals in dishwasher detergents can sometimes damage the patterns and trim of fine china. In many cases, china manufacturers will warn you that their dishes won't withstand the rigors of automatic dishwashing. The makers of most dishwashers also caution you to keep delicate china, glassware, and silverware out of the machines. Unfortunately, labels on the detergents aren't always so circumspect. Some carry the seal of the American Fine China Guild and claim to be "thoroughly tested for use on fine china patterns and fine glassware."

The most sensitive china has an "overglaze" pattern. Overglaze china has been glazed once before decoration, then put through the kiln a second time—at a lower temperature—after decoration. Examined closely, the overglaze decoration will appear less glossy than the rest of the dish, and the pattern will often be slightly raised above the undecorated surface. (Gold is always an over-glaze decoration.) If your everyday dishes are underglaze—deco-rated, then glazed once—they can safely be washed in an automatic dishwasher.

Any detergent will have a tendency to dull the overglaze gloss of colors. As a rule, detergents will do less damage to gold trim.

No dishwasher detergent should be considered completely safe for overglaze china, especially if you wash it very often. If you have delicate, decorated china that you value and use frequently, wash it by hand.

Safety

Dishwasher detergents have to be strong in order to get dishes clean. But that strength means they can irritate the eyes or be harmful if swallowed. Packages generally include appropriate warnings about those hazards. The products can also irritate the skin. If you should get a bit of powder on your skin, rinse it off thoroughly—especially if your skin is sensitive.

Some detergents may be scented. The reason isn't clear, be-cause the perfume vanishes during the dishwashing. A lemon scent could be a dangerous attraction to children.

Recommendations

Start out by trying a low-priced detergent. If you're not satisfied with the results, your problem could be hard water or a dishwasher that's not very effective. You could try another deter-gent, or try using more of the same detergent, but spotless dishes may be a goal beyond your reach with automatic washing.

There's no real cost advantage to buying a "family-size" package. In fact, you might do better to stick to the smaller boxes. Unless dishwasher detergent is stored in a cool, dry place *not* under the kitchen sink, it can lose both strength and dissolvability before it's used up. As a result, incompletely dissolved detergent could cake in the dispenser or leave a film of fine white powder on the dishes.

Dishwashing liquids

The selling price of a dishwashing liquid doesn't always reflect its cleaning power. In fact, a low-priced but inefficient detergent may cost more to use than an expensive efficient brand: You often have to use more of a cheap detergent and less of a high-priced one to do the same load of dishes. In effect, some cheap products are watered down and can end up costing more in actual use.

Not all cheaper detergents are inefficient, however. And you can't tell a "watered-down" product from a fuller-strength one just by looking at it. If you finish a bottle of one brand in half the time you use up another brand in the same size bottle, you might suspect that the first product is less efficient than the second. But you might not realize how much that lower efficiency will cost you.

Detergents compared

In the kitchen sink, a detergent works by loosening greasy soil and keeping the soil suspended in water so it can't be redeposited on the dishes. Eventually, the detergent traps all the soil it can hold. The suds disappear, and the grease-removing action ceases.

Consumers Union re-created what happens in the kitchen. The testers used the detergents in a concentration equivalent to the capful-per-dishpan often recommended on labels. They used hard water because that's what most people have. If you have soft water, you may need less detergent to get the same amount of cleaning power.

They measured each detergent into a container of water and whipped up plenty of suds. Then they added measured dollops of a lab-made kitchen grease—a mixture of fats and flours—to each container. After every addition, the suds were whipped again. When vigorous beating wouldn't bring back suds, they assumed the detergent had reached its grease-trapping limits. Some detergents lasted nearly five times as long as others. The high-priced national brands were very efficient cleaners. But so were a few store brands.

Efficiency

You don't have to buy an expensive national brand of dishwashing liquid. But what if you don't have a Safeway or a Kroger in your neighborhood?

Consumers Union assigned the best cleaners an efficiency factor of 1. The least-efficient cleaners gave up about five times sooner than the top-rated products; those were given an efficiency factor of 4.7. The groups in between were assigned efficiency factors of 1.4 and 2.7.

Given the efficiency factors and the average price paid for each detergent, you can figure real costs. (The Real-cost Calculator on page 7 shows how you can do the calculations when you shop.)

Here's how the efficiency factor works in practice: A detergent that's priced at $1.69 and that has an efficiency factor of 1 actually costs $1.69. But if its efficiency factor is 1.4, the real cost is $2.37.

Claims and scents

Dishwashing liquids aren't glamorous products. But advertising tries to lend them glamour. The products are often marketed as "skin softening," "gentle," or "mild."

It would be difficult, even for a dermatologist examining hands, to characterize a dishwashing product as being especially softening to hands—or for causing "dishpan" hands.

Naturally, individual users can be sensitive to an ingredient in a dishwashing liquid. If that happens, you should switch to another product. Other than that, the real trick to "skin softening" is using a hand lotion immediately after dishwashing or using rubber gloves to avoid contact with the dishwashing liquid.

The labels on some dishwashing liquids claim the products can be used for hand laundry. Even those liquids not labeled for hand laundering can probably be used safely on fine fabrics (see the section on Hand-laundry detergents page 90).

Dishwashing liquids have various scents—from lemon to herbal to floral. And they come in various colors. Some are clear liquids and some are lotions. However, no matter what a particular brand's variations in scent, color, or clarity, performance within the brand will usually be the same.

Recommendations

Real cost is the key to selecting a product. No matter which brand you choose, you can use it more efficiently if you measure doses. Most plastic bottles have a pull-up spout. Some have a snip-off cap. Squeezing out detergent tends to be wasteful: A single squeeze of the bottle can provide a lot more than the teaspoonful of detergent required for most dishwashing chores and tends to be wasteful. Only a few dishwashing liquids require unscrewing the cap and using it to measure out detergent. Squeezing the liquid into a teaspoon is a good way to get the most mileage out of the product.

Ratings of dishwashing liquids

Listed by groups in order of estimated cleaning efficiency in hard water. Within groups, listed in order of real cost. Unless otherwise indicated, all come in plastic bottle with pull-up or snip-off cap. And, except as noted, prices are as published in a July 1984 report for a 32-ounce bottle.

Product	Price	Real cost
■ *The following products had an efficiency factor of 1.*		
Kroger (Kroger), *A Best Buy*	$1.39	$1.39
Brocade (Safeway)	1.79	1.79
Ajax	2.09	2.09
Dawn	2.09	2.09
Ivory Liquid	2.09	2.09
Joy	2.09	2.09
Palmolive	2.09	2.09
Sun Light	2.09	2.09

(Continued)

Product	Price	Real cost	
■ *The following products had an efficiency factor of 1.4*			
Lady Lee (Lucky)	1.27	1.78	
Von's (Von's)	1.27	1.78	
Dermassage	1.69	2.37	
Dove	1.69	2.37	
White Magic (Safeway)	1.79	2.51	
Su-Purb (Safeway)	1.88	2.63	
■ *The following products had an efficiency factor of 2.7.*			
Octagon [1] [2]	.93	1.67	
Cost Cutter (Kroger) [3]	.64	1.73	
Lilac	.64	1.73	
Crystal White [1] [2]	.98	1.76	
Tryst (Lucky)	.68	1.84	
Ahoy (A&P) [4]	.79	2.13	
Econo Buy (Alpha Beta, Acme Stores)	.79	2.13	
Missy (Kroger) [3]	.84	2.27	
IGA (IGA)	.88	2.38	
Sweet Heart	.89	2.40	
Grand Union (Grand Union)	.98	2.65	
Gaylord	.99	2.67	
Gentle Fels	.99	2.67	
Janet Lee (Albertsons)	.99	2.67	
Pathmark (Pathmark)	1.06	2.86	
A&P (A&P)	1.12	3.02	
Trend	1.22	3.29	
Alpha Beta (Alpha Beta)	1.25	3.38	
Lux	1.69	4.56	
■ *The following products had an efficiency factor of 4.7.*			
No Frills (Pathmark)	.49	2.30	
Scotch Buy (Safeway) [3]	.94	4.42	

[1] *Purchased in 48-ounce size; price recalculated to 32-ounce equivalent.*
[2] *Has plain screw cap that must be opened for dispensing.*
[3] *Screw cap has snip-off tip for squeeze dispensing.*
[4] *Some samples have reclosable spouts; others, snip-off tips.*

Real-cost calculator

A dishwashing liquid's real cost is the average price paid by CU, multiplied by the efficiency factor determined by our tests of each product in hard water. Since prices vary, real cost will, too. But the following formula can be applied to any of the tested products using the price you find on the bottle:

$$\begin{array}{c}\text{Price} \\ \text{on bottle}\end{array} \times \begin{array}{c}\text{Efficiency} \\ \text{factor*}\end{array} = \begin{array}{c}\text{Real} \\ \text{cost}\end{array}$$

Efficiency factor: 1
Ajax
Brocade
Dawn
Ivory Liquid
Joy
Kroger
Palmolive
Sun Light

Efficiency factor: 1.4
Dermassage
Dove
Lady Lee
Su-Purb
Von's
White Magic

Efficiency factor: 2.7
A&P	Janet Lee
Ahoy	Lilac
Alpha Beta	Lux
Cost Cutter	Missy
Econo Buy	Pathmark
Gaylord	Sweet Heart
Gentle Fels	Trend
Grand Union	Tryst
IGA	

Efficiency factor: 4.7
No Frills
Scotch Buy

*As calcuated by CU, based on laboratory tests and average price for 32-ounce size. We found **Crystal White** and **Octagon** only in 48-ounce size. To compare their real cost with products in 32-ounce bottles, multiply their price by 1.8.

Machine dishwashers

If you wash dishes under a steadily flowing stream of hot water, you may be using even more hot water and therefore more energy, than if you wash dishes in a machine. An automatic dishwashing machine, however, will make life easier and establish a consistent level of dish cleanliness, even if it doesn't clean your dishes any better than if you wash them carefully by hand. You shouldn't count on a machine to cut down contagion in your household.

Features

Often, most dishwasher components are pretty much the same throughout several models of a manufacturer's line: the same basic cabinet, insulated to muffle noise and to prevent heat loss; the same wash arms, which protrude into the cabinet and spray water on the dishes; the same heating element, which usually heats both the wash water and the drying air; and the same pumps and filters, which circulate water and dispose of the water and soft food residue. Since those are the parts that most affect performance, a manufacturer's deluxe dishwasher may work no better than one of its more basic models. If you buy the deluxe machine, you may be buying more convenience than you need. The difference in price between a deluxe model and a basic one can be $100 or more.

Dishwasher cycles often have names such as "pot scrubber," "soak and scrub," and "china/crystal." The names may lead you to believe that a machine can wash all kinds of dishes, freeing you entirely from the chore. Unfortunately, that's not quite so.

A dishwasher cycle is basically a combination of washes and rinses. The typical "normal" cycle comprises two washes and two or three rinses. Then the heating element in the bottom of the cabinet dries the dishes.

To make a "heavy" or "pots and pans" cycle, a manufacturer might extend the wash periods, add a third wash period, make the water hotter, or combine those effects. A "light" cycle typically has one wash period instead of two. In a "china/crystal" cycle, water may shoot through the wash arms less forcefully.

The number of cycles may be increased by including a couple of optional phases and counting each cycle more than once or taking a part of the normal sequence of events and calling it another cycle. Dishwashers generally have a couple of nonwashing cycles, for instance. One is "rinse and hold," which rinses the dishes and then stops. A "plate warmer" cycle merely turns on the heating element.

A dishwasher can't always substitute for elbow grease. A machine run on its heavy cycle is likely to clean pots and pans little better than it does on its regular cycle. On either cycle, the machine will probably still leave the really burned-on food for you to scrub off afterward; heated drying may even bake the food on harder. Loading a dishwasher with lots of pots and pans and baking dishes also uses the space inefficiently.

A "china/crystal" cycle might seem useful if you give a lot of dinner parties, but you should think twice before subjecting good crystal or china to possible jostling within the dishwasher.

You should need only two or three cycles—normal, heavy, and perhaps light—to wash all the dishes you can reasonably expect a machine to wash.

Clean dishes

Consumers Union engineers determined the performance of dishwashers by loading the plates with beef stew, mashed potatoes, spaghetti, spinach, egg, butter, and other foods. They soiled bowls with chicken soup, cereal and milk, or stewed tomatoes. They poured milk, tomato juice, and orange juice into glasses and coffee into cups and saucers, and they dipped spoons, forks, and knives into the various foods. A good modern dishwasher should be able to clean unrinsed dishes without any problem (after you've scraped off bones and other hard debris, of course). Thereafter, the Consumers Union engineers let the dishes—enough for a family of ten—sit for an hour, scraped them lightly, and left them in the dishwashers overnight. The machines were turned on the next morning, using the setting the manufacturer had indicated as the everyday setting.

Each machine ran through this test several times; dishwashers designed to cope with 120°F water were tested with both 120°F and 140°F water. Some machines were run at cycles other than the normal one. After each cycle, every item in the dishwasher was examined for cleanliness. Many of the machines were capable of washing the load quite well.

Most of the dishwashers also did a good job of drying the dishes.

To use a dishwasher most efficiently, experiment with the cycles. If you habitually rinse the dishes or wash them right away, a light or low-energy wash may be all you need.

It's important that a dishwasher be easy to load and unload. Racks should move smoothly even when weighed down by dishes. Most dishwashers hold twelve full place settings of dishes but a few hold only eleven.

Most dish racks are designed for cups and glasses on top, plates on the bottom. On some machines, you have to watch where you put oversized items to avoid blocking the upper wash arm. A machine should be able to accommodate plates 10½ inches in diameter, and even large platters at the edges of the lower rack.

In some, though, larger dishes in certain positions may get in the way of the wash arm that spins just under the upper basket. If your plates are oversized or oddly shaped, take one along when you shop for the dishwasher to check clearances.

Dishwashers whose upper rack can be raised or lowered an inch or two are best at handling outsized plates or very tall glasses. Some upper racks can also be tilted, which helps water drain from the bottoms of mugs or glasses. Many machines have a rack that folds down or a special arrangement of supports, so you can double-stack cups. Other machines have a removable or adjustable set of props.

A nicety found on some machines is a covered basket or part of a basket for small, light objects—corn-on-the-cob holders or baby bottle nipples—that can be thrown around the cabinet by the strong spray of water.

Another nicety—a rinse conditioner dispenser—could be a necessity if you live where the water is hard and leaves spots as it dries. A rinse-conditioning agent, which helps water run off glasses, should improve the appearance of glasses washed in hard water.

Every now and then someone starts the dishwasher only to find that the wrong cycle has been selected. You can stop any dishwasher after it's started and restart it, but that's easiest on the less expensive, dial-controlled machines.

You can interrupt a cycle to load a dish you've overlooked or to rearrange the load if dishes start banging together simply by unlatching the door and waiting a moment before opening the machine. When you latch the door again, the cycle picks up where it left off.

If you do have to interrupt a cycle, be aware that the heating element under the lower rack can be very hot, especially if the dishwasher was in the heated drying phase. If you have to reach into that area during a cycle, or after the machine has shut down— to retrieve an item that's dropped to the tub bottom— be sure to let things cool off.

Other features

A feature that's common on dishwashers with electronic controls is a delayed-start timer. That feature probably shouldn't be used to run the dishwasher when you're away. It might come in handy if your household is chronically short of hot water, or it might save you a few dollars a year if your utility company charges a lower electricity rate during off-peak hours.

On some models you can boost the water temperature. On a few machines, this ability is similar to the automatic boost some machines offer so they can use 120°F water as a matter of course. The feature is sometimes called "assured wash temperature," and it ensures that the water used in at least one wash of a cycle is hot enough to clean the dishes. That might be useful if your hot water supply is unreliable.

Sometimes, however, the feature is presented as a health benefit, with a name such as "sani-cycle," "sani-steam," or "sani-scrub." On machines with those cycles, the final rinse cycle uses very hot water. A few brochures talk about "protection you'll appreciate during the flu and cold season" and "extra health protection." The feature is a waste of money to buy and use. Once you put "sanitized" dishes into the cupboard, they're repopulated with household microbes, a normal occurrence since microbes are also on everything else in the house.

Ratings of dishwashers

(As published in an August 1983 report.) Listed by groups in order of overall washing ability; within groups, ranked by energy-efficiency and convenience factors. Scores are based on performance with 140°F water and, except as noted, at cycle recommended by manufacturer for normal use. For models that can use 120°F water, performance with cooler water was about the same and energy efficiency improved. Price range is as quoted to CU shoppers; ✓ means yes and ✗ means no.

Better → **Worse**
● ◖ ○ ◑ ●

Brand and model	Approximate retail Price	Range	Washing ability [1]	Energy efficiency [1]	Heated drying	Noise	Time, min. [1]	Water consumption, gal. [1]	Can accept 120° water	Controls: Push button/dial	All push button	Cycles [2]	Advantages	Disadvantages	Comments
General Electric GSD 1200T	$525	$480 to $698	●	○	●	○	79	10½	✓	✗	✓	5	A,H,I,M	a	A,D
Kitchen Aid KDS-20	650	550 to 759	◖	◖	●	◖	69	8	✓	✗	✓	3	B,D,H,J,O	b,f	A,B,D
Kitchen Aid KDI-20	570	495 to 639	◖	◖	●	◑	73	9	✓	✗	✓	3	B,P	f	A,G
Maytag WU301	525	479 to 570	③	●	○		66	8½	✗	✓	✗	3	A,G,I	—	F,G

Brand and model	Price paid	Price range	Perf.					Water, gal				Cycles	Advantages		Disadvantages
Maytag WU901	615	549 to 680	③	●	●	●	○	66	8½	X X ✓			3	A,G,I	b	B,D,F,I
Whirlpool DU7900XL	465	390 to 529	○	●	●	●		55	9	X X ✓			4	D,H,K,N	—	B,E
Hotpoint HDA 865	415	355 to 530	○	◐	●	◐		76	9½	✓ ✓ X			3+	—	—	A
Magic Chef DU45	349	259 to 375	○	○	○	○		55	11	X X ✓			3	H	—	B
Tappan 61-1341	378	299 to 520	○	○	○	○		55	11	X X ✓			3	H	—	B
Thermador THD3500	600	510 to 682	○	◐	◐	◐		92	12	✓ ✓ ✓			2	C,E,I,L	c,d,e	A,C,H,I
Waste King WSK 3300	600	485 to 685	○	◐	◐	◐		92	12	✓ ✓ ✓			2	C,E,I,L	c,d,e	A,C,H,I
Wards 932	440	350 to 460	●	◐	●	●		64	9	X X ✓			3+	D,F,G,I	c,e	B
Frigidaire DWU44J	549	360 to 519	◐	◐	◐	◐		64	9	X X ✓			3+	F,H	c	B

① Measured with 140°F water at cycle recommended by manufacturer for normal use.

② Number indicates how many separate washing cycles are available; + indicates that portions of cycles can be selected by advancing dial.

③ Performance is based on cycle called "dual wash" by manufacturer, which is closer to cycle other companies designate as normal than the cycle recommended for normal use. When set that way, washing ability was ◐; that cycle, with only one wash and two rinses, redeposited tiny particles of food on dishes throughout the machine.

SPECIFICATIONS AND FEATURES

All: • Require about 34½ x 24 x 24 inches (H x W x D) for installation and 24- to 26-inch clearance to open door. • Have at least heavy wash, normal wash, and rinse-hold cycles. • Have switch to choose no-heat drying with any wash cycle. • Have heating element under lower rack that can pose burn hazard when energized: *Except as noted, all:* • Have dial that indicates progress through cycles. • Have rinse-conditioner dispenser. • Have one full or two half-size flatware baskets. • Have porcelain interior. • Have reversible front panel that allows choice of color. • Require 120-volt, 15-amp circuit.

(Continued)

KEY TO ADVANTAGES

A-Cup rack has one or more fold-down sections for double-stacking of cups.

B-Upper rack has adjustable dividers.

C-Upper rack has movable section.

D-Upper rack can be adjusted up and down to accommodate load.

E-Upper-rack dividers can be folded down to double-stack cups.

F-Upper rack has posts that allow double-stacking of cups.

G-Holds very tall glasses better than most.

H-Holds tall glasses better than others.

I-Flatware basket(s) has covered section(s).

J-Has additional small, covered basket.

K-May be set for delayed start of up to six hours.

L-Stainless-steel interior and door liner.

M-Solid-plastic interior and door liner.

N-Solid-plastic door liner.

O-Dual fill valves provide additional protection against accidental overfills and flooding.

KEY TO DISADVANTAGES

a-Timer can't be reset by hand; canceling a cycle takes about one minute and wastes all detergent in machine.

b-No timer dial; indicator lights give only rough idea of progress through cycle. Canceling to restart takes about fifteen seconds for **Maytag**, about two minutes for **Kitchen Aid**.

c-Door latch moved stiffly.

d-Upper rack moved stiffly when loaded.

e-Lower rack occasionally snagged on tub gasket and rolled out of tracks.

f-Upper-rack slides dripped a little water when pulled out.

KEY TO COMMENTS

A-If water is not automatically certain temperature for part of cycle, heater switches on.

B-Option provided to make sure water is certain temperature for part of cycle.

C-Option provided to boost water temperature to 175°F for part of cycle.

D-Has no plate-warming setting.

E-Removable flatware rack mounted on door.

F-Plate rack is on top, cup rack is on bottom.

G-Tested with optional rinse-conditioner dispenser.

H-Lacks reversible front panel.

I-Requires 20-amp circuit.

Ratings of alternate dishwasher models

Most of the dishwashers noted previously are loaded with features. The features may make dishwashing a little more convenient, but they don't improve washing performance in any significant way. From studying manufacturers' specifications, CU's engineers compiled a list of some more-basic models whose performance should be the same as that of the models tested. The dishwashers are listed by brand in alphabetical order. Within brands, they're listed in decreasing order of approximate retail price.

Brand	Approx. price	Difference from model tested
Frigidaire DWU55J	$689	Push-button controls; blower for drying; adjustable upper rack.
General Electric GSD 1000T	475	Button/dial controls; lacks "light" cycle.
GSD 900T	425	Button/dial controls; lacks "light" and "china/crystal" cycles; different upper rack.
Hotpoint HDA965	450	"China/crystal" cycle; option to boost water temperature.
Kitchen Aid KDS-60A	690	Convertible/portable version of **KDS-20** tested.
KDP-20	610	Similar to **KDS-20** tested, but lacks option to boost water temperature; small-item basket; upper rack not adjustable.
KDC-20	540	Similar to **KDI-20** tested, but lacks "soak and scrub" cycle.
Magic Chef DU55	415	Push-button controls; "plastic" cycle; blower for drying.
DU35	299	Lacks "heavy wash" cycle, option to boost water temperature, rinse-conditioner dispenser.
Maytag WU701	575	Similar to **WU301** tested, but has option to boost water temperature, rinse-conditioner dispenser; minor differences in controls.
WU501	575	Similar to **WU301** tested, except for minor differences in controls.
WC301	545	Convertible/portable version of **WU301** tested.

(Continued)

Brand	Approx. price	Difference from model tested
Tappan 61-1451	539	Different control layout.
61-1231	449	Lacks "heavy wash" cycle, option to boost water temperature, and tub insulation.
Thermador THD 4500	649	Push-button controls; "short" cycle.
THD 2500	549	Lacks option to boost water temperature.
Wards cat. no. 042	500	Electronic controls; extra indicator and warning lights; delayed start option.
982	470	Convertible/portable version of **932** tested.
Waste King WSK2200	549	Lacks option to boost water temperature.
Whirlpool DU9900XL	730	Electronic controls; "china/crystal" cycle; extra flatware basket.
DU8900XL	580	Push-button controls; "china/crystal" cycle; extra flatware basket.
DP6880XL	470	Convertible/portable version of **DU4000XL**, below.
DU5000XL	425	Lacks "low energy" cycle and delayed start option; different racks.
DU4000XL	405	Lacks "low energy" cycle and option to boost water temperature; different racks and basket.

Floors

Carpet shampooing

The most important tool in taking care of a carpet is a good vacuum cleaner—an upright or a canister vacuum with a power nozzle. Mechanical action is the only way to shake loose the grit that works its way deep into the carpet and grinds away at the fibers. A lightweight upright cleaner is all right, however, for quick pickup of surface litter.

Vacuum often. In a room that is used routinely, it's best to do the traffic lanes a couple of times a week and the entire carpet at least once a month. Move the vacuum slowly, giving it a chance to suck up the dirt it dislodges.

Spring cleaning

Even though regular vacuum cleaning is the best way to prolong the life and looks of your carpets, there comes a time when vacuuming just won't do the job. That's when you have to resort to chemical cleaners. You can forestall cleaning the entire carpet by cleaning just dirty areas. Dry carpet cleaning products are best for that. Some are powders, others are foams. You rub them in, let them dry, and vacuum.

Shampooing a carpet yourself is a tiring, somewhat tricky chore. Still, using a supermarket-variety cleaning shampoo can help keep carpets looking bright and stave off the need for commercial cleaning.

Most makers provide two types: a concentrated liquid that is diluted with water, and an aerosol spray foam. The liquids are applied with a sponge mop or an electric shampooer and worked into the carpet nap. Some foams also have to be worked in; others don't.

Cleaning effectiveness

Just about any product should produce a reasonable improvement in the appearance of your carpets. However, no product will remove all the dirt.

It's a good idea to consider a rug shampoo primarily as a surface cleaner. The main active ingredient is detergent, which is whipped into a froth by the scrubbing and left to dry. When you vacuum, you pick up dried detergent and whatever dirt it has trapped. The more thoroughly you vacuum, the more of the dirt and detergent residue you recover. Inevitably, some of the mixture will remain—and may foam up if you use a steam-cleaning machine later on.

Shampooing a relatively new rug can produce pleasing results. If the rug is in bad shape before you clean it, however, you may be disappointed with its appearance afterward. Worn areas and matted nap can become more obvious once the surface dirt has been removed.

Some shampoos claim to resist resoiling. At best, a shampoo can leave a residue that may help prevent a carpet from attracting and holding dirt. At worst, the residue can become a tacky glue that cements dirt to the fibers.

Time and effort

Shampooing any large carpet is a big job. The furniture should be removed or set up on foil or waxed paper "booties" to protect both the furniture and the carpet from stains. Applying the shampoo to a large carpet can take hours, and the carpet will be out of service until it dries—anywhere from a couple of hours to overnight. If you can't close off the room until the carpet dries, you'll have to shampoo in sections. Cleaning the carpet that way could be a two-day task.

Furthermore, rug shampooing takes a knack. Label instructions are simple enough, but you have to make allowances for the type of pile and the equipment you're using. For example, a high-pile rug should be stroked against the nap after shampooing to help the drying process and to restore the appearance of the pile. You have to learn through experience how big a patch you should tackle each time. And you have to take care not to soak the carpet, because that could induce shrinkage and might bring on stains or a mildew growth. It's easy to acquire the knack, but you ought to practice first on an area of the rug that is hidden from view. And try to keep the room well ventilated to accelerate drying.

It's also a good idea to choose an area of the rug that is inconspicuous to check the rug dye for colorfastness before trying a new shampoo. A simple test is to moisten a white rag with shampoo (diluted if you're using a liquid) and rub it against the rug. If the cloth does not pick up color, go ahead and shampoo.

Shampoo products are strong detergents that may irritate the skin or eyes. They should be used with caution and kept out of the reach of children. Check for spatters on furniture and woodwork. Wipe them up quickly.

Price

The price you pay for shampoos usually varies somewhat from store to store—much more so with the spray foams than with the liquids. The liquids are normally available in one-quart and two-quart bottles; the larger size is usually much cheaper per ounce.

Price has little to do with the real cost of the shampoo. That's because of the differences in the amount of shampoo it takes to do the job. The optimum amount of shampoo will produce an even application of foam, but that optimum amount can vary quite a bit from product to product. Deep-pile carpets, with their heavy dirt loads, usually require more shampoo than the label recommends, especially with a spray foam.

Recommendations

A basic recommendation for maintaining the life and good appearance of carpeting is to vacuum it thoroughly and regularly. Don't shampoo rugs more often than necessary, but do shampoo before they get very dirty or matted. Once rugs reach that state, it's unlikely that any cleaners will do a satisfactory job in one application. If your carpet is heavily soiled, you'd better call in a professional or rent a steam-cleaning machine from a local store.

If your carpeting isn't very dirty, then a shampoo may brighten it noticeably.

In order to make a difficult job more tolerable, consider renting a machine to work in the detergent foam, a wet/dry vacuum cleaner, or a machine that combines the functions.

How well the carpet is cleaned depends greatly on the skill of the operator—amateur or professional. Used carelessly, the rotating brushes of the carpet shampooer can abrade the pile. And if the carpet gets too soaked, it could shrink.

If you have an Oriental, antique, or costly varicolored wool rug, it's best to leave the cleaning to specialists in that type of rug. Rugs may shrink, and rug dyes are not always colorfast to cleaning chemicals; you would have no recourse if you damaged the rug when cleaning it yourself.

"Steam" cleaning is better than shampooing

For house calls, professional rug cleaning companies sometimes use a "hot water extraction" method that sprays hot, wet detergent solution into the rug and then vacuums away the solution and dislodged dirt. Smaller versions of this type of equipment can usually be rented from supermarkets and hardware stores. They are often called "steam" cleaning machines, even though they actually use hot water.

The typical machine has two reservoirs, one for cleaning solution, the other for the dirty liquid. Depending on the machine and the amount of soil in the carpet, a tankful of cleaning solution should last from fifteen to twenty minutes.

The machine you rent will take a little practice to handle. It is smaller than the professional variety, but still cumbersome. If you follow the instructions carefully, you should do all right. The machines usually don't require more effort than an electric rotary brush shampooer.

A steam machine should work much better on very dirty or

matted rugs than any ordinary rug shampoo but will probably not do as well as a thorough professional cleaning. For lightly soiled rugs, you'll probably be just as satisfied using a shampoo with a rotary brush shampooer and a good vacuum cleaner.

Carpet first aid for stains from spills

Clean up spills fast. With some spilled substances—children's fruit drinks, for instance—you have only minutes before the stain sets permanently. Here are some suggestions for carpet first aid: First, before using anything, test it on a carpet scrap or in an area hidden from view—in the corner of a closet, for instance.

Have on hand a dry-cleaning solvent (from the supermarket or hardware store) for greasy, oily stains. But be careful about using a solvent-based cleaner on a rug that has a plastic or rubber foam backing or separate padding. The solvent could soften such materials and ruin them. Use a detergent solution (one teaspoon dishwashing liquid per cup of water) for water-soluble spills. Some spills are both. For them, use the dry-cleaning solvent first and then the detergent solution. Do the same for unidentified spills.

Blot or scrape up as much as possible. Then cover the spill with a pad of several paper towels and stand on the towels for a minute or so. Then apply the cleaning solution—the dry-cleaning solvent to a rag or paper towel, the detergent solution directly on the carpet. Don't overwet the carpet. Blot, don't rub. Repeat those steps until the spill is cleaned up. Cover the wet spot with a half-inch pad of paper towels, weight it down, and let the rug dry.

For stains with an offensive odor such as pet urine, use a solution of one part white vinegar to two parts water, blot, then use the detergent solution. For acidic stains such as vomit or fruit drinks, use a solution of one tablespoon ammonia in a half cup of water to neutralize the acid (but don't use ammonia on wool, as it sets stains on that material).

Copious spills that penetrate through the carpet to the backing and even the floor are a special problem. If the substance is one that smells, you may have to have the carpet lifted and cleaned professionally.

Household products that contain bleach or some other oxidizing agent can cause irreversible damage. A leaking container of laundry bleach is an obvious villain. Other products are more insidious. The damage cause by acne medications containing benzoyl peroxide, for instance, often doesn't show up right way. Those medications, typically hard to wash off the hands, have ruined many a carpet. Other products to watch out for: swimming pool chemicals, mildew removers, liquid plant foods, and pesticides.

Floor polishers

An electric floor polisher is one of those appliances a lot of households can do nicely without, even if carpets do not cover most of the floor. There are, after all, workable alternatives. As a once- or twice-a-year proposition, floors can be polished with a rented machine, or a service company can be called in. "Self-polishing" floor wax may meet some people's standards all year round on floors that can take—and need—a water-based polish.

That's not to say an electric floor polisher is of no interest, particularly if you take pride in near-perfect floors and want to keep them buffed to a mirror sheen.

If you want a machine of your own, you should have little trouble buying one that works well enough at polishing bare floors or hard-surface floor coverings. Differences are more likely to be in convenience features than in performance.

Shampooing

Manufacturers of floor polishers usually offer devices for wet-shampooing rugs. These attachments can work quite well, but their use may entail some risk of damage to the rug from the brushes' abrasive action. Therefore, you should always try shampooing a small inconspicuous area of rug or carpet first to find out whether the rug can withstand the machine. Better still, rent one for a trial run. As well as checking for damage, see whether you're satisfied with the shampooing: You may find the shampooing technique difficult—and the results may not satisfy you.

Converting a machine from polisher to shampooer should be easy and quick. In shampooing, it's important to work a good thick foam into the pile of the rug to loosen the dirt. Moisture can promote mildew or rotting if it soaks into the carpet and underlay. Most shampooing machines have some means of agitating the shampoo into foam before it hits the rug.

If shampooing sounds like trouble, remember that rugs may not require shampooing very often. When they do, if you can take them up easily enough, they may be sent out for cleaning. Alternatively, a professional firm can shampoo them in place.

A floor-polishing machine, with or without special attachments, can be used for wet scrubbing on hard-surfaced floors. It can be a real boon on extremely dirty floors—much better than hand scrubbing or wet mopping. Damp mopping is easier and quicker for tidying up a slightly dirty floor.

A machine with vacuuming action offers a special advantage: It can suck up the dirty water, eliminating tedious sponge squeezing. Don't be surprised if the holes in the water-pickup entrance of these machines become blocked by particles of dirt. You can minimize this problem by sweeping or vacuuming the floor before you scrub. Dirty water may also continue to drip from the machine even after you have emptied it. Even a little water on a polishing pad or brush can smear a newly waxed surface. To help prevent this, be sure the machine has dried before you use it for polishing.

Waxing

Two-brush models, the most common type, tend to leave a narrow strip of less well-polished floor in the space between the brushes. To get reasonably even polishing, you have to push the machine through overlapping strokes.

Most machines have dispensers for such liquids as wax and sudsy water. A dispenser is likely to be much more useful for shampooing rugs or washing floors than for waxing. First, machines tend to spread wax unevenly. Second, a solvent-based liquid wax can clog a machine's dispenser and perhaps damage it.

If you do put wax in the dispenser, use a water-based emulsified liquid type. All factors considered, it's better to spread wax—liquid or paste—with an applicator and use your machine only for polishing and buffing.

Other factors

In general, the faster the brushes rotate, the more you can expect them to spatter wax, shampoo, or water. It would seem, then, that you'd want a machine with a fairly low speed for shampooing and scrubbing and a high speed for polishing after your wax is spread. Apparently with some such idea in mind, the manufacturers of many models provide two speeds. Such a machine isn't likely to perform noticeably better than a one-speed model.

A floor polisher often seems to have a mind of its own. If you aren't careful, it can spin out of your hand and go careening across the floor. This is most likely to happen when the handle is vertical, so keep the handle at an angle.

It helps if there's an indication whether the motor switch is on or off before you plug the machine in. With a push-button switch there may be no way to tell.

Recommendations

Price is not a guide to effectiveness since even a cheap polisher will do the job. As you move up the price ladder you get more accessories and more features. Whether these items are needed is best left up to the individual buyer, based on his or her needs and preferences.

Floor polishes

The introduction of no-wax resilient flooring about fifteen years ago promised liberation from the nuisance of periodic polishing, particularly important for people who insist on shiny floors in their home. Judging by the popularity of no-wax flooring—much of which is relentlessly shiny—consumers were glad to avoid the polishing chore.

But as more and more no-wax floors were installed in the kitchens of America, floor polish manufacturers saw their sales dip.

The companies found out from consumers that no-wax floors weren't shiny enough to suit some people, and there were complaints about dirt building up on such floors. People were using regular polish on no-wax floors.

A new product category emerged from the dissatisfaction: a combination cleaner and polish formulated for use on no-wax floor coverings.

The manufacturers of no-wax flooring were in a curious position. On one hand, they had to defend the no-wax qualities that sold their flooring. On the other hand, many of them sell a line of floor-care products, including their own polish for no-wax floors (because even a no-wax floor can lose some of its gloss in time).

The other polish manufacturers, according to one maker of floor coverings, made no distinction between no-wax floors with a polyurethane "special wear surface" and no-wax floors with a vinyl wear surface, which are a bit less shiny. The floor-covering maker recommended that owners of their flooring not use special clean-and-polish products because they were unnecessary. On vinyl no-wax floors, the use of such products isn't necessary for protection, said the floor covering representative, but would make the floor shinier.

No-wax waxes

If you have new no-wax flooring, you don't need to use a polish—even for cleaning.

On a very shiny, polyurethane-finished no-wax floor a polish won't make any real difference in appearance. On no-wax vinyl-surfaced floors, whose shine is a bit less glaring, a polish can add a touch of gloss. If you have a new vinyl no-wax floor and feel compelled to use a polish, you won't be doing anything but boosting the shine. The amount of protection offered by a thin film of polish is insignificant compared with the protection offered by the layer of vinyl on the flooring.

But even rugged plastics such as polyurethane and vinyl can get scratched and worn over time—probably years after the installation of the floor. And it is reasonable to assume that an accumulation of tiny scratches will eventually dull no-wax flooring a little.

Polishes do have some ability to fill in tiny scratches, which would tend to improve the shine of worn areas.

Until a no-wax floor is worn, however, floor polish is a waste of money. You'd be better off saving that money to make up for the extra cost of the no-wax flooring.

Although no-wax floors resist dirt well, they still get dirty. Should you buy a one-step, wash and wax product that "cleans as it shines," simply as a way to clean your no-wax floor? Products for no-wax floors are usually labeled as "self-cleaning"—that is, a new coat of polish wholly or partly dissolves the previous layer, and dirt is picked up on the mop along with excess polish. Products sold for no-wax floors are excellent at cleaning if the floor isn't terribly dirty to begin with, particularly if you damp mop once a week. That can make them quite clean. Damp mopping can make the untreated no-wax flooring look as clean as polished flooring.

When polish is first applied, it can be moderately slippery. We tested for slipperiness by putting a weighted cloth (the laboratory version of the foot on the throw rug) on a section of freshly polished flooring and seeing how far the flooring could be tilted before the cloth slid off.

We also tested how well the polishes resisted spotting when alcohol (in the form of vodka) and water were sprinkled on them. The products for no-wax floors were generally unmarked by water—most showed only a faint ring. All were severely marred by the vodka.

Floors that need waxing

While no-wax flooring has a smooth, sealed surface, the surface of conventional vinyl asbestos tiles and other plain resilient flooring is relatively rough and porous. On such floors, polish keeps a floor cleaner and shinier partly by sealing the surface.

Polishes for resilient flooring are water-based emulsions that impart more of a satin luster than a mirror finish to a dull surface like that of vinyl asbestos tiles. No product is likely to keep vinyl asbestos tiles pristine.

Like a polish for no-wax flooring, a product intended for regular flooring is usually resistant to water and vulnerable to alcoholic beverage spills.

Polishes that aren't good at self-cleaning require a clean floor before they're applied—otherwise, you encase the dirt and old polish in plastic.

Long ago, when floor waxes were really waxes, they required buffing in order to develop any shine at all. In the 1930s so-called self-polishing floor waxes came along. They were the waxes that dried to a satin luster without buffing. Today, self-polishing floor polishes may still have real wax in them, but more often they are principally vinyl, acrylic, or some other plastic that dries to an even shinier finish. The new formulations are better than the old waxes in one important respect: They are less slippery.

A few products say that you can use them diluted to restore shine in between full-strength applications. The diluted polishes add some shine, but not as much as a full-strength polish would. And diluted polishes remove some dirt, but not as effectively as at full strength. These products are useful as damp-mopping aids only if the floor were slightly dirty or dull.

Wax buildup

Technology has produced polishes that don't need buffing, but has been less successful in eliminating the chore of stripping off old polish as the layers build up. Even polishes labeled as self-cleaning leave a small amount of old polish behind. The problem is usually most noticeable in corners, where the polish isn't worn away by traffic. And while you may be content to let the layers of wax accumulate for a long time before trying to remove it, floor polish instructions generally say that "for best results" you should strip the polish after every five or six coats, or once or twice a year.

The typical recipe for removing old floor wax is one-half cup of powdered floor cleaner and two cups of ammonia in a gallon of cool water, some fine steel wool, and a lot of elbow grease. There are also several brands of wax remover on the market, which are often recommended on the labels of their brand-mate floor polish.

Recommendations

For taking care of new or fairly new no-wax floors, use a plain damp mop, or a little detergent and a rinse. When the floor is so worn that it looks like it really needs a polish, choose among the no-wax products by their price.

For taking care of a regular resilient floor, if shininess is important to you, buy a product that is known to give a high gloss.

Waxing wood floors

Wood floors are back in style. A lot of people have ripped up their carpets, rented floor sanders, and now have hardwood floors graced with area rugs.

But there's been no resurgence in the sales of waxes for wood floors. Most people who redo wood floors make them into no-wax wood floors by giving them several coats of polyurethane. The polyurethane finish requires nearly as little maintenance as a no-wax resilient flooring—vacuuming or dusting, and maybe a refinishing every few years.

Because water can damage and discolor wood, wood floor waxes are suspended in a petroleum solvent such as naphtha. Consequently, they are much more hazardous substances than water-based polishes and should be used with good ventilation. (A few water-based polishes claim to be usable on wood floors, too, but it's not worth the risk: If the finish has been breached for any reason, the wood could be damaged by the water.)

Stripping old wax from wood floors requires the use of a solvent such as mineral spirits. Fortunately, waxes are excellent at cleaning, so any buildup of wax will occur slowly.

Buffing waxes must be buffed after they have dried. Doing that by hand is theoretically possible, but using a machine is easier.

A one-step wood wax is likely to be noticeably duller and dirtier than a buffing wax after it's been on the floor for a while.

If you are willing to go to the trouble of moving the furniture to wax a wood floor, you might as well do it right. That would mean using a little extra effort and a buffing wax.

A wax with a coloring agent should be used only on very dark floors—those the color of end-grain walnut or rosewood. Otherwise, wax applied after some use can make scratches stand out because the wax is darker than the wood.

Hard-surface floor first aid for stains from spills

When using chemicals available from a supermarket or a drugstore, handle them with care and store them out of children's reach. Never mix chemicals with each other or with household cleaning products unless there are specific directions to do so. Wear rubber gloves when working with alcohol, hydrogen peroxide solution, household ammonia, acids, or chlorine bleach. Before using any chemical, test it on a small corner of the stain. If your procedure is wrong, the stain will not spread on the floor, nor will the floor be damaged further. If you apply steel wool to a stain, use grade 00 and rub gently. On wood, rub with the grain. To be on the safe side, it's a good idea to work in a well-ventilated room, keeping a window open.

After you have successfully removed a stain, rinse the area well and allow it to dry before you apply any new finish (polish, for example). The newly finished area should blend in with the rest of the floor within a day or two.

After you have tried ordinary liquid detergent (dishwashing liquid or laundry liquid) and water applied with a rag or sponge—or an all-purpose liquid cleaner sprayed from its container—here are some specific procedures that can help to remove a variety of potentially stubborn stains.

Alcoholic beverages. Try rubbing with a clean cloth dampened with rubbing alcohol.

Blood. Try clear, cold water first (before any detergent). If the stain remains, use caution in applying a solution of ammonia and cold water—and rinse quickly to avoid discoloration.

Candle wax or chewing gum. Chill the material to brittleness by using ice cubes. Then, carefully scrape the wax or gum from the floor, using a plastic spatula.

Cigarette burn. For heavy stains, try scouring powder and a piece of steel wool or plastic pad dipped in water. For hard-surface floors, rub with a cloth dampened with a solution of lemon juice and water.

Coffee or fruit juice. Saturate a cloth with a solution of one part glycerine to three parts water and place it over the stain for several hours. If the spot remains, rub it gently with scouring powder and a cloth dampened in hot water.

Dyes. Rub with a cloth dampened in a solution of one part chlorine bleach and two parts water. If this doesn't work, try scouring powder and a cloth dampened with hot water.

Grease and oil. Remove as much as possible with newspaper, paper towels, or a plastic spatula. On resilient tile, rub with a cloth dampened in liquid detergent and warm water (or an all-purpose cleaner). On wood and cork, place a cloth saturated with dry-cleaning fluid on the stain for no more than five minutes. Then wipe the area dry and wash with detergent and water.

Ink. Try a commercial ink remover, following instructions carefully.

Lipstick. Try steel wool wet with detergent and water. If the floor is hard surfaced or has a no-wax finish, or is embossed vinyl asbestos, use a plastic scouring pad instead of steel wool.

Mustard. Place a cloth soaked in hydrogen peroxide solution over the stain. Over that place an ammonia-soaked cloth. Leave in place until the stain has faded, sponge with water, and wipe dry.

Paint or varnish. On resilient tile, use liquid or all-purpose detergent with a cloth or sponge or steel wool applied very carefully. On wood and cork, rub with a cloth dampened in a solution of one tablespoon oxalic acid and one pint of water. On a hard-surfaced floor, scrub with a concentrated solution of powdered detergent and water, or liquid laundry detergent applied undiluted.

Rust. Use a commercial rust remover intended for your particular type of floor.

Shoe polish or nail polish. If concentrated detergent solution doesn't work on resilient flooring, try scouring powder or steel wool. On wood and cork, steel wool should do the trick.

Tar. Chill the tar to brittleness by using ice cubes. Then, scrape the tar carefully with a plastic spatula. To remove the tar stain, apply a damp cloth wrapped around a paste made of powdered detergent, calcium carbonate, and water. Leave the paste on the stain for several hours.

Tobacco. Rub with a cloth dampened in a solution of lemon juice and water. If that isn't effective, place a cloth soaked in hydrogen peroxide over the stain, and over that place an ammonia-soaked cloth. Leave in place until the stain has faded, sponge with water, and wipe dry.

Urine. Rub with a hot, damp cloth and scouring powder. For increased effectiveness, place a cloth soaked in hydrogen peroxide over the stain. Over that, place a cloth soaked in ammonia.

Vacuum cleaners

Though cleaners have begun to sport high-tech electronic gadgetry, the state of the vacuuming art remains imperfect. As of now, no one machine can handle all chores with equal ease.

Several kinds of vacuum cleaners are available. Lightweight "stick-type" uprights, for instance, are usually less expensive than full-sized uprights. However, the lightweights are useful mainly for picking up surface litter, not deep-cleaning a carpet or doing above-floor dusting. There are also little battery-powered models, but these are clearly closer to the dustpan and the handheld brush than they are to a full-sized cleaner. For general household use, your most practical choice is really between a full-sized upright and a canister cleaner—or perhaps one of their "compact" variants.

An upright, the most popular kind, is in its element on vast expanses of carpeting. Rotating beater brushes do the main part of the cleaning job: They are able to dislodge dirt up from deep in the carpet's pile. Suction from the cleaner serves mainly to carry the dirt into a bag on the handle. But uprights aren't very effective on bare floors, and they're awkward in tight places—too bulky to slide under the sofa, too ungainly for stairs. Many can be fitted with hoses and attachments to handle crevices as well as under-sofa and above-floor chores, but the arrangement is often clumsy.

Canisters can do jobs uprights can't do well. With a canister you push or aim only a nozzle assembly. The rest of the cleaner is a squat unit that trails along behind you. Canisters are generally easier than uprights to fit with cleaning attachments. They are agile when poking into tight spots, and most can sit comfortably on stairs, but unless you have the space to store a canister all set up, you'll have to cope with its wands, hoses, and specialized tools each time you use the machine. A standard canister relies on suction alone for cleaning; it picks up only surface dirt and debris from carpets, not the damaging deep down grit.

That's where a power nozzle is useful. It's an overgrown floor attachment with beater brushes driven either by air or by the nozzle's own small motor. A canister equipped with a power nozzle can combine an upright's deep-cleaning ability with a canister's convenience and versatility. Unfortunately, it also has the canister's drawbacks. Some assembly is always required, as is a tug on the hose every now and then to keep the canister trailing along behind you.

Full-sized vacuum cleaners have been joined by compact versions, promoted for general use but with emphasis on portability, light weight, and easy storage. Compact canisters are generally small enough to carry in one hand while you clean with the other. They're good in places where it's hard to take a full-sized machine—the stairs or your car, for example. Some models have a power nozzle.

Cleaning

The main test of a vacuum cleaner, of course, is how well it picks up dirt.

Deep cleaning. A carpet that looks well groomed isn't necessarily clean. Gritty soil that's allowed to accumulate deep in the carpet's nap will eventually abrade carpet fibers, causing them to break off. Many full-sized models do well at getting rid of this damaging kind of dirt. Compact models don't do as well.

Surface cleaning. Given enough patience and proper adjustment, any cleaner, including the compacts, should be able to handle surface debris such as popcorn, peanut shells, and pine needles. Some canister models may have trouble picking up toothpicks and the like. Thready debris tends to wrap around revolving brushes, a common problem for uprights and power-nozzle canisters alike on rugs or bare floors.

Suction. Cleaner makers have promoted "superior" suction by lifting everything from bowling balls to Volkswagens with their machines. Those feats, however, demonstrate suction with the intake closed off, and do not reflect performance under real working conditions, with the hose open and air moving through the cleaner.

The strength of a vacuum cleaner's suction doesn't tell you much about its carpet-cleaning talents, but it is a good indication of how well a cleaner and its various attachments will do on bare floors and in above-floor cleaning. With a clean bag, just about any canister should have at least satisfactory suction. Suction does have a tendency to drop off as the dust bag fills.

With uprights, suction usually isn't the main concern, since they're generally awkward to use with attachments. Nevertheless, some uprights do have pretty good suction.

A powered brush isn't really necessary when working on a hard floor. When using a power-nozzle canister, you can unplug or switch off the nozzle's motor and use the nozzle as a suction tool only.

High suction is fine until your vacuum pulls drapes or a scatter rug into its nozzle. Most canisters have some sort of air-bleed control—a ring, slide, knob, or lever—that lets you uncover a hole to reduce suction at the nozzle. A few models allow you to reduce suction by lowering the motor's speed. Several units (mostly compact canisters) have no means of reducing suction. That's a significant disadvantage.

Assembly

Getting ready. You may have to assemble a new upright, but thereafter it's ready to go when you wheel it out of the closet—if you want to clean carpets, that is. Attachments, usually optional, for other types of cleaning are a different matter entirely. You can buy most uprights with an optional adapter plate that snaps on underneath the cleaner, over the beater brushes. A hose then fits into the plate, the attachments fit onto the hose, and the body of the upright lumbers along behind you as you work.

A few uprights do provide an accessory port that lets you use cleaning tools while the machine stands squarely on its wheels. While plugging in the accessory hose and attachments is handy enough, using them is still fairly clumsy.

Setting up a canister involves inserting its hose into the housing, attaching one or more wands, and pushing the appropriate nozzle onto the wand's free end. The most convenient wands have segments that lock together with a positive click. Next best are plastic wands with latches. Wands and accessories held in place only by friction can be a problem. They sometimes fall apart as you use them, at other times they are hard to loosen for storage.

A canister's typical roster of attachments includes a rug/floor tool, a dusting brush, a crevice tool, and an upholstery nozzle, some or all of which store in or on the canister. (Much the same tools are available as options for uprights.) Power-nozzle canisters have, as well, the power nozzle for carpets.

Switch.   An inconvenient on/off switch is a nuisance every time you use the cleaner. The handiest models have a slide switch directly at hand when vacuuming. Almost as good are the few machines that turn themselves on when you lower their handle, and some others with a step-on switch or conveniently positioned toggle switch.

Don't use a vacuum cleaner on wet surfaces unless it is specifically intended for that kind of cleaning.

Noise.   Vacuums are typically noisy appliances. On models with multiple-speed settings, you can sometimes cut some of the noise by setting the cleaner at a lower speed, though you then lose some cleaning power.

Height adjustment.   Most uprights and a few power-nozzle canisters make you raise or lower the rug nozzle to suit carpets with high or low naps. That adjustment can be tricky. If you set the brush too high, the vacuum will be easy to push, but it won't get your carpets clean; too low, and the vacuum will be hard to push and may be hard on your carpet. Some models adjust "manually" with a foot lever or knob; others adjust automatically.

Once running and set at the proper height, a vacuum cleaner should be reasonably easy to push. A few uprights have a power-assisted drive that makes them very easy to push. But self-propelled models may take some getting used to. They also have some extra mechanical complexities that could be expensive to fix.

Maneuverability. Uprights are generally easy to wheel from one place to another.

Canisters follow a tug on the hose, but they tend to get stuck when you maneuver around things or make sharp turns. Some may tend to fall over when being wheeled. Those are presumably meant to be carried most of the time; some come with a shoulder strap for that purpose.

Stairs are easiest to vacuum with a compact suction-only canister, which you can carry with you as you clean. A full-sized canister should fit comfortably on a stair tread.

If you want to clean under a bed or sofa, you're better off with a canister. Upright cleaners have a high motor housing and typically need 6 to 7½ inches of clearance. As for canisters, all power nozzles and suction-only nozzles require less than 3½ inches of headroom.

Cord. The typical upright has a 20- to 25-foot power cord. Cords on canisters are usually shorter, possibly because their hose gives you some extra reach.

Models with a built-in cord winder and a release control generally afford the handiest cord storage; just press a button or a pedal and the cord reels itself back in.

Next best are automatic rewinders that work with a yank of the cord, like a window shade. Those are less controllable than the push-button type—the pronged plug can lash out at legs and furniture as it whips back into the canister.

Least convenient are the kind you have to wind up by hand. Of those, the uprights with at least one hook that swivels have a small advantage; they let you unhook the cord without unwinding it.

Getting rid of dust

If a cleaner has a large dust bag, that reduces the frequency of the messy job of changing dust bags. A large bag has another advantage: It's probably cheaper, size for size, than a small-capacity bag.

Full-bag alarms or other indicators on certain models are likely to be imprecise. Still, such devices do help you avoid overfilling the bag.

Uprights generally hold more dirt than canisters. The largest canister bags, in fact, hold less than half as much as the largest capacity uprights.

Electrolux models, upright and canisters, come close to having an ideal bag-cleaning arrangement. Their self-sealing bags are easily popped in and out. (All the **Electroluxes** have a convenient interlock that won't let the cleaner run without a bag.) Several other models have dust bags with plastic or cardboard collars for you to handle instead of the bag itself. Less convenient are the uprights that make you slip the bag's sleeve over the dirt tube and then stretch a spring around it.

It's messy to empty a bag that fills from the bottom in an upright model; the bag's open end is generally filled with dirt when you detach it. Several models don't use disposable bags; you must dump out a dirt receptacle to empty them. Bags with wide-open mouths tend to spill dirt.

Special features

If something gets caught in a vacuum cleaner's revolving brushes, the motor may overheat and burn out; at the least, the belt may break. Some cleaners have a self-protective shutoff mechanism for that situation, a distinct advantage. Another good feature, found on a few power-nozzle canisters, is a window that lets you monitor the condition of the power-nozzle belt.

Vacuum cleaners that convert to blowers are handy for blowing dirt out of hard-to-reach places (behind a radiator or around refrigerator coils) into the open where it can be vacuumed or swept away.

Recommendations

Uprights. The best for carpet cleaning because they have rotating brushes that beat the dirt out. But, with their low suction, they're not good at cleaning bare floors. And they can be clumsy in tight places or on stairs.

Suction-only canisters.   Do what uprights can't—easily lift dirt off bare floors. They're good in tight spots, and can be agile on stairs. But they can't deep-clean carpets, and their wands and hoses can be clumsy to store.

Power-nozzle canisters.   Good both on carpets and on bare floors because they combine the beater brushes of uprights with the suction of regular canisters.

Compact models.   There doesn't seem to be much point to buying one of the compact vacuum cleaners. They aren't all that much smaller than a standard-sized vacuum, nor are they necessarily less expensive. Furthermore, they don't perform as well or have as much dirt capacity as the better of their full-sized counterparts.

Ratings of vacuum cleaners

Listed by types. Within types, listed in order of estimated quality. Bracketed models were judged about equal; listed in order of increasing price. Prices are manufacturer's suggested retail as published in a May 1986 report; + indicates shiping is extra.

Legend: ● Excellent → ● Poor

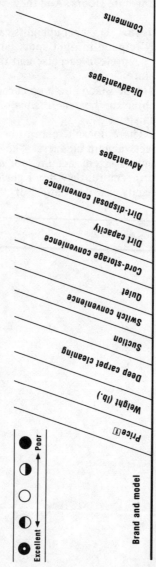

Full-sized uprights

Brand and model	Price	Weight (lb.)	Deep carpet cleaning	Suction	Switch convenience	Quiet	Cord-storage convenience	Dirt capacity	Dirt-disposal convenience	Advantages	Disadvantages	Comments
Panasonic MC6220	$210	16	●	—	○	●	○	◐	●	E,G,J,P,S,U,Y,Z	—	C,N
Whirlpool FV6000XM1	290	14½	●	—	◉	●	◐	○	●	A,E,G,M,U,Y	k	A,C,J
Hoover U3305030	330	20½	●	—	○	●	◐	○	◐	A,D,E	k	A,C
Kirby Heritage II	499	20	●	—	○	●	○	○	●	B,E,H,U,V,Y,Z	i	C,K,M
Whirlpool FV2000XM1	170	14½	●	—	○	◐	○	○	●	A,E,G,Y	—	J
Hoover U4381930	200	16	◐	—	◉	◐	◐	○	◐	C,U	—	C,F
Eureka 5060F	310	17½	●	—	○	○	◐	◉	○	D,F,U	r	C,R

Model	Price	Wt.													
Eureka 1425F	100	11½	◑	—	◑	●	○		q	○	◑	V	○	●	○	S
Hoover U4369	130	15½*	◑	—	◑	◑	●		—	○	○	C	●	○	○	C
Eureka 1945A	150	13½	◑	—	◑	◑	○		—	○	○	—	○	◑	○	C
Singer SST1000	170	14½	◑	—	◑	●	◑		c	○	◑	M	○	◑	○	A,C
Eureka 7575A	230	15	◑	—	◑	◑	○		—	●	◑	F	○	○	◑	C,H
Electrolux 1451E	500	24	○	[2]	◑	◑	●		v	●	○	G,M,S,T	◑	◑	●	K,R
Singer SST200	100	11	○	—	◑	◑	○		c,q	○	○	—	○	◑	○	C
Panasonic MC5130	150	12½	◑	—	◑	◑	○		—	◑	◑	G,P	◑	○	○	C,N
Hoover U4391	175	17½	◑	—	◑	◑	◑		—	○	◑	C,P	○	◑	○	B,C
Hoover U4365	100	14	◑	—	◑	◑	●		q,x	◑	◑	C	○	○	●	—
Royal M880	486	14	◑	—	◑	◑	○		—	○	◑	H,U,V	○	○	○	C,K

Compact uprights

Model	Price	Wt.													
Miele S125	215 [3]	12	○	[4]	○	●	○		v	●	○	F,G,I,P,V	●	●	◑	K,N,Q,T
Oreck XL100C	319	9½	◑	—	◑	◑	◑		s,v	○	◑	C,I,V	○	○	○	C,G,K,N,R

Power-nozzle canisters

Model	Price	Wt.													
Hoover S3281	460	30	◑	—	◑	●	◑		—	◑	◑	E,K,N,R,S,Y	◑	●	◑	C,J
Panasonic MC9420	250	23½	◑	—	◑	◑	◑		—	◑	●	E,H,P,S,X,Y	◑	◑	◑	A
Whirlpool FC7000	300	27½	◑	—	◑	◑	◑		—	◑	●	C,M,R,S,Y	◑	◑	◑	O
Singer CSS1000	270	25½	●	—	○	◑	●		u,z	○	○	C,R,S	◑	○	◑	—
Montgomery Ward 5046	279	27½	◑	—	◑	●	◑		u	◑	◑	H,O,P	●	◑	◑	C
Hoover S3271	280	22	○	—	◑	○	◑		—	◑	○	E,N,S,Y	◑	○	○	C
Eureka 1784B	370	28½	●	—	◑	●	◑		k,u	◑	◑	H,O,P	◑	◑	◑	C

(Continued)

Ratings key: Excellent ◉ — ◐ — ○ — ◑ — ● Poor

Brand and model	Price [1]	Weight (lb.)	Deep carpet cleaning	Suction	Switch convenience	Quiet	Cord-storage convenience	Dirt capacity	Dirt-disposal convenience	Advantages	Disadvantages	Comments
Eureka 1790A	430	29	◐	●	◐	○	◐	◐	◐	O,S	—	A,C
Miele S230i	435	23	●	◐	◐	◐	◉	◑	●	H,P	k,o,p,w	D,E,K
Electrolux 1521 Diamond Jubilee	639	26	○	◐	◐	◐	◐	●	◉	H,M,N,Q,T	j,m	E,K
Electrolux 1453 Special	349	23	○	◐	○	○	◐ [5]	●	◉	H,M,N,T	j,m	E,K,R
Royal M401PN	456	21	○	○	◐	○	◐	○	◐	H,L	e,g,m,o,v	K,M,D
Toshiba VC222	120	14	◐	◐	◐	◐	◐	◑	◐	P	a,e,g,n,p,v,z	B,D,E,K,P
Sharp EC7410	180	16	◐	●	◐	◐	◉	●	◐	J,S	a,e,h,n,p,v,w,z	B,J,K,P

Suction-only canisters

Brand and model	Price [1]	Weight (lb.)	Deep carpet cleaning	Suction	Switch convenience	Quiet	Cord-storage convenience	Dirt capacity	Dirt-disposal convenience	Advantages	Disadvantages	Comments
Panasonic MC7320	130	14	[6]	○	◐	○	●	◐	◐	L,S,W	p,t	—
Whirlpool FC5000XM	180	21½	[6]	◐	◐	◐	●	◐	◐	—	h	A
Sears Kenmore 25022	130	13	[6]	◐	○	○	◉	◑	◐	P,S	a,p,t,w	R
Hoover S3259	175	16	[6]	◐	◐	◐	◉	◐	◐	N,S,W	h	—

Brand and model	Price	Weight (lb.)											Comments
Sanyo SCP2000	110	11½	[6]	○	○	◐	○	○	◑	P,S	a,d,f,g,p,t	—
Eureka 3336A	140	16	[6]	◑	○	○	○	○	◑	—	a,h,k,l,u	—
Singer CSS500	150	18½	[6]	○	○	○	○	○	◑	H,J	f,h,j,k,u	—

Compact canisters

Brand and model	Price	Weight (lb.)											Comments
Toshiba VC420	100	9½	[6]	◑	◑	[7]	○	●	●	H,W	a,f,g,h,n,p,u,v,z	B,D,I,K,P
Hoover S1077033	110	12	[6]	[7]	◑	●	◑	●	◑	H,W	d,f,h,p,u	I,L
Eureka 3120B	120	11	[6]	◑	○	[7]	◑	○	◐	H	a,d,h,k,u	I
Sharp EC6310	100	9½	[6]	◑	◑	•	◑	●	●	—	a,f,g,p,w,z	B
Panasonic MC104H	66	6½	[6]	◑	◑	[7]	◐	●	●	—	a,d,f,g,h,p	B,H

1 Prices for canisters include attachments, except as noted.
2 Tested with standard roller-brush. Special roller-brushes of different design are available.
3 Includes cost of optional power nozzle.
4 Tested with optional power nozzle.
5 Judged without optional cord winder.
6 Judged unsuitable for deep-carpet cleaning.
7 Switch convenience judged while canister was carried during cleaning.

Specifications and Features

Weights are to nearest ½ lb.; those for canisters include stored tools, hose, and nozzle.

Except as noted, all models: • Have 1-speed motor. • Cannot be used as blower. • Use disposable dust bags.

Except as noted, all uprights: • Were awkward to use on stairs. • Require adjustment for carpet-pile height. • Have more than 2 pile-height adjustments. • Clean an 11-to-13-in. swath of carpet. • Require 6- to 7½-in. clearance to reach 1 ft. under furniture. • Have 20- to 25-ft. cord.

All canisters: • Have 16- to 23-ft. cord.

Except as noted, all canisters: • Have control for reducing suction. • Require 3½-in. clearance or less to reach 1 ft. under furniture. • Are fairly convenient to use on stairs. • Come with reinforced hose, metal wands with positive lock, floor/rug nozzle or power nozzle, wall/floor brush, upholstery nozzle,

(Continued)

dusting brush, and crevice tool. • Can store at least some tools in or on canister. *All power-nozzle canisters:* • Have means of running power nozzle on bare floor without brush revolving. *Except as noted, all power-nozzle canisters:* • Require no adjustment for carpet-pile height. • Clean an 11- to 13-in. swath of carpet.

Key to Advantages

A-Has both manual and automatic pile-height adjustment.

B-Has convenient mechanism for adjusting nozzle for different pile heights while cleaner is running. Highest suction of all uprights and judged most suitable of those models for use with above-floor attachments.

C-Revolving brush less likely than most to collect angel hair or other fluff.

D-Has power-assisted wheels; easier to push than most uprights.

E-Revolving brush is very close to one edge of nozzle housing, making it easier to clean carpet close to wall.

F-Somewhat higher suction than most other uprights.

G-Convenient, for an upright, to convert to suction-only use with optional accessories.

H-Can be used as blower.

I-Requires less clearance than full-sized uprights to reach under furniture, and was easier to use on stairs.

J-Has multiple speeds; lowest setting judged significantly quieter than highest.

K-Has main on/off switch and air-flow and motor-power indicator lights on canister, and has separate on/off switch with indicator light on power-nozzle handle. Has setting that changes motor power automatically in response to air-flow requirement. Handle is very comfortable.

L-Resisted clogging better than most canisters.

M-Overload protector guards against damage to cleaner if brush is jammed.

N-Overload protector guards against motor's overheating because of clog or overfull bag.

O-Power nozzle has window for monitoring condition of drive belt.

P-Has dirt-lever indicator gauge or (on *Hoover U4391*) transparent dirt container.

Q-Light goes on and unit shuts off when bag fills to preset level.

R-Has separate indicator to show blockage of wand, tool, or hose.

S-Indicator signals when dust bag or container is full.

T-Interlock prevents machine from operating without dust bag.

U-Long cord (30 ft. or more).

V-Brush is adjustable for wear.

W-Rug nozzle was easier to push on high-pile carpet than that of most suction-only models.

X-Red flag next to on/off switch indicates whether unit is switched on or off.

Y-Cleans relatively wide swath (13½ to 14½ in.).

Z-One of two uprights with convenient way to stop brush for bare-floor cleaning.

Key to Disadvantages

a-Has friction-fit wands that may be hard to pull apart; metal on *Eureka 3336A,* plastic ones on other models noted.

c-Changing pile-height setting judged inconvenient; control-knob settings not marked for height or carpet type.

d-Did not pick up thread from carpet readily.

e-Had difficulty picking up toothpicks from carpet.

f-Unlike most canisters, lacks means of reducing suction.

g-Tools cannot be stored in or on canister.

h-Pronounced tendency to clog with various kinds of litter.

i-Requires more clearance than other uprights to reach 1 ft. under furniture.

j-Stiff, unwieldly hose makes cleaner awkward to use in cramped quarters and to store.

k-Flimsy, unreinforced hose; on *Miele S230i* and *Eureka 1784B, 3336A*, and *3120B*, hose also tended to kink.

l-Canister does not stand on end; awkward to use on long staircases or to store.

m-Power nozzle has no detent to hold handle upright; handle often fell over.

n-Power nozzle's handle has no upright position; may be difficult to store fully assembled.

o-No positive lock between power-nozzle wand and hose; can come apart easily while vacuuming.

p-Lacks wide, bristled brush for walls and bare floors; available as option for *Hoover S1077033*.

q-Short cord for an upright (15 to 18 ft.).

r-Difficult to wheel about, especially on high-pile carpeting.

s-Revolving brush is farther from edge of housing than in other models; cannot clean carpet as close to walls.

t-Controls for turning unit on and off and for rewinding cord are poorly differentiated.

u-Exhaust poorly diffused and directed; especially likely to blow dirt about.

v-Cleans relatively narrow swath (9½ to 10½ in.).

w-Dusting brush has relatively narrow opening; likely to clog.

x-Has only 2 pile-height settings.

z-Suction fell off relatively rapidly as bag or dirt compartment filled.

Key to Comments

A-Has multiple speeds, but lowest setting judged not much quieter than highest.

B-Does not use disposable bags; has dust bin instead.

C-Has head lamp.

D-Comes with wall tool-rack (*Toshiba VC222* and *VC420*) or special radiator brush (*Miele S230*).

E-Comes with suction-only floor/rug nozzle in addition to power nozzle.

F-Comes with adapter, hose, and suction tools.

G-Initial assembly of vacuum cleaner difficult because of tightly fitting parts.

H-Cleaner does not wheel about; most conveniently used by holding motor unit in one hand and hose/nozzle in other.

I-Cleaner tends to fall over if wheeled about; most conveniently used by holding motor unit in one hand and hose/nozzle in other.

J-Has no bleed-type suction control, but suction can be reduced by lowering motor speed.

K-Brush-strip not replaceable as it is in most others; roller assembly must be replaced when bristles wear out.

L-Has plastic wands with positive-locking clamps.

M-*Royal M401PN* comes with cloth filter bag that can be used without paper bag; cloth filter bag optional on *Kirby*.

N-Unlike most uprights, has automatic pile-height adjustment.

O-Unlike most canisters with power nozzle, requires adjustment for cleaning carpets of different pile heights.

P-Power nozzle not electrically operated; powered by air flow.

Q-Hybrid model; comes with bare-floor, upholstery, and crevice-tool attachments that fit on end of motor or wands. Hose, dusting brushes, and power nozzle are optional.

R-Model discontinued or no longer listed in catalogue at the time the article was originally published in *Consumers Reports*. The test information has been retained here, however, for its use as a guide to buying.

S-According to company, a later designation is *1425G*.

T-According to company, available at $135 without power nozzle.

Furniture

Furniture polishes

Some say furniture should require an absolute minimum of care, maintaining that the oil or lacquer finish normally used on furniture protects the wood by sealing it. Others hold that the original finish itself needs a protective layer, usually a wax, that must be renewed periodically. Between those who recommend no wax and those who recommend lots of wax are those who temporize with a little wax sometimes.

The makers of furniture polish try to satisfy all the recommendations. Some products have no wax at all; others range from a little wax to nearly solid wax.

It doesn't matter much which you choose and use if your only aim is to keep the furniture presentable. But you should choose a polish that's easy to apply and that imparts only as much gloss as you want.

There are exceptions to that rule, however. If, say, your dining table shows signs of blotchy wax buildup, it makes sense to switch at least for a while to a product without much wax. Or if the table's finish has worn down so much that the raw wood is exposed to moisture and dirt, then a protective layer of wax would restore its appearance a bit and defer the day when refinishing is necessary. Antiques and pieces made of very expensive wood need special consideration, since the goal is to preserve the original finish or the pattern of the wood grain.

Keep your own needs in mind when you select a polish. Review the Ratings. But keep in mind that the addition of a lemon scent or a switch from aerosol to pump-spray bottle does not enhance the wood.

How much gloss?

The word "polish" implies that the product will impart a shine, but in truth the shine you get will depend not only on the nature of the polish, but also on the nature of the finish. For instance, no polish is likely to increase the gloss of a "piano top" high-gloss mahogany. It's already mirrorlike.

With lacquered walnut furniture that has a good-looking low luster, a "polish" should leave the wood looking just as it did when it started. That's an expectable result with a product that makes no bones about being a cleaner rather than a polish. It's also not so surprising with products that emphasize "no-wax" in their labeling. But many no-wax products can be buffed to a higher shine, too. No polish can turn a semigloss finish into anything like a high gloss, but some will provide a slight or moderate increase in gloss.

Since a change in gloss level, however subtle, is likely to be the most pronounced effect of using some furniture polishes, it makes sense to choose a product that will give you the gloss level you want.

Protection

A layer of polish should not only shine the wood but also resist staining, marring, and smudging.

Staining. You should be a little skeptical of claims that a polish "preserves all type of wood finishes," or "protects, beautifies fine furniture." It's really the furniture's finish and not the polish that provides the protection. Don't depend on a polish to provide any additional protection against staining.

Marring. A high-gloss surface can become marred when even something as unobtrusive as a coaster with a cup of coffee atop it is pulled across the surface of the polish. Most products won't mar, and those that do will be worse on very highly polished surfaces.

A polish that claims to hide scratches and nicks in furniture does so with the help of coloring material that darkens scratches to help disguise them. That works, but you shouldn't expect the polish to be an exact match for the color of the wood. The coloring may be too dark for use on light woods.

Smudging. Of all the problems that can affect furniture finish, smudges are the least severe. In fact, smudges often heal themselves and disappear. Smudging is usually more apparent on high-gloss panels; there should be none to speak of on oiled walnut finishes.

Polishes that retain smudges can be easily restored with a couple of swipes of a cloth. But that can become a daily chore if your furniture is heavily used, especially by children.

Effort

Polishes in aerosol containers are by far the easiest to work with. If anything, the aerosols apply polish too easily and too liberally, leaving too much polish on the wood and wasting too much on the cloth.

Pump sprays require a little more effort than the aerosols do, but provide better control. Pumps with a trigger in front are easier to use than those with a plunger on top.

Pourable liquids and paste waxes are meant to be applied with one cloth fairly soaked with the product, then wiped and buffed with a separate dry cloth. With several brands, you have to dampen the applicator cloth with water. Damp or dry, an oily, greasy applicator cloth coats your hands in no time at all; you can't touch anything without fear of smearing the stuff around.

The label on a few aerosols suggests a two-cloth application method: Spray some polish on one cloth, wipe on a thin coat of polish, then use a clean cloth to wipe off and buff. That's a good way to cut down on polish wasted or sprayed where you don't want it.

Any aerosol or pump-spray polish can also be used as a one-cloth dusting operation. When sprayed lightly on the cloth, any of the sprays will make the cloth tacky enough to pick up dust rather than just push it around. You're less likely to need a separate product for use between more thorough polishings.

Recommendations

If the oil or lacquer finish on a piece of furniture is worn and shabby, the cure doesn't lie with a furniture polish. What's needed is refinishing. But if the finish is in good shape, many polishes can help keep the piece looking presentable for a long time.

A good furniture polish should maintain the finish's original gloss, or lack of gloss: It shouldn't dull a high-gloss finish or put a hard, glossy shine on satin (semigloss), matte (no gloss), or natural finishes. A polish shouldn't affect the furniture's original color: A light finish should remain light and a dark finish should not be whitened. Polish should be easy to apply and rub up, and it should readily remove dirt in the process. It should form a coating that protects the finish from household stains—a coating that is itself stain resistant, that resists smudging, and doesn't give dirt much of a toehold. And, of course, any polish should be safe to use and store.

When using a product for the first time, try it out on an inconspicuous spot. Protect furniture finishes by making certain that lamp bases and *objets d'art* either have padded bases or are set on a cushioning material. Sponge up spills immediately to keep them from becoming stains or damaging the finish. When applying polish, it's easier and probably better to rub with the wood grain rather than against it. Use polish sparingly: You don't need to apply it each time you dust. That will help prevent unsightly polish buildup as well as make polishing easier.

Furniture polish won't protect against heat damage to the finish from hot items or from solvents such as the alcohol in a beverage, aftershave lotion, perfume, cough syrup, and the like. The best protection is a nonabsorbent barrier, such as a dish or coaster.

Ratings of furniture polishes

Listed by groups according to their effect on the gloss of unsealed, oil-finished wood; within groups, listed in order of estimated overall quality. Prices are as published in a January 1986 report.

Legend: ● ◐ ○ ◑ ● — Excellent ← → Poor

Brand	Price	Size, oz. or fl. oz.	Type①	Water resistance — Oil-finished	Water resistance — High-gloss lacquered	Alcohol resistance — Oil-finished	Alcohol resistance — High-gloss lacquered	Comments
■ The following showed a moderate increase in gloss on oil-finished wood.								
Favor Lemon	$1.49	7	A	◐	●	○	◐	C,D
Behold Lemon	1.38	7	A	○	●	○	●	C,E
Johnson Paste Wax	3.39	16	P	○	●	●	●	C,L
Butcher's Bowling Alley	3.59	16	P	○	●	●	●	C,M
Old English Lemon Creme	1.56	9	A	◐	●	○	◐	C,E
Pledge Lemon	1.63	7	A	◐	●	○	●	C,E,O
Pledge Original	1.72	7	A	○	●	○	●	C,E,O
■ The following showed a slight increase in gloss on oil-finished wood.								
Hagerty Vernax	6.22	16	L	◐	●	○	●	C
Parker's Lemon Oil	4.25	16	L	◐	●	○	●	A,M
Woolworth Lemon	1.46	14	A	◐	●	○	●	C,E
Old English Lemon	1.99	12	S	◐	●	◐	●	C,E
Goddard's with Lemon Bees Wax	4.49	10	A	◐	●	◐	●	C,D,O
Pledge Lemon	2.26	12	S	◐	●	◐	●	B,D,O
Old English Scratch Cover	2.86	8	L	◐	●	○	●	B,I,L,R
Kleen Guard with Lemon	1.19	7	A	◐	●	◐	●	C,E,H,O
Scott's Liquid Gold	3.51	14	A	◐	●	◐	●	A,G,Q
Scott's Liquid Gold	4.16	16	L	◐	●	◐	●	A,G,Q

Brand	Price	Size, oz. or fl. oz.	Type[1]	Water resistance — Oil-finished	Water resistance — High-gloss lacquered	Alcohol resistance — Oil-finished	Alcohol resistance — High-gloss lacquered	Comments
Trewax Tre Bien Lemon Oil	3.39	14	A	◐	◐	○	●	B,F,L,N
Guardsman Woodscent	3.99	16	L	◐	◉	◐	○	B,F,M,N,P
Guardsman Lemon	2.89	14	A	◐	○	○	●	B,F,N,P,R
Weiman with Lemon	3.02	12	A	◐	○	○	●	C,F,M,N,P

■ *The following showed no or almost no gloss increase on oil-finished wood.*

Brand	Price	Size, oz. or fl. oz.	Type[1]	Water resistance — Oil-finished	Water resistance — High-gloss lacquered	Alcohol resistance — Oil-finished	Alcohol resistance — High-gloss lacquered	Comments
Complete	2.36	16	S	◐	◉	◐	◉	B,K
A&P Lemon	1.38	14	A	◐	◉	◐	◉	C,D
Target with Lemon Oil	1.59	14	A	◐	◉	◐	◉	B,D
Wood Plus Lemon Scent	1.89	16	S	◐	◉	◐	◉	B,D,K
Endust	1.87	6	A	◐	◉	◐	◉	A,S
Amway Buff-Up	6.75	12	A	◐	◉	◒	◉	C
Wilbert Dri-Finish Lemon Oil	1.66	12	L	◐	◉	◐	◉	A,M,S
Furniture Magic with Lemon	2.79	13	A	◐	◉	○	◉	A,S
Safeway White Magic Lemon	2.09	14	A	○	◉	◒	◉	B
Old English Lemon Cream Wax	2.56	8	L	◐	◉	◐	◉	C,D,O
Formby's Lemon Oil Furniture Treatment	2.86	8	L	◐	◉	◐	◉	A,J,Q
Weiman Cream Lemon	2.96	8	L	◐	◉	◐	◉	A,M,N,P
Guardsman Lemon	3.24	16	S	◐	○	○	●	B,F,N,P

[1] *A = Aerosol spray. L = Liquid. S = Spray pump. P = Paste wax.*

Key to Comments

A- Caused no gloss increase on lacquered semigloss finish.

B- Caused slight gloss increase on lacquered semigloss finish.

(Continued)

C- Caused moderate gloss increase on lacquered semigloss finish.

D- Polish smudged on high-gloss finish.

E- Polish smudged on lacquered semigloss and high-gloss finishes.

F- Polished surface would mar when rubbed.

G- Label says product is for most natural-finished wood, which apparently precludes use on lacquered surfaces.

H- Label says not to apply product to unsealed surface, which apparently precludes use on oiled or Danish Modern furniture.

I- Contains dark pigment for help in hiding scratches. Not for light-colored woods.

J- Instructions say buffing isn't required, but buffing proved necessary.

K- Trigger-type pump easier to use than most other pump sprays.

L- Instructions call for separate application cloth.

M- Instructions call for separate, predampened application cloth; judged a bother.

N- Not as easy as most to buff.

O- Multiple coats tended to look uneven when applied to lacquered semigloss finish.

P- Tended to look scratchy when several coats were applied to high-gloss finish.

Q- Gloss diminished after 1 day on both oil-finished and lacquered semigloss finishes.

R- Gloss diminished after 1 day on oil-finished wood.

S- Gloss diminished after 1 day on lacquered semigloss finish.

Upholstery cleaners

Commercial cleaning services have the know-how and the hardware to rejuvenate upholstery that has lost its bloom, but commercial cleaning is expensive—it can cost close to $200 for a pair of large upholstered chairs and a matching sofa.

A cheaper alternative is to do the cleaning on your own, with a do-it-yourself cleaner.

Cleaning at home

Cleaning products' labels tell you how to apply the chemical and which fabrics it will work well on. Since some cleaners might alter a fabric's color or texture or make it shrink, be sure to test the one you buy before using it. Just apply a bit of cleaner to an inconspicuous patch of fabric, following the label instructions, and see what happens. Do that test no matter what the instructions say; the label may not tell you everything.

Convenience and safety

Most cleaners come ready to use, but a few liquids are concentrates and must be diluted.

To work a liquid into the upholstery you need a sponge, a soft-bristle brush, a clean cloth, or a piece of terry cloth towel. With some products, cleaner and soil are wiped off; other cleaners are vacuumed or brushed off when dry.

Some cleaners come with an applicator—usually a plastic brush or brush and sponge combination. Those applicators work well on vinyl, which surrenders dirt to bristles more readily than to cloth and is none the worse for rubbing. Brushes, however, can be hard on flat-surfaced textiles, especially after the yarn has been tenderized by wetting with cleaner. For those fabrics, an old terry cloth towel makes a gentle and effective applicator. After the cleaned upholstery has dried thoroughly, brushing won't hurt and may even help. With velvets and velours, brushing is essential to restore the fabric's nap.

A foam cleaner is simply sprayed on but you have to squeeze a liquid out of the bottle, which can be a problem. The cleaner's instructions may indeed warn against soaking the fabric. Despite the warning, it may not be possible to throttle the dribble once you stop squeezing. The result is soaked fabric, albeit cleaner, with wet padding that may deteriorate or smell bad later on. No such problem will arise with foam cleaners.

A powdered cleaner may go on dry. While it obviously won't soak fabrics, the powder is very powdery indeed; it gets on surfaces that you don't intend to clean, so you'll have to put in overtime with dust cloth and vacuum cleaner. As well as being messy to apply and remove, the powder may be an irritant: You should use a dust mask, safety goggles, and gloves when working with it. If you can move the furniture outdoors for cleaning, fine. If you can't, be sure the work area is well ventilated.

Recommendations

The most effective cleaners, applied with proper care to the proper fabric, will remove dirt and leave the fabric looking brighter. Even so, a good upholstery cleaner may cause unalterable changes in the feel, shape, texture, warmth of coloring, or overall look of the fabric. After cleaning, a flat-textured fabric might take on a blurry, plushy look because the cleaner has raised fibers here and there; plushy pile fabrics may become matted.

Try to get by with frequent dry brushing and vacuuming for as long as you can before using an upholstery cleaner. If you must use a cleaner, do the cleaning with all possible gentleness and use the least amount of cleaner that will do the job. It's far better to reapply a cleaner than to be overgenerous the first time. When applying cleaner, always wear rubber or plastic gloves to protect your hands.

House Cleaning

Air cleaners

Many years ago, opening a window to freshen room air was often unnecessary because the average house was so leaky that the air within changed a couple of times an hour. Today, that house, if it's been thoroughly weatherproofed, receives fresh air at half the old rate. That is still adequate ventilation, but smoke and smells linger much longer.

While smoke and smells may be unpleasant, at least they're easily perceived. Other pollutants are more insidious—gases such as combustion by-products from a gas range, formaldehyde from particle board, radon from some stone foundations or wells. These pollutants can become a concern in a new house built to be airtight; in such a house, the air may be exchanged only once every two or three hours.

In the late 1970s, a new product came along that promised to clear the air of tobacco smoke, odors, dust, pollen, and other pollutants—the tabletop air cleaner. Those early air cleaners worked by using a small fan to pull air through a filter.

The small fan/filter models paved the way for air cleaners using more expensive technologies. Some use a long-established method of removing particles from air, electrostatic precipitation. Others use a once-controversial device called the negative-ion generator. (The guide on page 55 explains those technologies.) Now, the range of designs and prices among air cleaners is wide.

Effectiveness

Any claim that an air cleaner can remove formaldehyde or other pollutant gases should be viewed with suspicion. In Consumers Union's tests, none of the air cleaners removed more than a trivial amount of formaldehyde gas. Studies have shown that reducing the level of gaseous contaminants in the air requires a much more elaborate filtration system than the ones these machines have.

Furthermore, air cleaners apparently aren't an effective way to deal with the health risk associated with radon gas and its by-products, a problem in some parts of the country.

If your windows can be opened and you can tolerate the chill, that may still be the best air cleaner of all. Contrary to popular opinion, opening a window in the dead of winter is not like shoveling dollars out the window. With the temperature 20°F outside and 70°F inside, opening the window a couple of inches—ventilation likely to be equivalent to that provided by a small exhaust fan—costs no more than a few cents an hour in lost heat.

Are air cleaners, then, completely useless? They certainly don't "purify" the air, but if all you want removed is smoke or dust, some can do a creditable job.

Tobacco smoke

The smell of tobacco smoke is one reason people buy an air cleaner. Getting rid of the smell, however, is more difficult than getting rid of the smoke. Smoke is particulate—resins and small particles are suspended in the air. Although the particles are as small as one one-hundredth of a micron (less than a millionth of an inch) in diameter, they can be trapped mechanically, in a filter—or in your lungs.

A small, inexpensive air cleaner—one with a small fan that draws relatively little air through a small, flat filter—is the least effective at removing smoke. Ion generators may be the most effective.'

Dust and pollen

An air cleaner can catch dust and pollen more easily than smoke because the particles are much larger—up to 100 microns (.004 inch) in diameter—but pollen and large dust particles are heavy enough that they don't remain airborne for long. They settle onto the floor and furnishings of a room until air currents or people stir them up. An air cleaner can remove dust and pollen only when they're in the air. It won't eliminate the need for dusting and vacuuming.

Airborne dust is a problem for many people, causing sneezing, wheezing, and other allergic reactions. A good air cleaner can be useful in treating dust allergy, especially if it's used during sleep. An air cleaner can also help those allergic to mold spores. An air conditioner is probably better than an air cleaner for people allergic to pollen. Unlike dust and mold spores, pollen originates outside the house, generally in weather warm enough for windows to be open. An air conditioner lets you circulate air without introducing pollen.

A guide to the three types of air cleaner

Fan/filter systems. Most air cleaners on the market use a fan to draw air through a filter. Fans' ability to move air varies a lot.

The filters vary, too. Granular materials—activated carbon, silica gel, a proprietary resin bead—are often part of the filter cartridge in an air cleaner. Such materials are supposed to interact with and trap various gases, but small-sized units probably can't use enough of the material to produce much effect.

Another type of filter is a web of synthetic or glass fiber. It works like a strainer, catching particles that pass through it. A fibrous filter can be made more efficient by increasing its surface area—typically, by folding it into accordionlike pleats. A "high-efficiency particulate air filter," or "HEPA filter," pleated and made of glass fibers, is the ultimate in fibrous filters; it has been used since World War II to filter air in hospitals and laboratories. Another way to increase the efficiency of a fibrous filter is to include fibers that have an electrical charge. The "electret" filter does this. Many particles in the air have a weak electrical charge, especially when the heating system has dried things out and the air is full of static electricity. An electret filter uses static electricity to catch small charged particles that otherwise would pass through. Electret filters are used in many top-rated models.

Electrostatic precipitators. Air cleaners using this technology draw in air with a fan past an electrode that gives airborne particles a relatively high electrical charge. Then the air passes a collector plate that has the opposite electrical charge, causing the dust and other charged particles to stick to it.

An electrostatic precipitator can be bought as a component to be built into a forced-air heating system (a method well worth considering if you want to clean the air in an entire house). Manufacturers such as Honeywell and Emerson Electric also sell room-size electrostatic precipitators similar in size and price to room air conditioners. Such models have been around for years, often purchased on an allergist's prescription. New, smaller models have been coming onto the market.

Negative-ion generators. Some twenty years ago negative-ion generators were sold as a miracle cure for just about any ailment, until the Food and Drug Administration called them quackery and halted their sale.

Now the negative-ion generator has been born again as an air cleaner. Negative-ion generators can be truly effective at removing smoke.

These devices spew a stream of electrons into the air, turning air molecules into negative ions. The ions apparently give airborne particles a negative charge. The particles than drift to grounded surfaces such as walls and ceilings, where they stick.

Negative-ion generators are also sometimes claimed to have a beneficial effect on people's minds. Some manufacturers mention the "revitalizing" effect of negative ions or the refreshing negative-ion charged air you find around waterfalls. Such claims have yet to be proven in well-controlled scientific studies.

Ratings of air cleaners

(As published in a January 1986 report.) Listed in order of estimated overall quality, based primarily on CU's tests for removal of tobacco smoke from the air. Models with a fan were tested at highest fan speed; effectiveness would decrease at slower speeds. None was effective at removing gaseous pollutants such as formaldehyde. Prices are suggested retail. + indicates shipping is extra.

Better ● ◐ ○ ◑ ● Worse

Brand and model	Price (replacement filter)	Type [1]	No. of fan speeds	Dimensions (H×W×D)	Weight	Smoke removal (room)	Smoke removal (desk)	Dust removal	Noise (high/low)	Airflow (high/low) [2]
Bionaire 1000	$299(16)	ION/PF	3	9×14×8 in.	13lb.	●	●	◐	○/◐	60/40
Pollenex Ionizer 1801	100(15)	ION/FF	4	11×13×9	8	●	●	◐	●/◑	100/30
Norelco HB9000	100(20)	PF	3	7×16×9	8	◐	◐	●	○/◐	80/50
Space-Gard 2275	140(12)	HE	2	14×12×12	12	◐	◐	●	○/◐	90/70
Oster 402-06	158(7)	EP	2	6×14×11	8	◐	◑	○	◐/◑	50/40
Pollenex 1099	60(15)	FF	4	11×13×9	7	○	○	○	●/◐	100/30
Norelco HB1920	36(6)	FF	2	7×7×7	3	◐	○	○	●/○	40/20
Ecologizer 8005	100(20)	HEPA	3	11×13×10	9	◑	○	○	○/○	100/80
Nature Fresh AP30B1	45+(5+)	PF	2	4×7×11	2	◑	◑	○	◑/○	20/10

(Continued)

Model										
Clean Aire 3	15(41)	FF	1	17×6[4]	◐	◐	◐	◐	○	20
Ecologizer 97305	29(5)	FF	1	9×5[4]	◐	●	●	●	◐	20
Pollenex 699	20(6)	FF	2	7×10×8	●	◐	●	◐	◑	20/10
Norelco HB1900	20(4)	FF	1	8×5×5	○	●	●	●	◐	10
Ecologizer 3605	40(5)	FF	2	8×7×9	◐	◐	●	●	○	20/20
Conair E3A	30(4)	FF	2	7×7×7	◐	●	●	◐	◑	30/20
Conair E1	22(4)	FF	1	8×5×5	●	●	●	●	◐	20

■ *The following models, all fanless ion generators, were severely downrated because they badly soiled walls in CU's smoke-removal test.*

Energaire	50	ION	0	9×3[4]	◐	●	•	●	●	—
Orbit	79	ION/C	0	8×3[4]	○	○	●	●	●	—
Amcor Freshenaire	44	ION	2	3×6×4	○	◐	●	●	●	—

[1] ION = ion generator; PF = pleated filter; HE = high efficiency; FF = flat filter; HEPA = high-efficiency particulate air filter designed to filter radioactive airborne contaminants; EP = electrostatic precipitator; C = collector.
[2] Cubic feet per minute.
[3] Continuously variable.
[4] Diameter; model is round.

SPECIFICATIONS AND FEATURES

Except as noted, all: • Have a fan. • Have plastic cabinet. • Have on/off switch.

Which machine cleans the most air?

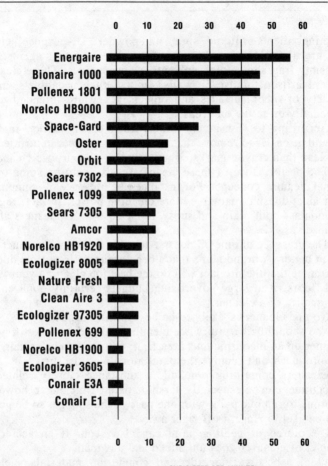

CUBIC FEET PER MINUTE

The graph shows the "effective cleaning rate" in cubic feet per minute (cfm) for each air cleaner running at its highest speed. The test room cleared itself at the rate of 2 cfm without an air cleaner at all.

All-purpose cleaners

The ingredients of liquid, spray, and powder "all-purpose" cleaners are a combination of detergents, grease-cutting agents, and possibly fragrance, color, solvents, or germicides. These cleaners are advertised for use on walls, floors, kitchen cabinets, and a variety of other surfaces and objects. They are intended to be especially effective on grease.

According to Consumers Union tests, pencil marks, in fact, should be easier to remove than grease. And grease, in turn, easier to clean than crayon marks, when using an all-purpose cleaner.

The performance of these cleaners casts doubt on some traditional cleaning concepts. For instance, the presence of ammonia in a product doesn't guarantee more cleaning power. In fact, regular ammonias, both plain and sudsy, don't do well as cleaners all by themselves.

The presence of pine oil doesn't necessarily mean a product will clean better. A brand name that's been around a long time doesn't guarantee that the product will do the best job cleaning your walls and floors. And large advertising budgets certainly don't ensure the quality of a cleaner.

No one cleaner is likely to be best for all purposes.

You should be careful when cleaning painted surfaces. Try the cleaner on an inconspicuous area first; you need to be certain that the product won't remove the paint along with the dirt.

Cleaners containing pine oil, a substance closely related to turpentine, can be especially harsh on paint. No cleaner, however, is prone to remove paint with one pass of the sponge, so be gentle and careful to rinse it off right away.

Discolored or peeling paint can also occur if an accidental droplet of cleanser goes unnoticed and unwiped.

Vinyl asbestos floor tile and countertop materials such as laminated plastic are highly resistant to marking by all-purpose cleaners, as is ceramic bathroom tile. But some sprays and liquids may turn glass frosty if not rinsed immediately. Metals are more vulnerable. Most cleaners leave marks on various metals common in the home—aluminum, copper, even stainless steel.

Many of the labels on these cleaners warn against using the cleaner on one or another surface, and the labels are nearly unanimous in warning against use on wood.

Cleaning cost

Since all-purpose cleaners come in three forms and have very different dilution rates, it's hard to make a meaningful price comparison using the price of the container alone. How much the cleaner costs to clean a given area is what counts.

Spray cleaners, as a group, are the most expensive cleaners to use. Cleaning a 10- × 10-foot kitchen floor with the average spray would cost at least $.60—four times the cost using an average liquid, six times the cost using most powders.

Sprays are expensive for two reasons—packaging and convenience. The pump-spray apparatus is a more costly package than a plain bottle or box. Refill bottles, available for some pump-spray cleaners, are a better value, since you don't have to pay for another spray attachment.

Some liquid cleaners may seem particularly cheap by the bottle, but their true cost is disguised because you dilute them less than you do other liquid cleaners.

Killing germs

A number of cleaners claim to kill germs. But routinely disinfecting the kitchen floor, the bathtub, or the sheets of a person sick with the flu does little to prevent the spread of germs. There are simply too many germs in the air and on everything in the house for the extermination of the odd hundred-thousand to have much effect. In circumstances that might require a germicide, follow a doctor's instructions.

Safety

The ingredients of all-purpose cleaners make a dangerous combination, especially if accidentally swallowed or splashed in the eyes.

They should be locked up if you have small, inquisitive children roaming about your house. Some spray cleaners can be turned to an "off" position, but that's hardly enough to keep a curious child from harm.

The labels of some cleaners advise wearing rubber gloves. More labels should give that advice; many products can be irritating to the skin. Cleaners that contain ammonia should never be used in combination with chlorine bleach, because the combination of ammonia and bleach can release hazardous gases.

Bathroom cleaners

A specialized bathroom cleaner won't clean bathroom dirt any better than an all-purpose liquid cleaner, and a bathroom cleaner doesn't fight mold and mildew as successfully as household liquid chlorine bleach.

Some bathroom cleaners are clearly a new product; a few are promoted, for instance, as "mildew stain removers." Others seem to contain variations on old all-purpose formulas, but like other specialized products, bathroom cleaners often cost more—as much as 50 percent more than all-purpose cleaners, ounce for ounce. The high unit price is somewhat disguised by the packaging (which also contributes to the extra cost). Bathroom cleaners generally come in pump-spray bottles or aerosol containers.

Special dirt

Inasmuch as bathroom cleaners are often labeled with a mild boast, such as "for the really tough jobs," Cosumers Union testers felt the stir of challenge in selecting a suitable test soil. They checked the new bathroom cleaners' mettle by concocting a laboratory version of soap scum, the kind of waxy gunk that accumulates persistently on bathroom tiles and fixtures.

Most bathroom cleaners should prove fairly potent. You can improve a cleaner's performance if you let it stand on a surface for a minute or so before wiping it off. Nevertheless, if a specialized bathroom cleaner does well, spraying on a good liquid all-purpose cleaner will do better, melting dirt away without any scrubbing.

Mildew

The inclusion of antimildew ingredients is one thing that makes a bathroom cleaner different from an all-purpose cleaner.

Cleaners that are likely to be most effective on mildew contain bleach, and undiluted chlorine bleach is, not surprisingly, the most effective mold-fighter of all.

Many cleaning products claim germicidal powers—a pointless boast even when true. Germs are everywhere, a condition of normal living. Killing them unselectively in an otherwise unsterile environment is futile. Any bacteria that a bathroom cleaner may wipe out will be replaced in short order.

Spots and stains

A bathroom cleaner isn't really strong enough to corrode common bathroom surfaces on mere passing contact, but it may mar certain materials if allowed to rest on them for some length of time, as might happen when spatters go unnoticed.

A cleaner won't do significant harm to tile, to acrylic plastic, or to a typical countertop material. Most cleaners will discolor aluminum and brass—particularly brass—and leave visible spots of reduced gloss on fiberglass. Note, however, that the potential exists only through oversight or misuse; products should not harm common bathroom surfaces if they're promptly rinsed and wiped off.

Much the same thing can be said about the cleaners' effect on human skin. Other tissues could be more seriously affected. Virtually all the products bear strong cautionary statements on their labels. Most advise keeping their bottles out of the reach of children. All the sprays can irritate the lungs, so some warn against use by persons with certain ailments—asthma and heart disease, for example. Ingestion is apt to lead to serious consequences; so may sprays or splashes in the eye, especially if you wear contact lenses. It's sensible to wear rubber gloves while using these products and to make sure the bathroom has good ventilation.

Recommendations

While a specialized bathroom cleaner offers respectable cleaning performance, a good all-purpose liquid cleaner costs less and does better.

Neither a bathroom cleaner nor an all-purpose cleaner is the most effective product for eliminating mold or mildew. If dampness and the fungal growth that accompanies it are particular problems in your bathroom, you may want to seek recourse in the best and cheapest mold fighter—ordinary household bleach.

Since bleach by itself isn't a good cleaner, there's a temptation to mix it with other products. Resist the temptation; it could prove quite hazardous. Bleach reacts almost instantly with acid to produce chlorine gas; and it reacts with ammonia and related alkaline substances to produce a combination of chlorine and other noxious gases. Never mix household cleaners or, for that matter, household chemicals of any kind.

Still, that's not to say that you shouldn't also use bleach in a room regularly scrubbed down with a cleaner. Just use the two separately. Make sure that you thoroughly rinse surfaces washed with bleach—something you'll want to do anyway because unwiped bleach can mar almost any smooth surface. What little bleach remains may soak into tile grout to prevent mold from taking hold again, but not in amounts great enough to hurt you when you next use another cleaner.

Ratings of bathroom cleaners

Listed in order of estimated overall quality, based primarily on cleaning ability. Prices are as published in a May 1986 report.

Better ◉ ◐ ○ ◑ ● Worse

Product	Price/size (oz.)	Cleaning ability	Mold-fighting ability	May mar these surfaces if left unwiped	Comments
Top Job All-Purpose	$2.07/28	◉	○	a,b,d	A
Tough Act Bathroom	2.09/17	◐	◐	a,b,d,e	A,E
Ajax All-Purpose	1.59/28	◐	◐	a,b	A
Mr. Clean All-Purpose	2.07/28	◐	◐	b	A
Boraxo Bathroom	1.99/17	◐	◑	b,e	A,E
Fantastik Bathroom	1.84/16	◐	◑	a,b	A,E
Tilex Mildew Stain Remover	2.54/16	○	◉	a,b,c,d,e	A,C,E
Lysol Bathroom	1.79/17	○	○	b,g	A,E
Dow Bathroom	1.69/17	○	◑	a,b,e	A,B
K Mart Bathroom	1.38/17	○	◑	a,b,e	A,B
Woolworth Bathroom	1.20/17	○	◑	a,b	A,B
Kroger Bright Basin, Tub & Tile	1.09/16	○	●	a,b,d	A,E
Carbona Tile & Bath	2.69/16	○	●	a,b	A,H
Chlorine bleach	.59 to 1.09/128	◑	◉	a,b,c,d,f	A,C
Easy-Off Mildew Stain Remover	1.99/16	◑	◐	a,b,d	A,C,E,F
X-14 Mildew Stain Remover	2.32/16	◑	◐	a,b,c,d,f	A,C,E
Lime-A-Way Bathroom/Kitchen	1.74/16	◑	◑	b,f,g	D,G
Scrub Free Bathroom	2.39/16	●	◑	b,e	D,E

Key to Surfaces
a-Aluminum.
b-Brass.
c-Chrome.
d-Semigloss enamel.
e-Fiberglass-reinforced plastic.
f-Phenolic laminate.
g-Stainless steel.

Key to Comments
A-Strongly alkaline.
B-Aerosol.
C-Contains bleach.
D-Strongly acidic. Should be somewhat better than most at removing hard-water stains.
E-Pump-spray bottle.
F-Dual safety closures, on nozzle and on neck of bottle.
G-Flip-top squirt bottle.
H-Squeeze bottle with brush applicator.

Drain cleaners

Chemical drain cleaners (or "drain openers," as many are now designated) are among the most dangerous products on the consumer market. Most drain cleaners are essentially lyes—caustic substances that, by definition, destroy or eat away material by chemical action. Others contain what amounts to a powerful mixture of poisonous solvents. Another type consists wholly of concentrated sulphuric acid, a very powerful corrosive.

Although chemical drain cleaners do promise a cheap, seemingly easy solution to what can be a serious household problem, they can be dangerous. It's better to consider these products only as a last resort.

Warnings

Caustic products containing lye should be properly labeled to indicate their hazards. The words "danger" and "poison" should appear repeatedly and conspicuously, as should the skull and crossbones symbol.

The emergency antidotes of choice for lye favored by public health authorities are extensive flooding with water after external skin contact, and one or two glasses of milk or water in the event the chemical has been swallowed. In either case, a physician should be called at once or the victim taken to an emergency care facility.

With some products the area in which the product is used should be well ventilated. In fact, it is prudent to leave the room during the time any chemical cleaner creates fumes.

Lye-based liquids usually come in a flexible plastic bottle that carries a warning to avoid squeezing the container when the cap is removed. Carelessness on that score could lead to a blinding squirt in the eye or a disfiguring splash on the skin.

Cleaners containing lye pellets can present hazards from accidental contact in yet another way: The labels sometimes recommend that you dole them out by the tablespoonful, but the opening in the can may be too small to admit a tablespoon; the pellets must be poured out, and they're easily spilled.

If a drain cleaner claims to be "noncaustic" or "noncorrosive," the label should state what the ingredients are; the product may still be poisonous if inhaled in heavy concentrations or if swallowed, and possibly hazardous to the environment once it enters a sewage system.

It almost goes without saying that any drain cleaner should have a child-resistant closure.

Recommendations

Chemical drain cleaners are dangerous to use, to be sure. To a grater or lesser degree, they can all attack human tissue in much the same way that they're expected to destroy and disperse organic matter in the drain. For that reason alone, they should be used with utmost care, precisely in accord with the manufacturer's instructions, and with the benefit of such commonsense protective measures as the wearing of safety goggles and rubber gloves. Furthermore, you should never use more than one drain cleaner at a time or mix it with other household chemicals.

Moreover, if a chemical drain cleaner doesn't work, it will remain in the plumbing system as a constant menace. Sink drains that have captured a ferment of lye, strong solvent, or sulphuric acid are too treacherous for a homeowner to tamper with further. Don't try to clear the drain by using a plunger or some pressurized drain opener; doing so only invites a dangerous splashback. There's no reasonable choice except to call for a plumber who must deal with a clogged and contaminated drain, and be sure to tell the plumber what's been added to the drain.

It may be wiser to rely on two tried-and-true plumber's aids before using chemicals: the old-fashioned rubber plunger and, for stubborn clogs, the plumber's "snake" or drain auger.

With a rubber plunger, available for a couple of dollars in hardware stores, you can generate as much as eight pounds of pressure on a drain blockage. There's not much to know about using a plunger: You remove the sink stopper and block up any overflow opening with a sponge or rag; leave an inch or two of water in the sink; depress the plunger in one corner of the sink (to get the air out of it), slide it over the drain, and pump it vigorously straight up and down. Once the drain opens, pour in a kettle of boiling water. (Many people pour boiling water down the drain every week or so to keep it clean; that's a good preventive measure).

You may also want to buy a small snake. It's a long, flexible steel cable that you feed into the drain. Its flexibility allows it to crawl to the site of the blockage. There it may break up the clog or grab unbroken fragments and pull them back out.

If you do not have great knowledge of plumbing you should be aware that there are still other avenues open for unclogging drains. For example, many sink traps have a threaded plug at the bottom of the U-bend in the pipe under the drain, where clogs are likely to occur. You can clear them by removing the plug and scraping out the debris.

Ratings of chemical drain cleaners

Listed, except as noted, in order of estimated overall effectiveness. Drain cleaners are among the most dangerous consumer products available. CU strongly recommends that nonchemical methods of unclogging drains be tried rather than one of these products. Unless otherwise indicated, all have child-resistant closure. Costs per use are for CU's tests on clogged drains as published in a March 1983 report.

Better ◉ ◖ ○ ◗ ● Worse

Product	Price	Type	Size (oz. or fl. oz.)	Clogged kitchen drain	Sluggish kitchen drain	Clogged bathroom drain	Sluggish bathroom drain
Lewis Red Devil	$1.07	Lye pellets	13	◉	◉	○	○
Crystal Drano	1.51	Pellets[1]	12	◉	◉	◗	◗
Double Agent	1.82	Liquid/pellets[2]	16	◉	◉	●	○
Servistar	3.19	Lye liquid	32	○	◉	○	◗
Liquid Drano	1.44	Lye liquid	32	◗	◉	◗	○
Plunge	1.01	Lye liquid	32	◗	◗	◗	◗
Mister Plumber	1.14	Lye liquid	32	●	◉	◗	●
Liquid-Plumr	1.43	Lye liquid	32	●	◗	●	◗

■ *The following product was downrated because package label lacked listing of ingredients and first-aid instructions; in CU's judgment, this invites improper, casual handling of hazardous chemicals. Only product tested that lacks child-resistant closure.*

Amway Drainmate	5.95	Solvent[3]	16	◗	◗	○	◗

■ *The following product was downrated because it was judged by far the most dangerous drain cleaner tested.*

Instant Plumber	4.20	Sulphuric acid	32	◗	◉	○	○

[1] *Product is mixture of lye and aluminum pellets.*
[2] *Sold as bottle of lye liquid and packet of aluminum pellets. Size given is for liquid only.*
[3] *Contains 1,1,1-trichloroethane as its major ingredient, according to CU analysis.*

Garbage and trash bags

You can spend a lot of time studying the packages of garbage and trash bags on the supermarket shelves and still make a mistake buying the kind you need.

The first mistake you can make is thinking that a bag of a certain capacity necessarily fits a container of the same capacity. In fact, that depends on how the capacity is measured. If a manufacturer wants to make the most of a bag's size, it measures capacity by filling the bag all the way to the top and says the bag "holds up to" however many gallons. An open bag may be a satisfactory way of packaging leaves, but it's hardly convenient or tidy for household garbage. Fortunately, most bags are described as fitting up to a certain size of container. Some package labels give both bag and container measurements. Either way, you do have to know the size of your container. Then there are the bags with built in "purse string" closures that permit closing the top of a full bag, providing you don't pull too hard and rupture the plastic.

A second mistake you can make in buying garbage bags is in misinterpreting refuse terminology. "Wastebasket" bag would seem to be a fairly straightforward designation, except when it's called a "large waste" or a "medium garbage" bag. According to some of the manufacturers, when you throw something away indoors, it's "garbage"—as in "tall kitchen garbage bag." Outdoors, a discarded item is "trash." A small trash bag is sometimes allowed to hold grass ("trash and lawn"). The largest bags are reserved for "lawn and leaf," sometimes condensed to "yard" or "lawn clean-up."

Clearly, when buying, you have to use the label terminology in conjunction with the dimensions given on the package, and you have to read the dimensions carefully. Some of the packages offer pictures to help you choose the right size, but since one size of garbage can often look like another, the pictures may add to the confusion.

Wastebasket. The category commonly includes bags that measure 22 × 24 inches, though the capacity given on the packages can be "28 quarts," "32 quarts," and "8 gallons." Some of the bags are called "large waste" or "medium garbage" instead of "wastebasket."

Tall kitchen. This group is 2 feet wide, and a typical bag in this group is about 2½ feet tall. Labeled capacity varies from 11 to 15 gallons.

Small trash. These generally measure 2 feet 4 inches × 2 feet 11 inches, though from the labels you might think there are two different sizes in the group. Some labels say the bags hold 26 gallons, and others say they fit up to 20-gallon cans. This size is intended for old style, small garbage cans with a nominal size of 20 gallons, and the bags fit those cans very tightly.

Large trash. This category comprises two sizes—bags that fit up to 30-gallon cans and bags meant for 32- or 33-gallon cans. The 30-gallon bags are the most popular size of all garbage bags. They work much better in small garbage cans than the bags in the previous category, as they leave plenty of extra bag to gather up, tie, and hold on to if you have to remove the bag from the can. Common dimensions for 30-gallon cans are about 2½ feet wide × 3 feet high.

However, 30-gallon bags may not fit 30-gallon cans. It depends on the shape of the can. If the can has a flared or squared top, the mouth of the bag may not be wide enough to go over it without ripping. In that case, you'll have to buy a 32- or 33-gallon garbage bag. These are about 3 inches wider and 4 inches taller than the 30-gallon bags, and they fit 32-gallon cans snugly.

Lawn and leaf. Most lawn and leaf brands are a few inches taller than the 33-gallon bags. Though their labeled capacity ranges from 39 gallons to 6 bushels (48 gallons), lawn and leaf bags fit nicely in 32-gallon garbage cans.

Thickness

Is there any way you can predict how good a bag is, short of conducting your own durability tests? Does the thickness of the plastic or the number of piles as given on the label tell you anything about the quality of a bag?

You really can't count on a correlation between thickness and overall strength. Plastics technology is such that very thin plastic,

1.5 thousandths of an inch thick (1.5 "mils"), can also be very strong. A bag made of it can hold a good load of garbage, perhaps as much as a thicker bag (e.g., a 3-mil bag).

A puncture often starts a bag breaking. When plastic film is punctured and then stressed, the hole tends to become a big split in one direction or another. A bag that's especially thick should be better at resisting punctures.

Holes are also apt to start at imperfections in the plastic, which can be caused if recycled polyethylene or low-quality ingredients were used in the manufacturing process. In theory, a garbage bag with more than one ply should have improved strength, since a split in one ply is contained by the other ply, and the chances of imperfection occurring in the same spot on both plies are quite small. Adding a third ply could further reduce the chances of a split bag.

That's the theory. It's hard to check if the theory is true because no manufacturer states on the label that its bag is only one ply, and you can't always tell how many plies a bag has just by looking at it. Many large trash bags are labeled as two ply, however, and there may be a few three-ply bags on the market.

Recommendations

No bag, however strong, will withstand pokes from broken glass, coat hangers, or sharp twigs. With that limitation in mind, start with a heavier-duty bag only if a lighter bag doesn't do the job at all.

Generic garbage bags

Generic products are the so-called "no-brand products" or, more recently, branded products whose packaging is intended to create a "generic," low-priced association in a shopper's mind. Generic products are based on the assumption that there are "price market" buyers who will forgo fancy or convenient packaging, and perhaps put up with lower quality merchandise, in return for a cheap price. Savings in promotional costs can be added to savings in the packaging and in the product itself because the no-brand products don't have to be advertised very heavily.

Unfortunately, it's difficult to know whether the generic bag you bought last month will be the same as the one you buy this month.

One way a distributor can sell inexpensive generic garbage bags is by purchasing odd lots, overruns of production from the many manufacturers that make plastic garbage bags. If this were a universal practice, quality would indeed be a chancy thing. More often, say people in the supermarket business, a distributor orders products from a particular manufacturer. Supermarkets have always been careful about the consistency of their own store brands, since these products are closely connected with the image of the supermarket itself! More and more stores have decided that their generic products should also be consistent in quality.

So today, there are both generics and there are "branded generics"—plainly packaged products with a brand name that's unique to a supermarket chain. Branded generics are really just another, cheaper store brand. As with a store brand, it's in the supermarket's own interest to maintain some kind of control over the quality of the branded generics. Sometimes the branded generics are segregated in their own aisle, as the original generic products usually are, or they may be on the shelves right beside the advertised brands.

Generic bags are often quite a bit cheaper than the name-brand bags, especially in the popular large trash size. In that category, you can save as much as 50 percent. The saving in the lawn and leaf and tall kitchen size is as much as 30 percent, while the saving in the small trash size is only about 10 percent. In order to be low priced, generic garbage bags are likely to be made of thinner plastic than a name-brand bag. Bear in mind that thick plastic isn't necessary for a good quality garbage bag. Many of the name-brand bags may actually be too good for your garbage.

Experimenting with a generic garbage bag or two may be worthwhile. A good place to start experimenting is with one of the branded generics.

Glass cleaners

Judging by the number of glass-cleaning products on the market, each apparently formulated specifically for the purpose, it would seem that washing windows and mirrors is akin to the fine art of restoring old paintings. In fact, glass is hard and doesn't absorb dirt. Its smooth surface should be easy to clean.

The trick with any pump spray, aerosol, cream, or home-made mixture is to use it sparingly to avoid streaks and spots. Any unsightly residue that remains is easily removed by wiping the glass with a damp towel.

Side effects

Simple as they may seem, there are a few things you should be aware of when using glass-cleaning products.

Effects on nonglass surfaces. Although the chemicals in cleaning substances may not harm glass itself, they may damage more vulnerable surfaces. (A number of glass cleaners are labeled with cautions to that effect.)

No glass cleaner is completely safe on all surfaces. For example, colored liquids (most are tinted blue) may stain white enamel, and all cleaners temporarily soften the paint at least a bit. Varnished surfaces, aluminum, and automobile paint are generally unaffected by cleaners, but wood coated with furniture-grade lacquer can be somewhat vulnerable to all types of cleaners. Therefore, with any product, you should quickly remove drips or spray from surfaces around the glass.

Antifogging properties. A few products claim to deter fogging of glass, but a few drops of liquid dishwashing detergent applied with a damp paper towel also prevent fogging.

Safety. Although a glass cleaner is not likely to be more than moderately alkaline, an inadvertent splash in the eye can be irritating and should be flushed away promptly with fresh water. A swig or two of a glass cleaner by a curious child might cause gastric distress or perhaps worse. (All cleaning products, of course, should be kept well out of reach of small children.) Some products have first-aid instructions on the label to help you cope with such accidents; some have warnings only.

Packaging and labeling. Cleaners generally come in or are packaged with a container that provides a convenient means of application—a push-button can for the aerosols and a pump spray or trigger pump-spray container for the liquids.

Recommendations

Try water first. Plain tap water should clean dusty glass in your home as effectively as any commercial product.

If the glass you want to clean has accumulated layers of stubborn grime, you might try a thick liquid cleaner that you apply, allow to dry, and then wipe off. The mild abrasive action has much more effect on tough soil than the chemical action of other cleaners.

There may be a middle ground in which neither water nor an abrasive cleaner suits your needs exactly. If, for instance, you have a lot of glass that hasn't been washed in a long while but isn't caked with soil, consider mixing up a batch of your own cleaner.

One old home brew is a half-cup of vinegar per gallon of water, but this mixture is really no more effective than water. Another home concoction is a half-cup of "sudsy" ammonia in a gallon of water. It's better than vinegar in water, but still not perfect.

A third do-it-yourself mixture is much better. Its formulation is only slightly more complicated than those of the other two: a half-cup of "sudsy" ammonia, a pint of common 70 percent isopropyl rubbing alcohol, a teaspoon of liquid dishwashing detergent, and enough water to make a gallon in all.

This effective brew—mixed from pint and quart quantities of ingredients bought at undiscounted retail prices—can be made cheaply if you don't count the cost of your own labor and the price of a spray container to dispense it. It contains all the effective ingredients—ammonia, alcohol, and detergent—found in many commercial preparations, although commercial manufacturers may vary the proportions.

Oven cleaners

There are only two effective ways to clean an oven that isn't self-cleaning. You can scrub it clean—a difficult, messy, and tiring job—or you can reduce the drudgery quite a bit by using a chemical cleaner. In either case, oven cleaning ranks very high on the list of onerous household chores. It's dirty. It's undignified. It's hard on your back and it's usually hard on your skin and lungs—as well as on any inanimate objects that get in the way.

Most oven cleaners are aerosols, a few are pump-operated sprays or brush-on pastes.

In their last tests, Consumers Union's chemists turned up an interesting result: a nontoxic aerosol that is safe to use and that does a good job of oven cleaning and needs only one or two applications to do the trick.

Safety

When you roast a duck in orange sauce, you may don an apron and, perhaps, an oven mitt. When you clean the oven, you may want to wear an apron, rubber gloves, safety goggles, and a face mask. That's what you really should protect yourself with when using a caustic chemical cleaner, a category that includes just about every brand except the nontoxic **Arm & Hammer**. A typical cleaner contains lye—one of the most dangerous substances you can use around the house. The labels on toxic cleaners appropriately state that the products can burn skin and eyes. Most labels warn about the hazards of inhaling fumes (although some of the cleaners are lemon-scented, a strange state of affairs for a toxic product). They warn about ingestion. They outline first-aid treatment in case an accident occurs.

Not only do you have to worry about protecting *yourself* from a toxic oven cleaner, but you must also take care to protect nearby floors, counters, and other surfaces. Spread newspaper on the kitchen floor as most of the cleaners' labels correctly advise. Be careful not to splash the cleaner on aluminum, chrome, baked enamel, copper, or painted surfaces.

Arm & Hammer carries no such warnings—and needs none. It contains no lye. It does contain nontoxic ingredients that, when heated, work as lye does to loosen oven grime by reacting with the fats and oils in the grime. **Arm & Hammer** can be safely used without rubber gloves or other paraphernalia. It won't irritate your eyes or nose, and it won't damage kitchen surfaces.

Cleaning

The instructions for use on most oven cleaners vary. You apply some products to a heated oven, others to a cold oven. With some, you wait just ten to thirty minutes, then wipe off; others must remain on the oven surface for hours, or even overnight. Many labels give more than one method.

Products whose labels give alternate methods will sometimes be more effective in one mode than in another.

Convenience

From a convenience standpoint, the most important consideration is getting the task over with quickly. Aerosols are the quickest and easiest to apply. Repeated pumping of a pump spray can be a bit tiring and brush-on pastes are tedious to apply.

Wiping away the soil is the messiest part, no matter what product you use. With most of these cleaners, you can use a damp or water-soaked rag or sponge. Some brands may recommend using a vinegar and water solution, which only complicates matters.

The containers of toxic cleaners have the appropriate warnings about safe use, but the containers *themselves* can present safety problems. Some may not have a child-proof closure, for instance, and a pump spray may not have a locking mechanism.

Recommendations

Arm & Hammer is safe to use. It's easy to apply, and it does a very good job.

If you have to choose a product other than **Arm & Hammer**, make it easy on yourself and choose an aerosol. The pump-operated sprays aren't as easy to use. The brush-on pastes are difficult to use and not very effective.

What the price means in terms of the cost of cleaning your oven really depends upon how dirty the oven is. Few labels state how many cleanings you can expect from a container. Most would probably allow two cleanings of a moderately grimy oven.

Paper towels

A lot of paper towels are store brands, sold by regional supermarket chains. That's partly because paper is bulky and therefore expensive to ship over long distances.

Many name-brand towels, are also sold to only part of the country. Even a brand that's advertised nationally may not be the same paper towel from one place to the next. The differences between the "same" products can be so great that you'd think they were different brands.

Strength and absorbency

The ideal paper towel absorbs a lot of liquid and stays strong when wet. Some paper towels do well in both types of tests. That's a tribute to paper manufacturers, because processes that make paper absorbent tend to make it weak and those that make paper strong tend to make it nonabsorbent.

Various techniques to overcome the weakness of absorbent paper have been developed. Some paper towels for example, are hybrids of cloth and paper. A few have two plies of paper sandwiched around a netting of nylon threads, and a few may have three plies of paper.

In general, two plies are better than one, and three better than two. The exceptions to the rule are the exceptional towels: those that are very thick, for instance. But there are other exceptions: Some two-ply towels have plies that are flimsy.

It shouldn't be surprising, then, to find that the differences between what towels can do are great. A "thirsty" towel may soak up about fourteen times its weight in water. A towel with poor absorbency will hold about six times its weight, or about one-half ounce of water. Another aspect of absorbency is how fast a towel absorbs liquids. A towel with a high-absorption capacity is not truly helpful if the carpet soaks up the spilled coffee faster than the towel can.

The best towels soak up water drops in less than a second; the worst take more than thirty seconds. For oil absorbency the range can be from two seconds to more than four minutes.

Linting and colorfastness

Paper towels shouldn't deposit patches of lint when you're washing windows.

There's another problem possible with paper towels—wet towels that leave some of their color behind when used to wipe white place mats or white walls. A great many towels come in colored patterns, and most also come in solid colors. Sometimes the colors rub off, sometimes they don't. Yellow, blue, green, and pink are most likely to come off at least some of the time. The obvious solution if colorfastness matters to you: Stick to white paper towels.

Tearing off

Some paper towels consistently refuse to tear at the perforation. Admittedly, towel-tearing problems may not always be the towel's fault. If the entire roll often pulls out of the towel holder and falls onto a frosted cake or into pancake batter, the holder may be too loose. It's also possible to get rogue rolls of a brand of paper towel that has never given trouble before. The perforations between towels are cut with a blade before the towels are rolled up in the paper factory. If the blade isn't kept sharp, those towels won't tear off correctly. At times, though, no matter which direction you pull or where you grab, you get only a piece of a towel. That's not your fault, nor is it when a downward pull changes a roll into a sinuous snake of paper. A side-to-side pull produces the largest number of intact towels in that situation.

Recommendations

Paper towels that are strong and absorbent are generally the most expensive.

Are strength and absorbency really worth double the money in a throwaway product? You may decide those qualities are not that important. You don't need the best towel to wipe up a small spill or even to dry your hands between cooking chores; the cheapest paper towel you can find may be good enough for that. You might consider keeping a roll of good paper towels on hand for the chores that are made much easier with a quality paper towel—washing windows, for example—and using an inexpensive towel for day-to-day cleanups. You may even decide against disposable paper towels entirely when sponges, dishtowels, rags, and old newspapers still work as they did in the past.

Price shopping among towels of similar quality can be difficult. Towels come in too many different sizes and quantities for easy comparison. If you frequently substitute paper towels for a mop or for blotting up large spills, buy by the square foot. They're not as great a bargain by the towel, since the individual towels may be quite long. Large towels may be fine for doing windows and big jobs, but they're a lot of paper to use for blotting up the wet ring left on a table by a glass of iced tea.

If you generally use paper towels for cleaning up a dribble of oil here or a smudge of jam there, you'll get best value with a cheap towel.

Be aware of towels packed two or more rolls to a package. Buying towels that way is often more expensive than buying single-roll packages. Compare prices and packages for yourself in the store.

Scouring cleaners

All scouring products—both liquids and powders—are abrasive, and a little bit of abrasion goes a long way. A really abrasive scourer can make the job of removing baked-on grime from ovens and barbecue grills (where appearances aren't important) easier. The same abrasive scourer will play havoc with the shine of expensive stainless steel cookware, or with the unmarred surface of a new porcelain enamel sink. The bigger and harder the gritty abrasive particles in a product, the more likely it is to damage the surface being cleaned.

Most scouring powders use silica, a quartz dust so hard it can scratch glass, plastic, and the enamel surface of your sink. Many of the "soft" liquid and powder cleansers use milder abrasives such as feldspar or calcium carbonate, but even the softest will do some damage.

Effectiveness

Cleansing powders, generally, are a mixture of abrasives, soaps, detergents, bleaches, and alkaline or acidic chemicals. The abrasives help to lessen the labor needed to remove grime. The detergents or soaps help to wet the surface being cleaned, cut grease, and suspend some solids. The bleaches help to remove stains, particularly from old, abraded surfaces. The alkaline or acidic chemicals enhance the cleaning action of the detergent and have a cleaning action of their own (removing aluminum pot scrapes from porcelain enamel, for instance).

Few products claim disinfecting ability, although cleansers containing bleach are likely to have some degree of disinfectant power. Disinfecting doesn't mean much, however. Germs are everywhere. A disinfectant will kill germs, but they'll be back again as soon as you finish cleaning.

Grit

Regular use of any abrasive scouring product will gradually scratch the shiny surfaces of sinks, bathtubs, porcelain enamel, and kitchen appliances. Harsh abrasives can also damage plastic, glass, paint, and polished metals.

The least abrasive products will leave only a satiny glaze on porcelain after a good deal of rubbing. The average will leave it moderately abraded. The most abrasive products will dull porcelain quickly.

Overall, powders are more abrasive than liquids, but not always. Just about any cleaner will scratch acrylic plastic and aluminum; none can be safely used on mirror-finish metal. Generally, a scouring product that is gentle on porcelain is also gentle on plastic and aluminum.

Whatever product you use, remember that the effects of abrasion are cumulative. You might not scuff up the tub right away even if you scrub like blazes, but light scrubbing over twenty years will eventually ruin the finish. To help minimize these effects, don't apply scourers with a heavy hand and a hard pad. Use a sponge or a soft cloth at first, and use a rougher applicator only if you can't get the cleaning results you want.

Stains

A powerful, abrasive cleaner that's good for general cleaning may not be the best for getting at stubborn stains. Stain removal depends on chemical action, usually the action of bleach. Most products are alkaline, meaning they are best at removing dirt, grease, grape juice, and other organic stains. The few acidic cleansers are useful for dissolving hard-water stains or metallic, colored spots.

Scouring products vary in their ability to remove common stains:

Aluminum scuffs. Some sinks, especially older ones with a bit of their enamel worn off, tend to collect scuff marks from aluminum pots and pans. A good cleanser should remove those marks readily after being allowed to be in contact with the stain for approximately fifteen minutes.

Rust. Only the special-purpose product discussed on page 84 is likely to be effective on rust or green metallic deposits.

Tea. Chlorine bleach products should remove tea stains readily. Nonbleach products won't do it at all.

Safety

Cleaning products that contain chlorine bleach or acid should not be mixed with other cleansers. Chlorine bleach reacts with ammonia or acid and produces dangerous gases.

When you're cleaning, take off jewelry or wear rubber gloves. These scouring cleaners can dull the polish on a ring, scratch soft gems such as pearls and opals, and the chlorine bleach in some of the products can discolor silver.

Pads and sponges

Many scouring pads claim they can do almost any scrubbing chore. Some bill themselves as products that can handle the "tough" jobs, suggesting they are quite abrasive.

In fact, some are gentle, some are tough—too tough, in fact, for many jobs.

Abrasives

Light-duty plastic mesh pads or reinforced sponges are probably the best choice for cleaning highly polished metals. Light-duty pads are generally safe to use on plastic countertops. Light-duty products are often labeled as well for use on nonstick-coated cookware, but repeated scourings may reduce the nonstick properties of the coated surface.

It's safest to clean porcelain enamel with a cellulose sponge and powdered or liquid cleanser than with any kind of scouring pad.

Cleaning ability. Overall, light-duty pads require a lot more rubbing than the heavy duty. They are less efficient with baked-on oven grime than powdered cleaners.

Removing gooey food residue is a different kind of chore—messy, but light duty. Plastic mesh pads and metal spirals are the most suitable type of pad for this job; they pick up the gloppy remnants and part with them easily when they are rinsed. Heavy-duty, abrasive-faced sponges and steel-wool pads are the least suitable. The former are more inclined to spread mess than pick it up; the latter won't let go of it in rinsing (and they lose any soap they contain—and therefore rust resistance—in the bargain).

Thorough cleaning of porcelain enamel sinks is a job usually relegated to powdered cleaners. Light-duty scourers (plus detergent) are suitable for cleaning porcelain in good condition. Heavy-duty, abrasive-faced sponges and pads are much too abrasive for such cleaning and will prematurely age the finish. On an abraded surface, however, pads aren't able to get into the tiny hairline cracks that only a fine, powdered cleanser can reach. On that type of surface, too, metal pads are likely to leave marks.

Recommendations

You probably need more than one scourer, depending on what you have to clean. A new porcelain enamel sink or tub, for instance, doesn't want a highly abrasive, powdered cleanser; such a cleanser will erode the surface and make it look old before its time. In fact, if you can clean that sink with just a wet sponge, some detergent, or a nonabrasive, all-purpose household cleaner, or a product specially formulated for the purpose—all the better. On the other hand, an old, abraded porcelain surface may require a more abrasive powdered cleanser with chlorine bleach to get into tiny cracks where the stains are.

To clean highly polished stainless steel or aluminum cookware, try the least abrasive product—a plastic mesh pad—first. (Although here, too, if a soapy sponge or cloth will do the job, that's preferable.) Matte-finished metals can stand a little more abrasion than shiny metals. Cleansers can actually help to brighten matte-finished stainless steel, and steel wool can do some of the same for matte aluminum. Rub with the grain to minimize any abrasion.

Nonstick cookware and laminated countertops fare best with a soapy sponge or gentle abrasion—a plastic mesh pad or mesh-covered (reinforced) sponge. Save highly abrasive scrubbers for the nasty chores, like cleaning the oven.

Zud

Scouring cleansers generally can't remove hard-water stains, rust, or the green stains that appear below the faucets in some houses with copper plumbing, but **Zud**—a special-purpose powder—claims it "works where ordinary cleansers fail."

Zud is, in fact, able to remove some rust stains that other products can't even touch. **Zud** can also remove tea stains as well as a good regular cleanser. It can also do a respectable job of dissolving aluminum scuff marks without scrubbing.

Zud doesn't work well on ordinary grime that accumulates on porcelain. Furthermore, it is quite abrasive.

Zud gets its stain-fighting power from oxalic acid, a very toxic chemical that attacks rust stains. Use **Zud** with care, and keep it safely out of the reach of small children.

Powered scrub brush

The #50 **Black & Decker Scrub Brusher Model 9385**, a rechargeable, battery-powered brush, is supposed to clean tubs, floors, refrigerators, carpets, whitewall tires, and more.

The **Scrub Brusher** comes with two bristle brushes that snap in and out easily. The larger brush, which looks like the type used on a vacuum cleaner, is intended for the bulk of cleaning chores. The smaller brush is for hard-to-reach areas and corners.

The **Scrub Brusher** effectively cleaned finger marks from test panels used to simulate painted walls in Consumers Union's tests. It was also very good at cleaning a painted brick wall, a sealed concrete floor, a refrigerator, and a car's wheels and wheel covers. It was quite good at removing surface dirt from sheet-vinyl flooring.

But the **Scrub Brusher** didn't do very well with some fairly difficult chores: cleaning vinyl asbestos floor tiles, whitewall tires, and shower tiles. Scouring by hand worked better.

Although the scrubber can be a labor saver for light, quick cleaning, holding and guiding it for extended periods proved to be tiring. It had one other problem, especially on vertical surfaces: The **Scrub Brusher** made liquid cleaner foam and spatter.

Black & Decker says that 20 percent of the batteries' capacity can be restored with two hours of charging. (A full charge takes at least sixteen hours.) The manufacturer also claims up to thirty minutes of scrubbing on a single charge. That claim may be realistic for light cleaning jobs, but not for moderate or heavy tasks. In a test simulating a heavy hand on the scrubber, the motor stopped after twenty-two minutes. After a two-hour recharge, the motor ran only three minutes, then stopped.

If age or infirmity makes cleaning a painful chore, or if you just want a little help with some light cleaning, the **Scrub Brusher** can be useful. In other situations, it doesn't have much of an advantage over a hand brush or a scouring pad.

Ratings of scouring cleansers

Listed in groups in order of cleaning ability; within groups, listed in order of increasing abrasiveness and then in order of decreasing stain removal. Products judged equal in those qualities are listed alphabetically. Prices are as published in a September 1985 report.

Legend: ● ◑ ○ ◐ ● Better ← → Worse

Product	Price	Size	Cost per oz.	Powder/liquid	Cleaning ability	Abrasiveness	Stain removal	Comments
Bon Ami Polishing Cleanser	$0.86	14 oz.	6¢	P	●	●	◐	A,C,F
A&P	0.29	14	2	P	●	●	○	B,C,F
Ajax (with phosphates)	0.44	14	3	P	●	●	○	B,C
White Magic (Safeway)	0.49	14	4	P	●	●	○	B,C
Bab-O	0.41	14	3	P	●	●	◐	B,D,F
Comet (new formula)	0.38	14	3	P	◑	●	◐	B,C,F,G
Soft Scrub	1.19	13	9	L	◑	○	●	C,G
Ajax (without phosphates)	0.49	14	4	P	◑	●	◐	B,C
Bright (Kroger)	0.43	14	3	P	◑	●	◐	B,C
Woolworth	0.49	14	4	P	◑	●	○	B,C
Acme	0.89	26	3	L	○	●	●	D,G,H
Sierra	1.50	26	6	L	○	●	●	D
Comet (with phosphates)	0.44	14	3	P	○	●	◐	B,C,F
Old Dutch	0.39	17	2	P	○	●	○	B,D
Lady Lee (Lucky)	0.31	14	2	P	○	●	◐	B,C

Product	Price	Size	Cost per oz.	Powder/liquid	Cleaning ability	Abrasiveness	Stain removal	Comments
Comet	1.66	21	8	L	◒	◉	◉	B,C,F,H
Bon Ami	0.84	12	7	P	◒	◉	●	D,H
Woolworth	1.00	26	4	L	◒	◉	●	D,G
Lady Lee (Lucky)	1.39	26	5	L	◒	○	◉	E,H
Shiny Sinks	1.52	26	6	L	◒	○	◉	E,H
Comet (without phosphates)	0.46	14	3	P	◒	●	◐	A,B,C,F

Key to Comments
A-Contains oxygen bleach.
B-Contains chlorine bleach. **Bab-O** has less than most; **Comet** (without phosphates), **Lady Lee** powder, and **Comet** liquid have more than most; bleach content of **Ajax** with phosphates varied from sample to sample. None should be mixed with ammonia.

C-Highly alkaline.
D-Moderately alkaline.
E-Acidic; contains citric acid.
F-Better than most at removing aluminum potmarks.
G-Scratched acrylic plastic less than most.
H-Scratched aluminum less than most.

Toilet-bowl cleaners

Supermarket shelves sport a variety of bowl-cleaning products, some for bowl scrub-outs, but most hinting that they will clean toilets "automatically."

There are relatively few pour-in-the-bowl scrubbing varieties, perhaps because their very nature indicates you have to do some work to use them. The majority of products are made to be placed in a toilet's flush tank, whence they dispense cleaning solution into the bowl every time you flush.

In-bowl cleaners

The hard-to-remove soil that collects on toilet bowls is, in most cases, made up of minerals derived from the water itself and from human waste. Acid softens or makes soluble such deposits, which you then swab off; cleaners are strongly acidic.

The labels of cleaners give the acid concentration. The liquids, which are used at full strength, all contain hydrochloric acid. Granular cleaners are based on sodium acid sulfate. Granulars must be dissolved in the bowl's water for use, which considerably dilutes their acidic concentration.

Even a weak acidic cleaner will do a better job than ordinary chlorine bleach or an all-purpose cleaner that claims to be able to clean toilet bowls.

Toilet bowls sometimes acquire rust stains from iron in the water. Liquid in-bowl cleaners should do a better job than the granulars at rust removal because of their chemical properties and method of application. They should do best at removing hard-water stains, too.

In convenience, as in performance, the liquids have an edge on the granulars. It's easier to squirt a liquid onto a sloping bowl and up under its rim than it is to apply granules which you drop in, allow to fizz, and then use for scrubbing. The liquids come in plastic squeeze bottles.

A common claim for toilet-bowl cleaners is that they disinfect toilet bowls. There's little if any medical importance to such a talent.

In-tank products

Most in-tank products consist of a detergent, a fragrance, and a dye that turns the toilet water blue or green. These "cleaners" really do little more than add a bit of color to the bathroom and startle guests who aren't used to blue toilet water. The products won't clean an already soiled bowl, or even spare you the need for a periodic scrubbing. At best, they will merely slow the rate at which soil accumulates, and disguise existing soil to some extent.

Typically, an in-tank product is a cake in a container with vents that allow some water to enter and dissolve a bit of the colored cake. With each flush, some of the resulting solution comes out into the toilet bowl.

Most in-tank products are liquids that deliver the colored product through a metering valve as the tank empties itself during a flush.

Some are colorless solids that contain a granular bleach as their active ingredient. There have been some reports that extended use of these products can damage the mechanisms in some toilet tanks.

Recommendations

There's no way to keep a toilet from getting dirty and no alternative to cleaning it by hand. An in-tank "cleaner" will only postpone the chore, and not for long, if you're meticulous.

Sooner or later, it's on with the rubber gloves and out with the scrub brush. A liquid household cleaner should easily do the job if the bowl is lightly soiled.

A specialized in-bowl toilet cleaner will clean the toilet better if the soil and stains are stubborn.

Be careful how you use any in-bowl cleaner. These products contain acid and can be harmful when they get into the eyes or onto the skin or clothing. They can also do damage if swallowed. The labels properly urge caution, and all warn you to keep the products out of the reach of children.

In-tank products offer very little for the money. Still, they may slightly extend the time between swabbing. Most of them appear innocuous, but they can present special hazards in their concentrated condition. There may be a germicide that's potentially harmful if swallowed. Powerful chlorine bleach can be possibly fatal if swallowed and is also able to release a toxic gas if mixed with ammonia or an acid. It would therefore be wise to avoid cleaning your bowl with an in-bowl cleaner if you also have a chlorine-bleach cleaner in the tank.

Once in the tank, the bleach cleaners shouldn't produce a chlorine concentration higher than what you'd get if you added a chlorine bleach to your washing machine. A splash of it, then, shouldn't be harmful to clothing or to your skin if rinsed promptly. The water isn't apt to be safe for pets to drink, though, so keep the toilet lid closed.

Laundry

Hand-laundry detergents

There are a number of clothing items that require special laundering care—silks and woolens and delicate synthetics that can't safely suffer the rigors of regular washing machine agitation. In addition to being sensitive, such items are often likely to be expensive. The usual routine is to hand wash these garments in cold water with a detergent formulated for the purpose.

Label instructions on special-purpose products usually tell you how much detergent and water to use and how long to wash—or, more precisely, soak the garments. Hand washables call for almost no agitation. Most labels suggest three to five minutes of soaking. Soak time is important. The less time a garment has to spend in the bath, the better. If you decide to use an ordinary dishwashing liquid, 1 to 2 teaspoons for each 2 quarts of water and a four- or five-minute soak time should be just about right.

Just about any special-purpose product or liquid dishwashing detergent is likely to be quite acceptable.

In most cases, coffee and smudge stains are easiest to remove. Tea and wine present the greatest challenge. Chocolate is in-between. Red wine is a particularly tough stain. While most products do an excellent job of removing it from triacetate, only a phosphate-containing laundry detergent is likely to be able to do an excellent job at getting it out of acrylic.

While phosphates have a variety of talents, they are cleaners in their own right and they help to soften water so other cleaners in a product can be more effective. They are also forbidden in certain parts of the country. Phosphates have been accused of causing rapid growth of algae in lakes and ponds, resulting in the premature demise of the body of water.

Whether or not a garment maintains its shape when you wash it has more to do with water temperature and handling than with detergent.

Alkalinity

Some of the specialty detergents boast about their gentleness. The dishwashing liquids generally say they are kind to hands.

Highly alkaline products tend to be harsh. Products that are low alkaline or neutral tend to be more mild. Since laundering time for hand washing is so short (five minutes or less), the difference in alkalinity (or pH) from one product to another is unlikely to have much effect on fragile fabrics.

Recommendations

There's really nothing special about specialty products. Other products, including ordinary laundry detergent and dishwashing liquids, can clean just as well or better and for much less money. You may find a dishwashing liquid convenient to use. The small bottles are easy to store under the kitchen or bathroom sink and, of course, they're good for dishes.

Before laundering any garment, it's wise to check the fabric care label sewn into it. Even if a garment is washable, you should check to be sure it's colorfast before laundering the first time. Dip a small, hidden section in water to see if the dyes run.

The directions on specialty laundering products call for soaking. Most advise against rubbing. All advise to gently squeeze suds through. You may be tempted to scrub a stubborn spot, but resist that temptation. Rubbing can damage delicate fibers; so can wringing or twisting.

These cleaning products, like any household chemicals, should be stored where children can't get at them.

Ivory Snow for hand laundering

Ivory Snow is one of the few laundry products available that's pure soap. Detergents have taken over the laundry room. They're generally more efficient than soaps in hard water and in cold water. **Ivory Snow**, however, purports to be gentle.

The results are very good, using up to 4½ teaspoons in 2 quarts of water. You may want to dissolve the powder in warm water before adding it to the cold-water wash, and if your water is hard, you might add a small dose of powdered softener.

Laundry bleaches

Today's assortment of natural and synthetic fabrics are washed in water that's warm or cool, with a detergent that's most likely phosphate-free; sometimes a fabric softener is added. Now, as in the past, clothes eventually become dingy and stained—particularly whites. The solution now, as in the past, is laundry bleach.

Laundry bleach can be either chlorine or nonchlorine. Liquid chlorine bleach is the old stand-by, having earned its place in the laundry room as well as in the bathroom and kitchen for whitening, disinfecting, and removing stains and mildew.

Chlorine bleach also has its problems. The telltale signs of misuse or overuse of chlorine bleach are splotches of faded color or white where undiluted bleach has splashed, fabrics that have faded from vivid to dim, fraying collars, stitching that has dissolved, and sometimes the appearance of small holes in the fabric.

Excessive use of chlorine bleach can cause additional problems if your home has a septic tank for sewage disposal. Too much chlorine in a septic tank may slow down the natural decomposition of the sewage and necessitate more frequent servicing of the tank.

Nonchlorine, "all-fabric" bleaches promise the benefits of chlorine bleach without the risk, but it's easy to make a claim about a bleach. The real story unfolds in the laundry room.

Both chlorine and nonchlorine bleaches use an oxidizing agent (usually sodium hypochlorite or sodium perborate) that reacts with and, with the help of a detergent, lifts out a stain. Liquid chlorine bleaches all have about the same amount of active ingredient and there is little difference from one brand to another.

The whitest white

Chlorine bleaches have always been better than all-fabric bleaches at whitening clothes. They still are.

All-fabric bleaches, especially the powdered products, do whiten, but not nearly as well as chlorine bleaches. In fact, all-fabric liquid bleaches whiten hardly better than detergent alone. If you wash the laundry load successive times with an all-fabric bleach, the whitening process continues, but even four applications won't match the whitening power of a single use of chlorine bleach.

If you double the recommended amount of all-fabric powder bleach, there's some improvement. The bleach's whitening power doubles, at least for the first washing, but still falls slightly behind chlorine bleach. A second washing with a double dose of all-fabric powder won't show such dramatic results. It whitens clothes only a little bit more.

If you use hot water (140°F) rather than warm water (100°F) the bleaches will show little, if any, improvement.

Tough stains

Some stains, such as spaghetti sauce, red wine, blood, and motor oil, seem to have an affinity for clothing and, once entrenched, leave with great reluctance, particularly with a fabric such as nylon knit.

Neither chlorine nor nonchlorine bleach can completely remove spaghetti sauce. In general, however, a good all-fabric powder surpasses chlorine bleach at removing greasy stains. That's because a powdered product contains detergents and chemical "builders" of its own and acts as a detergent "booster" as well as a bleach. Chlorine bleach removes most blood stains, but won't do well at removing wine and oil spots.

Color fading

Bleach, especially chlorine bleach, can cause colors to fade.

Initially, bleach has no noticeable effect on the brightness of colors. Chlorine bleaches may not seem harsher that an all-fabric product. After a few washings, however, the chlorine begins taking its toll. Slight fading becomes evident and then, after more washings, objectionable. An all-fabric bleach, however, will continue being kind to colors.

Another concern with chlorine bleach is its tendency to gradually weaken a fabric. You would have to wash repeatedly in chlorine bleach to seriously weaken a fabric—a routine you should avoid.

Recommendations

Chlorine bleach, when used properly, is the most effective way to whiten fabrics, including many synthetics. It's ideal for the occasional whitening your wash may need, but knowing how to use chlorine bleach is essential: Improper and long-term use will take its toll on colors and fabric life. Using chlorine bleach may be tricky, but buying it is simple. The only real difference you are likely to find is price.

All-fabric powdered bleaches have the advantage of being safe with most fabrics and dyes, even over the long term. They're a lot more expensive to use than chlorine bleaches, and aren't as good at whitening. If you prefer them, you can get extra whitening performance out of powdered all-fabric bleaches by doubling the recommended dose. Of course, you also double the average cost per use.

A more reasonable and less costly approach might be to incorporate both chlorine and all-fabric bleach into your laundry routine. Occasional and cautious use of chlorine bleach on chlorine-safe white fabrics will deliver the whitening you need. Use all-fabric bleach to brighten colors without fading, whiten fabrics that aren't safe with chlorine bleach, and remove greasy stains.

When you do use chlorine bleach, follow these guidelines:

1. Bleach only when necessary, or you will get color fading and fabric deterioration.
2. Before you bleach, read the garment's care label.
3. Don't use chlorine bleach on wool, silk, mohair, or noncolorfast fabrics or dyes. If you're unsure about a garment's fabric content, experiment with a diluted solution of bleach on an inside seam. Any discoloration should appear in a minute or so.
4. If your washer has a bleach dispenser, use it according to the manufacturer's directions. If there's no dispenser, you can add the bleach full-strength to the wash water *before* you add the laundry, or dilute the bleach with a generous amount of water and add it to laundry that is already immersed in wash water.
5. *Never* use chlorine bleach with ammonia or toilet cleaners. That combination can produce deadly fumes.

Ratings of laundry bleaches

Listed by types; within types, listed in order of bleaching ability. Bracketed products were judged equal and are listed alphabetically. Differences between closely ranked products were small. Prices are as published in an August 1985 report.

Rating scale: ● Excellent ◀——▶ ● Poor (◉ ◐ ○ ◑ ●)

Product	Size (fl. oz. or oz.)	Price	Cost per use	Whitening	Red-wine stains	Motor-oil stains	Blood stains
Liquid chlorine bleaches [1]							
Clorox	64	$.94	6¢	◉	◐	●	◐
Purex	64	.91	6	◉	◐	●	◐
Powdered all-fabric bleaches							
Clorox 2	40	1.79	20	○	◐	●	◐
Lady Lee	61	1.51	9	○	○	●	○
Alpha Beta	61	1.61	12	○	○	◐	○
P & Q	40	.87	11	○	○	◐	○
Bright	40	1.29	14	○	○	◐	●
Purex	40	1.34	15	○	○	◐	◐
Acme	40	.99	11	○	◑	○	◐
White Magic	40	1.51	17	○	○	●	◐
A&P	40	1.17	13	○	○	○	○
Cost Cutter	61	1.39	9	○	○	○	◐
Scotch Buy	40	1.59	16	○	○	○	◑
Biz	30	2.77	23	○	○	●	◐
Econo Buy	61	1.45	12	○	●	◐	◐
Climalene	55	1.59	12	◐	○	◐	◐
Snowy	40	2.94	13	◐	◐	◐	○
Borateem	40	1.77	16	●	◐	●	○
Liquid all-fabric bleaches							
Snowy	64	2.24	14	●	●	●	◑
Vivid	64	2.31	14	●	●	●	◑

[1] There is no real difference among brands, so judgments of **Clorox** and **Purex** apply to other brands CU bought and analyzed: **Acme, Alpha Beta, A & P, Bright, Cost Cutter, Econo Buy, Grand Union, Hilex, Lady Lee, P & Q, Pathmark, White Magic**.

Laundry boosters

Anyone who does laundry knows that some stains don't come out in an ordinary detergent wash. Hence the occasional need for products called laundry boosters. Some boosters are included as a component of regular laundry detergent. Others are separate products used as pretreatments or included with the detergent as the laundry is washed.

Not many boosters are more effective on protein stains (for example: blood, egg, milk) than a good laundry detergent used alone in the wash cycle. No booster is likely to be superior in cleaning up sandwich and party stains like red wine, dark beer, cola, purple grape juice, or pink lemonade. For soiled rags, the kind used for cleaning up around the house or for washing the car, just about any booster should be effective—but so should a regular detergent used as a presoak, or simply used in the wash cycle.

TV commercials have left the impression that "ring around the collar" is one of the toughest laundry jobs since the invention of dirt. That just isn't so. A good detergent should do the job nicely.

Convenience

Boosters are often meant for presoaking. Though that doesn't mean a lot of manual labor, it does tie up the washing machine. You could, of course, do the soaking in a bucket, but transferring the sopping laundry into the machine is messy.

Aerosols and pump sprays are easier to use. You simply spray those products on the stain, then throw the item into the machine with the rest of the wash.

Directions for other sprays call for you to rub them into the stain. That's a small chore when you're faced with one stained shirt, but think of rubbing these boosters into: five shirts, grass-stained trouser knees, a cola-stained T-shirt, and other assorted stains. Rubbing can become a big chore indeed.

Hazards

If there's a chance that a booster or a boosting detergent is going to come in contact with your skin (as it would in rubbing a stain), you might want to wear rubber gloves. Gloves are almost a necessity if you have a skin rash or cuts, which can be particularly irritated by contact with one of these products. If, despite careful handling, any laundry booster product gets into an eye, rinse immediately and thoroughly with water.

Children and boosters don't mix; keep boosters and other laundry products out of their reach. In addition to the hazards of contact, there are hazards of ingestion. Few of the products have child-resistant packaging.

All boosters can damage some household surfaces if not wiped up quickly. Aluminum and paint seem most vulnerable, with stainless steel the most resistant to staining or damage.

Recommendations

Laundry booster ads often seem to promise miracles. Some boosters do work very well on most stains, but most aren't much more effective at stain removal than detergent alone—and some are worse.

Choose a laundry booster based on its effectiveness and on your idea of convenience. Presoaking is probably the least convenient method. If you don't agree, any of the powders that are presoaks should do.

Liquid boosting detergents claim to do two jobs. They do the job of a detergent well enough, but as boosters, they are at best only average.

Laundry detergents

Laundry detergents come in almost stupefying variety. There are powders that resemble old-fashioned soap and liquids introduced for easier dispensing and pretreatment of tough soil. Some detergents contain phosphates to boost cleaning power; others are made without phosphates to avoid possible harm to lakes and streams. There are products with a variety of stain-attacking enzymes, mixtures of cleaning agents, and fluorescent dyes. There are low-sudsing and concentrated formulations.

The abundance of formulas and brands is only partly the work of merchandisers looking for something more glamorous to sell than a washboard. It is also the result of a decades-long struggle between chemists and hard water.

Hard water, the bane of laundry soap, was also the bane of early synthetic detergents. The mineral content that makes water "hard" deposits itself on the wash, leaving a grimy curd known as "tattletale gray." After World War II, chemists discovered that they could overcome those mineral deposits with water-softening chemicals called "builders." Phosphates served that purpose well and soon came into heavy use.

Unfortunately phosphorus (phosphates are compounds of that element) from detergents and other sources found its way into lakes and streams. There it was blamed for encouraging an overgrowth of algae that left mats of green slime on the water's surface—the acceleration of a natural process that eventually turns many bodies of water into bogs. To minimize that pollution, legal restrictions in localities where some 40 percent of the U.S. population lives now ban or limit the use of phosphate detergents.

Phosphate-free detergents can solve the hard-water problem in several ways. Some use "precipitating" builders. Those soften wash water by making dissolved minerals in water settle out, or precipitate, as particles. Extra cleaning agents are then added in those products to keep the particles from depositing themselves on clothes. Alternatively, detergents can employ "nonprecipitating" builders. Those soften wash water by inactivating hardness ions, freeing the cleaning agents for full-time attention to washing. Alternatively, a product can simply avoid builders and substitute a high dose of cleaning agents; such products may be labeled "concentrated."

Some cleaning agents ("surfactants") are more sensitive to deactivation by minerals than others. Detergent makers usually match the type of softening agent to the type of surfactant, or combine several surfactants for cleaning ability on various soils and fabrics. The manufacturers further tailor their formulas by geographical area, to account for differences in the mineral content of water.

Some cleaning agents are high sudsing and others are low sudsing. Those characteristics have no connection with a detergent's cleaning ability. The misconception that they do is a holdover from washboard days. With soap, you had to use enough to get suds before cleaning began.

The newest detergents contain enzymes. These are complex proteins, produced by living cells, that can break down stains produced by other proteins or by carbohydrates. There are many different kinds of enzymes in use, each specific for a kind of stain. Some detergents contain several enzymes; they're the substances with the suffix "-ase" in the label's ingredients list.

Enzymes found their way into this country's detergents a few decades ago, but were dropped in 1971 because they sometimes caused skin rashes and respiratory problems in the workers who handled them. Today's enzymes are granules with a low-dust coating that eliminates the former industrial health problems.

Enzyme products never posed the threat to consumers that they did to workers. Still, if you or a family member notice skin irritation after wearing garments washed with a detergent with enzymes, you'd be wise to switch to a nonenzyme product. Further, it's also a good idea to protect your skin from contact with any heavy-duty detergent.

Brightness

Most laundry detergents leave colorless dyes in the wash that glow in the near-ultraviolet wavelengths in fluorescent lighting and sunlight. The effect is sometimes used by actors on stage under black light to impart an illusion of disembodied animation to white gloves, masks, shoes, or the like. In the home, the effect is to mask dinginess, making laundry look whiter or brighter than it is.

Soil loosened during washing and redeposited on clothes can also affect the look of a wash load. Accordingly, detergents usually contain special antiredeposition agents.

Recommendations

A few cautions, not disclosed on some of the labels, are in order with any detergent. Care is needed to avoid contact with eyes or mucous membranes. Accidental ingestion will do the stomach no good. Detergents should, of course, be kept out of the reach of young children.

A detergent is unlikely to make wash water more than moderately alkaline, so it's not a threat to a general family wash.

Before pretreating a new, colored garment—or, indeed, tossing any garment of unknown colorfastness into a general wash— you'd be wise to check your detergent on an inconspicuous section of the fabric. Children's sleepwear and other items with a flame-retardant finish may need a special washing regimen. Check the garment's care label for specific laundering instructions.

Ratings of laundry detergents

Listed in order of estimated overall quality, based on effectiveness in removing fresh stains in regular laundering (without pretreatment) in

Excellent ◄────► Poor

Product	Type (liquid or powder)	Price	Size (oz. or fl. oz.)	Dose (cup)	Cost per dose	Blood	Chocolate syrup	Spaghetti sauce
New Liquid Tide	L	$3.99	64	1/2	25¢	●/◐	●/◐	●/◐
Sears Heavy Duty	P	2.49	48	1/2	10	◐/◐	◐/●	○/◐
Concentrated All	P	2.14	49	1	24	◐/◐	◐/◐	○/◐
Tide New Denser Formula (with phosphates) [2]	P	2.19	49	1	15	●/◐	●/◐	○/◐
Tide New Denser Formula [2]	P	2.29	49	1	15	◐/◐	◐/◐	◐/◐
Wisk Heavy Duty	L	3.99	64	1/2	25	◐/◐	◐/◐	◐/◐
New ERA Plus	L	3.97	64	1/4	12	○/◐	◐/○	◐/◐
Fresh Start New Scent (with phosphates)	P	3.99	34.5	1/4	16	◐/◐	◐/◐	○/◐
Dynamo Action Plus	L	4.02	64	1/4	13	○/◐	◐/○	◐/◐
Fresh Start New Scent	P	4.24	34.5	1/4	17	●/◐	◐/○	○/◐
Purex New Dense Formula	P	1.69	42	1	13	◐/◐	◐/◐	○/◐

[1] Comments for **Wisk Heavy Duty**, **New ERA Plus**, and **Dynamo Action Plus** apply to 32-fl.-oz. size tested. Price and cost per dose for those brands are stated for 64-fl.-oz. size, to allow ready comparison with **New Liquid Tide**.

Key to Comments

A-Contains enzymes.

B-packed in cardboard box without spout or other leakproof provision for reclosing.

C-Comes in convenient transparent-plastic botle with screw-on measuring cap.

D-CU's samples came in relatively in convenient bottle. Now available in same convenient bottle as **New Liquid Tide**, see Comment F.

E-Comes in opaque-plastic bottle with screw cap; has no provision for measuring.

F-Comes in wide-based opaque-plastic bottle with convenient drip-free nozzle and screw-on measuring cap.

Ratings of laundry detergents

warm, hard water. Except as noted, products contain no phosphates. Prices are as published in a February 1986 report.

Stain-removal (from polyester-cotton/from nylon)							Fluorescent whitening		
Grass	Mud	Grape juice	Makeup	Tea	Black ballpoint ink	Motor oil (used)	Polyester-cotton	Nylon	Comments [1]
●/◐	●/◐	●/◐	◐/◐	○/◐	◐/◐	●/●	◐	○	A,F,G
◐/○	◐/○	○/○	○/◐	●/○	◐/◐	●/●	◐	○	B,H,I,L
◐/◐	○/○	○/○	○/◐	●/○	◐/○	●/●	◐	○	B,H,I,K,L
○/○	●/○	○/◐	◐/○	●/◐	●/◐	●/●	◐	○	B,H,K
○/○	◐/○	○/○	◐/○	●/○	◐/○	●/●	◐	○	B,H,K,L
○/○	○/○	◐/○	◐/○	●/○	◐/○	●/ [3]	◐	○	E,G
◐/○	○/○	○/○	◐/○	○/○	◐/◐	◐/◐	◐	○	A,D,G,J
○/○	◐/○	◐/○	●/○	◐/○	◐/○	●/◐	◐	○	A,C,G
◐/○	○/○	◐/○	◐/○	◐/○	◐/○	●/◐	◐	○	A,G,J,M
◐/○	◐/○	◐/○	●/○	●/○	◐/○	●/◐	●	○	A,C,H,L
○/○	○/○	◐/◐	●/●	◐/◐	●/◐	●/◐	◐	◐	B,H,L

[2] A new product, containing enzymes, is labeled **New Tough Cleaning Tide**.
[3] Variable among samples. Performance ranged from fair to very good.

G-Not alkaline when diluted in wash water, a possible advantage for delicate fabrics.

H-Slightly or moderately alkaline when diluted in wash water.

I-Strongly alkaline if wetted with water as a paste; avoid personal contact.

J-Allowed more soil to redeposit on nylon than most.

K-Labeled with appropriate test for colorfastness of fabrics.

L-Darkened tea stain on polyester-cotton.

M-32-fl.-oz. size tested comes in opaque-plastic bottle with dispensing cap; cap was slow in dispensing, has no provision for measuring, and dripped when bottle was set down.

Washing machines

The latest crop of washing machines is very versatile—you can have a great deal of control over the way the laundry is handled.

There are a variety of top-loading, front-loading, regular-size, large-capacity, compact, portable, or stackable machines. Then there are a multitude of features and combinations of features, cycles, temperatures, speeds, and water levels, and a further choice between dial controls, push buttons, or electronic touch controls. Knowing a few basics will help you narrow the choices.

Type. Washers can be either top or front loading. Top loaders are by far the most popular in this country, while the European favorite is the front loader.

Aside from the differences implicit in the names, the two types of washers differ in the way they agitate clothes. Top loaders circulate clothes up and down and back and forth; front loaders tumble clothes up and around, much the same way that a dryer does.

An advantage of loading from the front is that the top of the washer can be used as a work area all the time.

Size. The size you choose depends on how much laundry you do and how much room you have. The most versatile machine is one that offers large capacity but adjusts to small loads. The most generous sizes of the large-capacity models are top loaders, some of which take as much as 16 pounds of mixed, dry laundry. In general, front loaders hold less than top loaders.

"Stackables" are compact washers that are available separately or as part of a unit that includes a dryer. Some are small enough to fit inside a closet.

Water level. You can adjust the amount of water to the size of your wash. On most large-tub models the minimum fill takes about half as much water as the maximum fill. The difference can amount to 20 or 30 gallons of water in a single wash.

The fill level is regulated by a pressure switch rather than a timer. So, even if you live in an area where your water pressure is low or irregular, your machine will continue to fill until the water reaches the level you've selected.

Adjusting the water level to the load will help you save water, energy, and detergent. But the most economical way to use your machine is to accumulate enough laundry to run the machine only with a full load.

Water temperature.   You can control the temperature of the wash water and the rinse water separately. These are the standard options for wash and rinse; hot/warm, hot/cold, warm/warm, warm/cold, and cold/cold.

The less hot water you use, the cheaper the machine will be to run. The only time you need a hot wash is when you have a load of very dirty clothes. Otherwise, a warm or cold wash will do. And always use a cold rinse because warm water won't rinse any better, and it may help wrinkle permanent-press fabrics.

Speed-control.   Separate or built into the cycle selector, these differing speeds are part of the typical top loader. This feature allows for gentler handling of delicate fabrics such as silk and for fewer wrinkles when spinning out permanent-press fabrics. Front loaders do not offer multiple speeds. They run at a slow speed for wash and a higher speed for spin.

Performance

There are a number of characteristics to consider.

In absolute terms, front-loading machines use the least water. Fully filled, a front loader uses 25 to 30 gallons; top loaders anywhere from 40 to 57 gallons. But top loaders can hold as much as 50 percent more laundry than a front loader. So one has to compare the gallons used with the laundry done to arrive at an efficiency judgment. As it turns out, a front loader is still the most efficient, using less water per unit of laundry than even the most efficient top loader.

Hot-water efficiency is a measure of how costly a machine is to operate. That's because the greatest cost of running a washing machine is the cost of providing the hot and warm water it uses (the cost of electricity to run the motor is negligible).

Again, a front-loading machine is the most efficient. For example, in a typical front loader, heating the water for what the U.S. Department of Energy considers a typical year's worth of laundry would cost about $40 in electricity or $15 in gas (assuming a rate of 7.75 cents per kilowatt-hour and 62 cents per therm).

Other machines can cost considerably more. To do the same amount of laundry in an efficient top loader would cost $75 in electricity or $30 in gas. With a relatively inefficient top loader it would cost about $110 in electricity or $45 in gas.

If you're concerned about cutting down on water consumption, you might consider buying a "suds-saver" model that allows you to store the wash water and reuse it later on. Some people are skeptical about reusing dirty, cooled wash water. But many consumers seem to be interested in this feature.

Suds-savers can cost $20 to $40, but not all manufacturers promote suds-savers.

Permanent-press handling. If you dry your clothes on a line, it's important to have a machine that cools the clothes effectively before the spin-dry phase. That will help keep wrinkles from setting in permanent-press fabric. But if you use a clothes dryer, you don't really have to worry about how your washer handles permanent-press items; the dryer's permanent-press cycle should remove most wrinkles.

How the washer handles permanent press is important mainly for those who line-dry their laundry. A washer with at least two speeds minimizes compaction of the clothes by using a slow spin. And a machine with a permanent-press cycle cools down the wash with sprays of water or with rinses before it goes into the final spin. The extra-rinse method on some models is even more effective.

Unbalanced load. A washing machine will operate best when its load is spread evenly around the tub. With an unbalanced load, some machines show no signs of stress; others stop automatically when the load is even moderately unbalanced; still others don't spin properly. The best solution to the unbalance problem is to redistribute the wash load manually as soon as the problem occurs.

Water extraction. The amount of water left in your clothes after they're spun out determines drying time, whether in the dryer or on the clothesline.

Linting. The amount of lint left in your wash can depend on what you wash, the degree of agitation, and the machine's method of lint disposal. Front loaders and the most effective top loaders will leave only slight deposits of lint.

Lint filters vary somewhat in convenience for emptying, but not enough to be significant. A few washers flush the lint out with the wash water, which may pose a problem for drains that are already partially blocked.

Most models have a bleach dispenser. Its job: to channel the bleach into the outer tub instead of onto the clothes in the inner tub; the bleach is diluted before the water reaches the clothes. Therer's no dispenser on front loaders.

Sand disposal. Most machines do a good job of getting rid of any sand that's collected in beach towels and clothing.

Oversudsing. Some machines, especially front loaders, tend to froth when you use a high-sudsing detergent, especially if the water is soft. You can get around it by using a low-sudsing detergent.

Features

Top-of-the-line washers are all loaded with features, many of them similar. Still, the design and execution of a particular set of features might give you reason for choosing one washer over another.

Controls. These can usually be found on a console at the back of the machine and are clearly marked.

The controls generally consist of conventional rotary dials. Most of the washers prevent you from moving the dial forward while the machine is running, saving you from needlessly wearing out components.

An electronic touch panel may prove intimidating to first-time users. And resetting or advancing from one cycle to another may require turning the power off and on again and then pressing the desired function, a small inconvenience.

Dispensers. With any washing machine, you can put the detergent in the tub before you put in the laundry. A few machines, however, have a dispenser that releases the detergent when the water circulates—handy if you're using the soak cycle.

Higher-priced machines generally can add fabric softener automatically.

Safety. Tangling with a washer's spinning tub and oscillating agitator is a losing proposition. Most washers minimize the risk by stopping the spinning within a few seconds of the lid being opened. Some reduce the risk by locking the door or lid during spin.

Special features. Some models have a prewash feature that provides an extra period of agitation. Most also have a soak cycle, which provides the soaking and spin-out that might be necessary for heavily soiled clothes.

Some less-expensive washers don't have the soak feature. But you can accomplish the same result manually; you turn off the washer after a few minutes of agitation in the regular cycle, let the wash soak about half an hour, and then set the machine to spin before the regular wash cycle.

Extra rinses are available on a number of models. They are useful for washing heavily soiled items and they can also be important for people who are allergic to residues of laundry products.

Recommendations

If conserving water or energy is a primary concern, choose a front loader. Most people, however, would probably prefer a top loader. Top loaders hold more laundry and they can also adjust to small loads. The best of them are even efficient in using water.

Another consideration should be a brand's reliability. Consumers Union's Annual Questionnaire surveyed subscribers to *Consumer Reports* to see how often brands they own have been repaired. The latest data indicate that **Maytag** models continue to be the most trouble-free. Better than average in frequency of repair are washers from Hotpoint, General Electric, Sears, and Whirlpool.

Ratings of washing machines

(As published in a June 1985 report.) Listed by types; within types, listed in order of estimated quality.

Prices are average and range for white models, as quoted to CU shoppers in a fifteen-city survey.

Legend: Better ◉ ◑ ○ ◐ ● Worse

Water efficiency [2]

Brand and model	Average price	Price range	Dimensions (HXWXD), in. [1]	Lid opens	Total, regular cycle	Total, perm. press cycle	Hot, all cycles	Capacity	Unbalanced-load handling	Water extraction	Linting	Noise	Brand frequency of repair	Advantages	Disadvantages	Comments
Top loaders																
Maytag A712	$586	519-655	43¾(51¼)X25½X27¼ [3]	Back										B,D,L,P,R	f	A,C
Whirlpool LA9800XM	547	439-669	43½(50)X29X26	Back										M,R	n	A,G,I,J,L
Sears 23921	574	490-669	43(52¾)X29X26	Left										J,M,O,R	d,j	A,F,I
Gibson WA28D7WP	450	389-540	43(54¼)X28¼X27¼	Left										F,H,L,P	d	—
Speed Queen HA7001	516	459-600	43¼(51)X25¾X28 [3]	Back									[5]	D,G,L,P,R	b	I
Kelvinator AW800A	448	369-539	43½(54¼)X28¼X27¼	Left									[5]	F,L,P	d	B
General Electric WWA8480B	493	420-600	43(50½)X27X25	Back										A,D,N	e,m	C,G,K
Hotpoint WLW5700B	476	388-589	43¾(50¼)X27X25	Back										D,N	m	C,G,I
Wards 6841	567	479-609	44(55½)X27X27¼	Left										C,E,I,M,P	d,h,i	B,D,E,K

(Continued)

Rating legend:

Better ●——————○ Worse
(◉ better, ◐, ○, ◑, ● worse)

Brand and model	Average price	Price range	Dimensions (HxWxD), In. [1]	Lid opens	Total, regular cycle	Total, perm. press cycle	Hot, all cycles	Unbalanced-load handling	Capacity	Water extraction	Linting	Noise	Brand frequency of repair	Advantages	Disadvantages	Comments
Norge LWA9120s	461	400-515	43½(55½)X27X27	Left	◐	○	○	◐	◉	◐	◐	◐	E,M,P [5]	d,h	B,D,K
Admiral W20B8	458	396-520	43¼(55½)X27X27¼	Left	◐	○	○	◐	◉	◐	◐	◐	E,M,P [5]	c,d,h	B,D,K
Frigidaire WCIM	481	390-598	44¼(54)X27X26¼	Left	◐	◐	◐	●	○	◐	○	○	F,L,M	o	B,D
White-Westinghouse LA800E	470	420-520	43¾(53½)X27X27	Left	●	●	●	●	◐	●	◐	○	F,L,M	I,o	B

Front loaders

Brand and model	Average price	Price range	Dimensions (HxWxD), In. [1]	Lid opens	Total, regular cycle	Total, perm. press cycle	Hot, all cycles	Unbalanced-load handling	Capacity	Water extraction	Linting	Noise	Brand frequency of repair	Advantages	Disadvantages	Comments
White-Westinghouse LT800E	577	470-699	43¾X27X27(39¼) [3]	Down	●	●	●	◉	●	◐	●	◉	C,F,K,M,P,Q [5]	a,e,g,k,l	C,H,I
Wards 6514 [4]	602	490-680	36¼X27X26¼(39¼) [3]	Down	●	●	●	◉	●	◐	●	◉	C,F,P,Q [5]	a,e,g,i,k	A,C,H,I

Water efficiency [2] (Unbalanced-load handling, Capacity columns)

[1] Parenthetical figure is height or depth with lid open. Leveling legs can add up to 1½ inches. Additional depth may be needed for hoses.

[2] Measured at maximum fill for cycles indicated.

[3] Can be flush with wall; others need up to 4 inches clearance.

[4] Stackable model; requires painted top (approx. $20 extra) to be free-standing.

[5] Insufficient data.

SPECIFICATIONS AND FEATURES

All have: • Presetable water-level control. Except as noted, all: • Were judged average in handling permanent-press clothes for line-drying. • Were judged average in sand disposal. • Have 40-45 min. regular cycle. • Have 335-45 min. permanent-press cycle. • Have no special prewash setting. • Have safety switch on lid that stops spin action only. • Have timer that can't be rotated when machine is on. • Have top, lid, and tub finish of porcelain enamel; rest of cabinet, baked enamel. • Have lint filter that must be cleaned periodically by user.

KEY TO ADVANTAGES

A-Can be set to use less water than others for small loads.
B-Uses less electricity to run motor than others.
C-Safety switch on lid or door stops all action.
D-Safety switch on lid stops agitation and spin.
E-Safety switch stopped tub faster than most during spin.
F-Lid or door locks during spin.
G-Stainless-steel tub.
H-Plastic tub.
I-Has top-mounted detergent dispenser.
J-Has top-mounted dispensers for detergent, bleach, and softener; convenient, but side-by-side position could cause mix-ups.
K-Has top-mounted bleach and softener dispenser.

L-Washer speeds, temperature combinations can be set independently of chosen cycle.
M-Has prewash setting.
N-One cycle has automatic second rinse.
O-Water-temperature selection manual or automatic.
P-Allows front access for repairs.
Q-Better than average in sand disposal.
R-Judged better than average in handling permanent-press clothes for line drying.

KEY TO DISADVANTAGES

a-Range of fill controls very narrow.
b-Range of fill controls fairly narrow.
c-Controls poorly marked and difficult to set.
d-Timer can be rotated forward with machine on, causing wear and tear on components.
e-Low-sudsing detergent may be required by **GE**, likely to be required by front-loading **White-Westinghouse** and **Wards**.
f-Tub took longer to stop than others when lid was opened during spin.
g-Noisy when changing action.
h-Makes loud clank at end of spin cycle when tub brakes.
i-Front-mounted controls may require stooping to set.
j-Lid does not lie flat, so access from left is hampered.
k-Top has painted finish, easily scratched.
l-Top has intrusive projections.

m-Changing cycle speed while machine is running may damage machine.
n-Can't be set for slow agitation/fast spin.
o-Worse than average in sand disposal.

KEY TO COMMENTS

A-Regular cycle shorter than most.
B-Regular cycle longer than most.
C-Permanent-press cycle shorter than most.
D-Permanent-press cycle longer than most.
E-Has "pre-spot" feature, a minor convenience.
F-Agitator's top and bottom sections move differently.
G-Manufacturer offers manual or toll-free number for do-it-yourself repair.
H-No choice of speed; same speed for all washing, higher speed for extraction.
I-"Self-cleaning" lint filter convenient, but lint discharged into partially blocked drain may promote blockages.
J-Has electronic touch-panel controls; although well thought out, they're not as flexible as other controls and may confuse first-time users.
K-Model discontinued at the time the article was originally published in **Consumer Reports**. The test information has been retained here, however, for its use as a guide to buying.
L-According to manufacturer, a later model is **LA9800XP**, similar except for control panel.

Washing machine features

Brand and model	Price [1]	Normal/normal	Normal/slow	Slow/slow	Slow/normal	Hot/cold	Warm/cold	Cold/cold	Hot/warm	Warm/warm	Fill options	Timed soak	Extra rinse	Bleach dispenser (wash)	Softener dispenser (rinse)	Other
		Speed options [2] (agitation/spin)				Temperature options (wash/rinse)						Cycle options [3]				
Top loaders																
Admiral W20B6	$570 [4]	Automatic				✓	✓	✓	✓	✓	3	–	–	✓	–	–
•Admiral W20B8	620 [4]	Automatic				✓	✓	✓	✓	✓	Cont.	✓	–	✓	–	–
Frigidaire WCDM	425	Automatic				✓	✓	–	–	–	Cont.	–	–	✓	[8]	A
Frigidaire WIM	470	✓	✓	–	✓	✓	✓	–	✓	✓	Cont.	[7]	–	✓	[8]	–
•Frigidaire WCIM	525	✓	✓	✓	✓	✓	✓	–	✓	✓	Cont.	[7]	✓	✓	✓	–
General Electric WWA8320B	450	✓	–	–	✓	✓	✓	✓	–	–	4	✓	–	✓	✓	B
General Electric WWA8350B	475 [5]	✓	✓	✓	✓	✓	✓	✓	–	–	Cont.	–	–	✓	✓	B
•General Electric WWA8480B	520 [4]	Automatic				✓	✓	✓	✓	✓	Cont.	–	✓	✓	✓	–
Gibson WA28D5WP	405	Automatic				✓	✓	–	✓	–	Cont.	–	–	✓	✓	–
•Gibson WA28D7WP	435	✓	✓	✓	✓	✓	✓	–	✓	–	Cont.	✓	–	✓	–	–
Hotpoint WLW3700B	434	✓	–	✓	–	✓	✓	–	–	–	Cont.	–	–	✓	✓	C

Model	Price														Notes
Hotpoint WLW4700B	449	✓	✓	—	✓	✓	✓	✓	—	Cont.	—	—	✓	✓	C
•Hotpoint WLW5700B	499	Automatic	✓	✓	✓	✓	✓	✓	✓	Cont.	✓	✓	✓	✓	C
Kelvinator AW60DA	490	Automatic	✓	✓	✓	✓	—	✓	✓	Cont.	—	✓	[8]	—	—
•Kelvinator AW800A	540	✓	✓	✓	✓	✓	✓	✓	✓	Cont.	✓	✓	✓	✓	—
Maytag A612	569	✓	—	—	✓	✓	✓	✓	—	Cont.	[7]	✓	✓	✓	—
•Maytag A712	614	✓	✓	✓	✓	✓	✓	✓	—	Cont.	[7]	✓	✓	✓	—
Norge LWA7120S	570[4]	Automatic	✓	✓	✓	✓	✓	✓	✓	Cont.	—	✓	✓	✓	—
Norge LWA9120S	620[4]	Automatic	✓	✓	✓	✓	✓	✓	✓	Cont.	✓	✓	✓	✓	—
Sears 23721	450	Automatic	✓	✓	✓	✓	✓	✓	✓	3	✓	✓	✓	✓	A
Sears 23801	480	Automatic	✓	✓	✓	✓	✓	✓	✓	Cont.	✓	✓	✓	✓	—
•Sears 23921	570	Automatic	✓	✓	✓	✓	✓	✓	✓	Cont.	[7]	✓	✓	✓	—
Speed Queen HA6001	529	✓	✓	—	✓	✓	✓	✓	—	Cont.	—	✓	✓	✓	—
•Speed Queen HA7001	569	✓	✓	✓	✓	✓	✓	✓	—	Cont.	✓	✓	✓	✓	—
Wards 6542	[4]	✓	✓	✓	✓	✓	✓	✓	—	Cont.	—	✓	✓	✓	—
Wards 6641	[4]	Automatic	✓	✓	✓	✓	✓	✓	✓	Cont.	—	✓	✓	✓	—
•Wards 6841	[4]	Automatic	✓	✓	✓	✓	✓	✓	✓	Cont.	[7]	✓	✓	✓	—
Whirlpool LA5800XM	489[6]	Automatic	✓	✓	✓	✓	✓	✓	—	Cont.	—	✓	✓	—	—
Whirlpool LA7800XM	519[6]	Automatic	✓	✓	✓	✓	✓	✓	✓	Cont.	—	✓	✓	—	—
•Whirlpool LA9800XM	599[6]	Automatic	✓	✓	✓	✓	✓	✓	✓	Cont.	✓	✓	✓	✓	D
White-Westinghouse LA600E	459	✓	—	—	✓	✓	✓	—	—	Cont.	—	✓	[8]	—	—
White-Westinghouse LA700E	499	✓	✓	✓	✓	✓	—	✓	—	Cont.	✓	✓	✓	✓	E
•White-Westinghouse LA800E	559	✓	✓	✓	✓	✓	—	✓	—	Cont.	✓	✓	✓	✓	C,E

(Continued)

Brand and model	Price [1]	Speed options [2] (agitation/spin)				Temperature options (wash/rinse)					Fill options	Cycle options [3]				
		Normal/normal	Normal/slow	Slow/slow	Slow/normal	Hot/cold	Warm/cold	Cold/cold	Hot/warm	Warm/warm		Timed soak	Extra rinse	Bleach dispenser (wash)	Softener dispenser (rinse)	Other
Front loaders																
•Wards 6514	680	—	—	—	—	✓	✓	✓	—	✓	Cont.	—	—	—	—	A
White-Westinghouse LT600E	589	—	—	—	—	✓	✓	✓	—	—	3	—	—	—	—	A
White-Westinghouse LT700E	659	—	—	—	—	✓	✓	✓	—	✓	Cont.	—	—	✓	—	A,E
•White-Westinghouse LT800E	689	—	—	—	—	✓	✓	✓	—	✓	Cont.	✓	✓	✓	✓	A,E

[1] Manufacturer's approximate retail; see Ratings for indication of actual prices.
[2] Manually selectable speeds; automatic models may have some or all speed combinations.
[3] All models have regular, permanent press, and delicate cycles.
[4] Model discontinued at the time the article was originally published in Consumer Reports. The information has been retained here, however, for its use as a guide to buying.
[5] Manufacturer says model replaced by WWA8350G, similar except for color changes on control panel.
[6] Manufacturer says model replaced by -XP line, similar to -XM line except for design of control panel.
[7] Can advance automatically to regular wash cycle.
[8] Optional.

KEY TO OTHER FEATURES
A-Top not porcelain-coated.
B-Has built-in small-load wash basket.
C-Has separate agitator for small loads or gentle action.
D-Has electronic touch-pad controls.
E-Has built-in weighing scale.

Metals

Metal polishes

There is no one polish or polishing method that will do for all household metals. Although many metal polishes make broad claims, none are likely to be outstanding for use on brass, copper, stainless steel, aluminum, and chrome. In fact, very few would be worth buying for stainless steel, aluminum, or chrome. Ways to handle these metals are given on page 117.

As for copper and brass, some polishes must be washed off thoroughly because they are acidic and can stain or etch some metals if left in contact with them. Others, however, may be wiped or rubbed off, for they leave at most only a slight stain if they are not completely and immediately removed. It's a good idea, therefore, to restrict your choice to a wipe-off polish for objects that can't be readily rinsed or submersed.

A good polish should make it easy to remove tarnish. It should leave an appropriate gloss and not rub off excessive brass in the process.

As a group, wipe-off brands produce a better shine. Wash-off products, however, require less elbow grease to remove tarnish than do those of the wipe-off type—a difference that you might consider important if you have to clean a heavily tarnished surface. (If you want to give a high gloss to a heavily tarnished surface, you can, of course, use both types of polish, a wash-off brand followed by a high-shining wipe-off brand.) Another advantage of a wash-off product is that, on the whole, it causes less wear than most polishes of the wipe-off type.

Wear may not be a factor if you're cleaning a solid metal; but for things that may be only thinly coated with brass or copper, you should use the mildest cleaning method possible. This means a cloth with detergent or a wipe-off brand that's low in abrasion. Then it might be a good idea to protect the surface with a spray-on finish for brass or copper. You can usually find out whether the object to be cleaned and polished is solid or coated by holding a magnet against it. Objects that have a ferrous base coated with brass or copper will attract the magnet; solid brass and copper will not. Before any brass polish can work, the metal surface must be free of any lacquer. You'll have to use a special cleaning solution to do that. You can also use nonoily nail polish remover—or acetone. Any of these products is toxic and/or flammable. They must be applied cautiously and sparingly.

When the metal is clean, and after it has been polished, it's a good idea to recoat it immediately with a spray intended for the purpose.

Copper-bottomed cookware

The qualities of wash-off products are particularly suited to cookware, which can be washed easily and isn't necessarily required to have a high gloss. These products should be able to remove light tarnish with little or no rubbing, and with less effort on heavy tarnish than a wipe-off material. Even with the most efficient product, however, considerable elbow grease is still called for to clean a heavily coated blackened pan bottom. Steel wool will do the job more easily than polish, but leaves scratch marks on the copper. If your pans are in bad shape but you are display conscious, you might first scour the worst of the dirt off with bronze wool and then finish the job with a wipe-off polish. That will reduce the scratch marks and rub up a good gloss.

If you are looking for an excuse to avoid cleaning the tarnish off copper-bottomed cookware, you can find one in the fact that the darkened surface is more efficient for cooking than a shiny one; it absorbs heat better.

Safety

Polishes, like other household chemicals, should be kept out of the reach of children. Some brands (most often the ones labeled as containing petroleum, mineral spirits, or kerosene) carry appropriate warnings required by law.

This doesn't mean, however, that you can depend on a polish without warnings to be safe.

How to polish stainless steel, aluminum, and chrome

Stainless steel, aluminum, and chrome aren't entirely impervious to soiling, stains, or corrosion, whatever their names may imply or the claims state. Stainless steel may stain with heat; aluminum becomes discolored with use, and its polished surface may dull; chrome doesn't tarnish, but it can become dirty and splotched.

Stainless steel. Ordinary cleaning in the sink will do for stainless steel cookware except for an occasional stain from heat. To remove heat stains from the matte-finish inside of a saucepan or fry pan, a wash-off polish can do a competent job, at least as good and maybe better than soapy steel wool. If the pan's polished exterior is also stained, your choice is more limited. For polished stainless steel, use a polishing product cautiously, and work as quickly as possible to avoid leaving chemicals in contact with the metal for any length of time.

Aluminum. You shouldn't expect to be able to restore a polished aluminum finish to its original glossiness. Soapy steel wool, besides being better overall in cleaning and polishing, will probably do a better job of restoring at least some of the luster than will a special aluminum cleaner. Rubbing the metal with straight, back and forth motions, rather than in circles, helps to maintain a uniform appearance.

Chrome. A chrome finish may be so thin that it is best not to use any abrasive polish on it at all. The mildest cleaning method possible should be used for chrome-plated utensils, starting with detergent and progressing to nonabrasive plastic scouring balls. Stubborn food residues that resist this treatment can be tackled with an oven cleaner, following label instructions.

On the chrome trim of a car, periodic applications of car wax can hold corrosion at bay. If the surface is already corroded and gentle cleaning methods don't work, you will have to resort to a moderately abrasive chrome cleaner, available in automobile supply and hardware stores.

Silver care

A silver-care product can do three jobs simultaneously: It removes tarnish, polishes, and treats silver with chemicals that retard further tarnishing. There are also two-way products that clean and polish but don't claim to provide tarnish retardance. Both types of product include a mild abrasive. You rub the polish on, wipe it off, and then buff the finish to the shine you want.

One-way products are only cleaners. All are liquids and don't require tedious rubbing to remove tarnish. You just dip the silver in them or spread them onto silver surfaces. Because of the acid in the liquids, you have to handle them carefully to prevent skin irritation, rinse cleaned silver thoroughly, and tolerate a disagreeable odor as you work.

Special problems

Antique finishes.   Dark-looking silver with an antique or "oxidized" finish is often deeply patterned. Silver polish is almost certain to remove some of the finish. Dip cleaners damage antique finishes, too, even when you wipe the liquids carefully onto the silver.

Satin finishes.   Dips are the only cleaners that remove tarnish from satin, or low-luster, finishes without making them shinier to some degree.

Staining.   If you accidentally allow drops of polish to fall on silver pieces, dip cleaners are likely to leave pale stains, and some other products may leave dark stains. You have to repolish to remove the stains. Many silver table knives are made with stainless steel blades, and—just as the label warns—drops from dip cleaners can permanently spot or even pit stainless steel if allowed to dry on the surface. Rinse such knives off promptly after using a dip cleaner on their silver handles to avoid damage.

Acidic dip cleaners, as a class, have some inherent hazards that the label may or may not mention. For example, some labels don't suggest using plastic or rubber gloves to protect your hands while cleaning, even though prolonged contact with the cleaner may irritate the skin. Some labels don't warn of the danger of getting a cleaner in the eyes. Some labels fail to mention the necessity for proper ventilation when using dip cleaners—excessive inhalation of their sulfide fumes can cause headaches.

Recommendations

As a class, three-way products are higher priced than other products. Nonetheless, a good three-way product is to be preferred. Although they won't clean silver as easily as a good one-way product, they also do the polishing job—and do it well. What's more, because of their tarnish retardance, you won't have to clean the silver again quite as soon.

Dip cleaners work fast but you still may need to use a polish afterward, and polishing, after all, is like cleaning all over again.

Two other ways to clean your silver

Cleaning and polishing heavily tarnished silver with a stick of jeweler's rouge entails coating a piece of flannel with rouge, rubbing silver surfaces with the flannel until they are tarnish-free, then buffing the silver with a piece of clean flannel. The result will be silver just about as clean and bright as you can get with the best silver polish. This method has two drawbacks: You have to rub a lot more, and the process is messy, producing quantities of red particles that can smudge clothes and furnishings. Rouge, however, is much cheaper than regular polish. Cleaning cloths are reusable until they start to come apart. You can get rouge from hobby shops or firms that supply professional jewelers. Look in the *Yellow Pages* under Jewelers' Supplies and Craft Supplies.

There is also a cheap and easy way to untarnish silver without rubbing—by a chemical process known as electrolysis. First you put the silver in a well-scoured aluminum pot (or in a nonaluminum pot with a piece of aluminum foil). Then add ¼ teaspoon baking soda and ¼ teaspoon salt dissolved in one quart of boiling water. If the tarnished objects are completely immersed and are touching the aluminum, electrolytic action will clean them in minutes. Then be sure to rinse them off well.

Electrolysis should not be used on satin or antique finishes that you want to preserve. Electrolytic cleaning may leave a dullness on silver that only a silver polish can remove. Of course, electrolysis is just for cleaning, not for polishing. One additional caution: Do not use electrolysis on tableware that may have hollow handles. The boiling solution may soften the cement and loosen the handles.

Miscellaneous

Audio/video recording and playback equipment: compact discs

Despite the proliferation of compact disc cleaning devices on the market, care for CDs is easier than for LPs. Just remember that the most serious damage to a CD is a scratch in the direction the disc spins. Small scratches in the *radial* direction, across the "grooves," are completely ignored by the CD player; therefore, always wipe a CD in the radial direction. Light dust will not harm play; heavier dust can be removed by light strokes with a soft cloth. Smudges or deposits should be washed off under running water, with a little liquid dishwashing detergent if needed, then rinse the CD and allow it to air-dry on edge or *carefully* pat it dry with a soft cloth.

LP phonograph records

You can reduce the need for cleaning the phonograph cartridge stylus if your discs are free from dust, and dust-free records last longer. Records can be cleaned with a cloth-pile brush before you play them; electronics stores sell such brushes. Keep the turntable's dust cover closed except when changing records, and handle records only by the edges and the label area to prevent perspiration and body oils from attaching dust to the record's vinyl surfaces. When returning a record to its album, make sure that the opening in the inner sleeve doesn't coincide with the opening in the outer cover and leave the record case wide open for dust to enter. Always store records vertically to reduce the likelihood of warping and keep records away from direct sources of heat.

Phonograph stylus

Cleaning a stylus is neither difficult nor time-consuming. It's important to keep the stylus free from accumulated dust and dirt, which accelerate record wear and can cause mistracking and distortion.

Clean the stylus with a fine camel's hair brush lightly moistened with a little rubbing alcohol. Brush lightly from the rear to the front of the cartridge; brushing backward or sideways could bend the delicate stylus.

Tape deck recording and playback heads

The quality of sound you hear when you play an audio tape depends to a great extent on the condition of the tape machine's heads. Clean the delicate recording and playback heads periodically for the best sound by following the manufacturer's instructions (if any are given). Use a small cotton swab, or, even better, a lint-free piece of cotton cloth wrapped around the swab. Lint-free cloth doesn't have as much of a tendency as cotton to release tiny fibers that might get into the moving parts of the machine. The swab or cloth should be lightly moistened with a cleaning agent. You can use isopropyl alcohol (rubbing alcohol), but it is probably safer and better to buy "tape head" cleaner from an electronics supply store. That should ensure getting a product with a formulation developed specifically for the purpose. Such a cleaner is most likely to contain solvents that are safe for use on the heads as well as for the materials around the heads. Clean everything in the tape path, not just the heads: the capstan (the rotating metal shaft that moves the tape past the heads), the pinch roller (the rubberlike roller that contacts the capstan), and the tape guides.

If the deck or tape player is built so that the heads are not accessible for cleaning, you might try a special head-cleaning tape. Follow the instructions explicitly. Never use any kind of abrasive material to clean the heads.

Clean as frequently as necessary, based on how often you play tapes, the quality of the tapes, and any evidence of dirt accumulation. Once a month is probably a reasonable interval.

VCR recording and playback heads

A video head is the device that picks up the video signal from the tape. Video heads are abraded and pick up iron particles as they rub against the tape; eventually they wear out.

In tests of a VHS model and a Beta model running continuously for an extended period, with tapes changed every 200 hours, Consumers Union engineers found that the picture began to deteriorate after about 2,500 hours of play.

VCRs come with two or more heads. The presence of more than two heads usually doesn't improve picture quality but it does improve the VCR's ability to produce cleaner still pictures or slow-motion pictures.

Replacing the heads can be expensive, running to a considerable fraction of the cost of the entire machine. There's not much you can do about normal wear of the head resulting from its spinning at high speed against the tape, and the tape moving past the head. You can try to keep the machine as free of dust as possible by covering it when the VCR is not in use and by storing tapes where they aren't likely to gather a lot of dust or other debris.

Sooner or later, however, the head will get dirty and the picture will become "noisier" and/or fuzzier than it was when the machine was new. Cleaning the head is no easy chore. It is very delicate and often accessible only through a maze of delicate wiring and mechanical components.

When the picture becomes annoyingly deficient, you might try a special VCR cleaning tape, using it very cautiously and strictly in accordance with its manufacturer's instructions.

Auto polish

Polishing your car may not be worth the time and effort, given the excellence of modern auto finishes.

Nevertheless, plenty of people do take the time and effort to polish their car. That's not because polishes shine or protect better than they used to. Rather, it's likely that the car polishers are trying to protect a sizeable investment. It obviously can't hurt to preserve a new car's finish, and a glossy finish may well enhance the resale price of an older car.

Despite advertising claims to the contrary, auto polishes can't endow your car with eternal good looks. To appreciate why that's so, consider the physical realities involved in protecting the sheet metal on a car.

Automotive finishes are precisely formulated to present a relatively long-lasting coating that protects against all kinds of weathering. Even so, the coating is necessarily thin—only about four-thousandths of an inch on most cars. Water, dust, sunlight, soot, road grime, and the like slowly combine to break down the top layers of paint, opening microscopic cracks that deaden the gloss and diminish the paint's water repellency.

Against such constantly abusive forces, auto polishes start out severely disadvantaged. Polish is buffed down to a thickness measured in microns, or thousandths of a millimeter. There's really not much of anything deposited during a polishing operation that can protect for very long.

Nevertheless, *something* is deposited. The abrasives in most polishes can smooth off the degraded top surface of a car finish. The waxy ingredients in most polishes fill microscopic cracks and renew the surface's water repellency, at least temporarily. Finally, buffing the newly smoothed surface can restore gloss to the finish, at least temporarily.

Before you apply any polish, the car should be thoroughly cleaned with water and detergent to remove road dirt and with a car-cleaning product that's formulated to remove road tar.

One indication of a polish's presence is beading, the water repellency that a wax or oil can confer on a surface. If the waxy film is intact, water will skitter about the surface in nervous droplets. As the film wears away, the droplets will appear to relax and settle down, eventually forming broad pools or sheets.

Another sign that auto polish is holding up is, of course, gloss. A smooth, unbroken film can present a mirrorlike surface. As the film erodes, blemishes coarsen its surface, scatter its reflected light, and deaden its gloss.

Shine durability

Whenever you try to show off the thin film of an auto polish by washing it, you necessarily remove some of it. On the other hand, if you *don't* wash, the elements that have dirtied your car will probably degrade its finish more than a wash will.

For all practical purposes, even the most durable polish will be gone after about ten car washes. A typical polish won't last through half-a-dozen washes.

If you're a meticulous car owner, you may well want to repolish long before it becomes absolutely necessary. If water splashed on the car beads up, you can postpone polishing, but if the water runs off in sheets, get out the polish.

Rubbing it in

You should apply polish according to label instructions, using any special applicator that comes in the package. Otherwise, use soft, prewashed T-shirt material. It's generally a good idea to polish a car in the shade even though some manufacturers' instructions don't require it.

Liquids have a reputation for going on easier than pastes, but you're not likely to be able to detect a really appreciable difference between types, or even between soft pastes and hard pastes.

Buffing usually involves wiping off the haze that forms after the polish has dried. If you use a polish that doesn't form a haze, that's a step-saving convenience you may not find convenient. On already shiny surfaces, it's not easy to tell where you've polished and where you haven't.

Pastes are packaged in familiar-looking wide-mouthed tins. Some liquids come in metal cans, others in bottles that are usually plastic. These products should be kept out of the reach of children and used with the normal precautions you'd observe with other cleaning chemicals.

Recommendations

Although it's doubtful whether new or nearly new cars will really benefit from polishing, there are other points of view. Certainly, no car will suffer from a careful polishing now and then, and devotion to a regular polishing schedule may eventually pay off by enhancing a car's resale value. (Don't overdo it. Polishing too often can remove a car's finish down to the primer.)

If your car badly needs a shine—if its finish is completely dull, chalked, or bronzed—consider using a special polishing or rubbing compound first.

Drinking water

Impurities in water aren't necessarily bad. The "clean, delicious" taste of bottled spring waters often comes from the beneficial minerals they contain, such as calcium and magnesium. In fact, chemically pure water tastes quite flat and unappealing.

Nevertheless, Americans are becoming increasingly concerned with the quality of their water, as the booming sales of bottled water clearly show, but paying a lot for water from bottles isn't the only way to get good-tasting water. Many people have turned to activated carbon filters to upgrade their drinking water.

The carbon material is formed by exposing a carbon-containing material (usually charcoal) to high temperatures and steam in the absence of oxygen. The resulting material is honeycombed within by minuscule branching and twisting channels. The channels greatly increase the surface area to which the water is exposed and thereby account for activated carbon's impressive filtering power. As water passes through this microscopic labyrinth, contaminants stick to the walls of the channels. "Adsorption" is the technical term.

Some homestyle activated carbon water filters are sink mounted and attach to the faucet outlet, others go under the sink and are connected to the cold water line there, and a few are independent of the house plumbing. Most manufacturers of home-use filters claim only that their products improve the taste and odor of water. A few claim that their products will remove toxic chemicals.

Limitations of filters

There are some important water problems that activated carbon filters will not affect. They won't help against:

Hard water. This contains large amounts of dissolved minerals, mainly magnesium and calcium. A water-softening device is needed to remove those minerals.

Other dissolved minerals. Activated carbon filters will remove dust particles, but they have only a small effect on dissolved metals such as iron, lead, manganese, or copper. They won't remove chlorides, fluorides, or nitrates at all. An "ion exchange" device, available at plumbing supply stores, can be used to remove most of those minerals, as can a "reverse osmosis" device. "Reverse osmosis" is a much more complex procedure.

Hydrogen sulfide. This chemical gives water the taste and odor of rotten eggs. Chlorination usually takes care of the problem; carbon filters can remove only small amounts of hydrogen sulfide.

Filtering

Despite their limitations, activated carbon filters can significantly improve water quality. First, the filters can quite effectively remove many objectionable tastes and odors. Second, they can also help clear sediments (turbidity) from tap water. Third, many home filtering units can effectively remove organic chemicals, such as chloroform, which belong to a family of chemicals known as trihalomethanes (THMs).

Three important filter characteristics are the following:

Organic chemical removal. Chloroform is known to cause tumors in animals and is suspected to be a carcinogen for humans. It provides a tough test of a filter's ability to remove organic chemicals because activated carbon filters don't retain chloroform as well as they do more complex organics such as pesticides. To prevent chloroform absorbed by the filter from being returned to the water later on, avoid models that used powdered activated charcoal in a pad. Granular activated carbon is much more effective.

Chlorine removal. This indicates a filter's ability to remove a chemical that contributes heavily to water's taste and odor. Chlorine is added at water treatment plants to protect public health—usually in sufficient quantity to maintain a residual amount at the tap. Even moderate amounts of chlorine can contribute to characteristic and often disagreeable tastes.

Useful flow rate. As a general rule, filtration ability depends on the flow rate of the water. Gushing water isn't filtered as well as water flowing at slower speeds. Some filters are effective only when water trickles through; others can handle much faster flow rates. A filter's "useful flow rate" is the flow rate it can tolerate while still removing contaminants adequately.

Under-sink filters

Under-sink units are the larger and generally more expensive type. Their size is also one of their main advantages. Most are effective against chloroform for extended periods. They all do well at removing chlorine.

A good cartridge design is essential for effective filtration that keeps the filtered contaminants within the filtering device and doesn't return them to the water later on. The most effective units use granular carbon in a cartridge with hard plastic sides. This design forces the water to travel the length of the filter, ensuring longer contact time with the carbon. Some filter cartridges with mesh or wound-string sides allow water to pass through the sides of the filter, permitting much less contact with the carbon, but a wound-string type can incorporate the desirable features of long-time carbon contact.

To take advantage of the high useful flow rate of an under-sink filter and extend the life of the filter cartridge, connect the unit so it operates from a separate faucet. That permits running cold water through the filter only when you need filtered water for drinking or working.

Sink mounting

Sink-mounted filters are generally smaller, easier to install, and cheaper than an under-sink variety. They also perform more modestly. Typically, they have a lower useful flow rate than an under-sink unit and their filter lifetime is also shorter, which is understandable in view of the smaller size. The **Hurley**, which contains much more carbon than the other sink-mounted models, is a notable exception.

The **Hurley** is unique, too, in that filtered water comes out of a spigot on the filtering unit and not out of the tap. That requires the filter to be positioned right at the edge of the sink.

The **Hurley** has another distinctive feature: It can be cleaned by "backwashing," a reverse-flow procedure in which hot water is run through the filter spigot and out the bottom of the filter. Backwashing flushes out some contaminants and can help to reduce bacterial levels for up to several days. You have to back-wash regularly, however, to maintain the effect, and there is one possible hitch: The **Hurley** requires 145° F water for backwashing your water isn't that hot, backwashing might not do much good.

Taste

If you ask people to compare two versions of heavily chlori-nated water—one version unfiltered, the other filtered—the panel-ists are almost certain to prefer the filtered water overwhelmingly.

Evidently, an activated carbon filter does help improve the taste of water; what's more, it doesn't have to be very effective to make the improvement noticeable.

Safety

A filter traps many contaminants, but it isn't effective against bacteria. In fact, a filter can allow the bacterial levels in water to multiply many times over. Wet activated carbon, richly infused with trapped organic matter, provides an ideal breeding ground. High bacterial levels are most likely when a filter has a saturated cartridge and when some time has passed since the filter's last use.

Tests run by the U.S. Environmental Protection Agency showed that periods of stagnation—up to five days of nonuse—will increase bacterial counts in filtered water. (A filter can go unused even in a busy household, for instance, when the family takes a weekend outing or a vacation.)

Bacteria get into the filter in the first place because disinfection at the water treatment plant doesn't kill everything. A certain number of bacteria survive and end up in tap water.

The digestive system usually adapts to the low level of "harmless" bacteria found in drinking water. Common sense suggests that drinking large doses of unidentified bacteria is best avoided.

One thing is certain: If bacteria don't get into the filter in the first place, they can't multiply inside. For this reason, filters should only be used to treat water that is microbiologically safe. (If you have questions about the safety of your water, you should ask the water company for its latest test report; if you use well water, you'll need to have it tested yourself.)

Some filters contain silver and claim to discourage growth of bacteria within the filter; but don't be impressed by any filter's "bacteriostatic" claim. The EPA has concluded that silver compounds in water filters show "no significant bacteriostatic effect" on drinking water.

Using a filter

How to use your filter is almost as important as which brand you buy. If you follow these suggestions you can maximize your filter's performance.

1. Flush out the filter before the first use of the day. Open the

faucet wide and let the water run for at least fifteen seconds for an under-sink model, at least five seconds for a sink-mounted filter. When you install a new cartridge, flush for several minutes to remove fine carbon particles.

2. Change filters regularly. A heavily used filter is more likely to contain high bacterial levels and to discharge organic chemicals previously trapped. An exhausted filter is worse than useless.

3. Don't filter hot water. A filter on the hot water faucet won't remove contaminants very well. And the hot water may liberate chemicals previously trapped on the filter.

4. Use the slowest flow rate you can tolerate. The longer the water is in contact with the filter, the more impurities the carbon can attract and the cleaner your water will be.

5. After installing a new cartridge, circle the date for the next replacement on your calendar. Stick to your schedule.

Recommendations

An activated carbon water filter will remove chlorine and other chemicals that impart taste and odor to water; some filters are also effective at removing organic chemicals, including chloroform and others that have little taste. Unfortunately, a wet carbon filter makes an excellent breeding ground for bacteria that can find their way into your drinking water. The potential for bacteria demands that you buy a filter only if you're willing to change the cartridge regularly.

If you simply want to clear your water of rust and dirt, then a sediment filter may suit you just fine. Such a filter contains no carbon.

If your complaint about tap water is mainly esthetic—an objectionable taste or odor—then a sink-mounted carbon filter would probably suit you.

An under-sink unit is for more serious problems such as water that tastes awful unless it's treated, or water that contains small amounts of harmful organic chemicals. These units must be permanently connected into the cold water line; this means some effort if you do it yourself and may be costly if you hire a plumber.

There are also large, whole-house units with over 30 pounds of carbon that are used when a serious pollutant has been identified. Such units have a provision for regular backwashing. Check the *Yellow Pages* for Water Treatment Equipment.

Ratings of water filters

(As published in a November 1983 report.) Listed by types; within types, listed in order of estimated number of gallons of water effectively filtered to reduce chloroform. Bracketed models are judged similar in ability to remove chloroform and are listed in order of increasing price. Estimated filter lifetime is for guidance; actual lifetime may vary greatly according to local water quality. All come with installa-tion instructions and mounting hardware. Under-sink models may require installation by licensed plumber. Except as noted, sink-mounted models fit on faucet end. Prices are suggested retail and do not include cost of installation; prices in parentheses are for replacement filter cartridges; * indictes that price is approximate; + indicates that shipping is extra.

				Chloroform removal				
Brands and models	Price	Dimensions (W×H) (in.)	Estimated filter lifetime [1] (gal.)	Effectiveness	Useful flow rate	Chlorine removal [2]	Carbon type [3]	Comments
Under-sink models								
Culligan Super Gard SG-2	$175* ($23*)	5×16	3000	◐	◐	●	G	A,B,O
Sears 3464	23*(7.50)	5×12	1200	◐	●	●	G	D,P,S
Amf-Cuno AP50T	67(12)	4½×14½	1200	◐	●	●	G	H
Seagull IV X-1F	290(40)	5×6½	1200	◐	○	●	Pb	A,B,C,E,F,K
Fulflo WC-12	51(8.85)	5×13	300	○	●	◐	G	D,H,J,R

Excellent ◀ ● ◐ ○ ◑ ● ▶ Poor

Brands and models	Price	Dimensions (W×H) (in.)	Estimated filter lifetime [1] (gal.)	Chloroform removal		Chlorine removal [2]	Carbon type [3]	Comments
				Effectiveness	Useful flow rate			

■ *The following 3 models were judged much less effective than those preceding. In addition, they "unloaded" or returned, some chloroform to tap water when used for more than 300 gallons. All may be satisfactory for removing some tastes and odors, however.*

Brands and models	Price	Dimensions (W×H) (in.)	Estimated filter lifetime (gal.)	Effectiveness	Useful flow rate	Chlorine removal	Carbon type	Comments
Aqua Guard AGT200	37+(6.25+)	4¼×12½	150	◑	◉	◉	P	H,R,T
Keystone 3121	44(6.75)	5×13	150	◑	◉	◉	P	H,R
Filterite 1PC	55(9)	5½×12¼	150	◑	◉	◉	P	H,J

■ *Sink-mounted models*

Brands and models	Price	Dimensions (W×H) (in.)	Estimated filter lifetime (gal.)	Effectiveness	Useful flow rate	Chlorine removal	Carbon type	Comments
Hurley Town & Country	190(47+)	6½×10½	3000	●	◉	◉	G	A,L,M,N,O
Ecologizer Water Treatment System 5505	35+(10+)	4×6	250	○	◑	◑	G	A,H,I,L,U
Pollenex Pure Water "99"	35(4.95)	5½×5	150	◑	○	◑	G	A
Aqua Guard AGT300	30+(3.50+)	4×4½	100	◑	○	○	G	H,T

■ *The following model was judged much less effective because it never achieved chloroform-removal level of 50 percent in CU's tests.*

Brands and models	Price	Dimensions (W×H) (in.)	Estimated filter lifetime (gal.)	Effectiveness	Useful flow rate	Chlorine removal	Carbon type	Comments
Peerless RP5506	20(4)	3½×3	—	●	◑	◑	P	F,G,K,Q

[1] *Lifetime, as determined by CU, is number of gallons during which removal of chloroform is expected to be greater than 50 percent. Lifetimes of 1,000 gallons or more are combination of CU and EPA test results.*
[2] *Chlorine removal judged with unused cartridge for first few gallons only.*
[3] *G, granular; Pb, powder in block; P, powder in pad.*

Paint-removing tools

You don't have to remove old paint every time you repaint. Before repainting any surface, however, you should get rid of bits of loosened paint and make sure the remainder isn't greasy or dirty.

When you have to deal with a paint in really poor condition, you may have to go beyond just stripping away the flaking and peeling paint. If you don't, the surface—whether that of furniture, the walls of a room, or the side of a house—may continue to deteriorate. You'll usually end up with far better-looking results if you strip off *all* the old paint.

What kind of paint-removing equipment should you use? Chemical paint removers are poisonous or highly flammable—or both. They are among the most dangerous products you can have around the house. Blowtorches and other devices that soften old paint by heating it pose a fire hazard. That leaves scrapers and sanders that you use by hand or as an accessory for an electric drill. Finishing sanders can also be used to remove paint. These methods are all slow and often strenuous to use, but for the most part they are safer.

There's a wide variety of paint-removing tools available from hardware stores, home centers, and by mail order, but no single scraper or sander will handle every paint-removal job. You may eventually need three or four different types, depending on the jobs you tackle.

Hand tools—for small jobs

There are a large number of hand tools available—scrapers, rasps, and sandpaper substitutes. Each type has its uses, however specialized. Since none is really expensive, it's a good idea to keep more than one type in your tool kit: one or two scrapers, along with a rasp or a sandpaper substitute. Within types, differences from one brand to the next are usually minimal, so you can choose according to price and availability at hardware stores and home centers.

Hook scrapers. A hook scraper is best suited for removing loose paint from flat surfaces. It looks something like an extra-large razor with a stiff, fairly dull blade, and, like a razor, it's pulled along the work surface so the edge of the blade scrapes away the paint.

The blade on a hook scraper usually has more than one usable edge. By loosening a screw, you can bring another edge into the working position. The more usable edges a scraper has, the longer you can work without having to sharpen it. A tungsten carbide blade is far harder than a conventional metal blade and will hold its edge much longer. If such a blade gets dull, you'll have to replace it or have it honed by a professional. Other blades can be resharpened simply by filing them lightly, a job you may do quite often.

Push scrapers. These resemble the familiar-looking putty knife, though they vary in details. Some have a long handle, others a short one. Some have a blunt edge; others are sharpened. You have your choice of stiff or flexible blades in several widths. The differences are of minor importance. You should try to match the shape and size of the scraper to the job at hand—a narrow-bladed scraper, for example, will be best for working in and around window frames.

Push scrapers are useful on flat surfaces and for digging paint out of corners, but they are not meant to be used on curves. In general, they are less effective than hook scrapers on all but the loosest paint. It's harder to push a scraper than to pull it.

Rasps and abrasive blocks. These devices can scrape and sand and are generally available in a variety of sizes and abrasive grades. Rasps and blocks can also be used for sanding wood. Their shape limits their use primarily to flat surfaces, however.

Sandpaper substitutes. Unlike rasps and sanding blocks, sandpaper substitutes are fairly flexible, so they can get into places the others can't. They may be rectangles of tough cloth coated on both sides with sheets of abrasive-coated nylon mesh, or possibly a thin sheet of metal punched with ragged holes.

The substitutes are durable and fast cutting and can be wrapped around a dowel to sand a concave surface or can be used with a sanding block. Some may leave the surface rather rough, making it necessary to do some light sanding before painting.

Sponges and glass blocks. To sand moldings and other

complex shapes, woodworkers often wrap sandpaper around a sponge. Sanding sponges come essentially prewrapped, with an abrasive coating covering four sides. They are springy and flexible, as you'd expect a sponge to be. They can also be rinsed out to unclog the abrasive.

Foamed glass blocks resemble chunks of hardened plastic foam. They wear away quite rapidly as they're used, leaving a residue of glass dust in the work area. What's worse, they may give off the stench of rotten eggs as you work. Sandpaper is better, and less offensive to the nose.

Drill attachments—for larger jobs

A majority of drill attachments are simply variations on the standard sanding disk, the difference being the kind of abrasive supplied. Most disks use cloth or stiff mesh coated with grit. Others are metal circles punched with holes to form a rasplike cutting surface. Yet another type is a "flap wheel" attachment, which consists of a hub fringed with flaps of abrasive paper on cloth. Some oddball attachments consist of a stiff wheel with a texture much like that of a natural sponge, stiff rubbery disks impregnated with abrasive, and a disk of material that's similar to a kitchen scouring pad.

Powered by a drill, these accessories have the ability to remove paint fairly quickly from large, reasonably flat surfaces, such as garage doors and boat hulls. These attachments can also be used to remove rust, but a hard-edged disk is suitable for use only on nearly flat surfaces. Disk attachments generally perform better than flap wheels primarily because they work faster. Wire brushes, the kind found in many drill kits, take a long time to remove paint and have a tendency to scratch wood surfaces.

A fast model should be able to strip away a square foot of paint in a little less than a minute. Even with the fastest tool, however, it would take you more than twenty hours, working strenuously, to strip a one-story house that measured 30 feet by 40 feet. That's not a weekend job.

Although speed is an important factor, there are other things to consider in choosing a drill attachment for paint removal:

Condition of surface. Some of the fastest attachments are also the harshest, leaving cleaned surfaces quite rough. If you're removing paint from a piece of furniture or a door, where appearance matters, you should look for an attachment that's reasonably gentle. One that's both fast and rough might be suitable for stripping paint from steel, concrete, or other surfaces that are hard to scratch.

Effort and comfort. All attachments produce some noise, but the disk rasps are especially loud. Other types, including most of the flap wheels, are heavy and tend to slow a drill down, making them a chore to use.

Safety

Paint removal, especially with power tools, requires certain safety precautions. To guard against the obvious hazard—flying chips of paint or grit—you should wear safety goggles or a face shield, work gloves, and a heavy jacket. Hearing protectors are also advisable.

You should also guard against health hazards that may not be immediately apparent. Older houses may have some lead-based paint on them. Removing it with a hand tool or a drill attachment will disperse small particles into the air, where they can be inhaled. Likewise, "antifouling" paints often used on boats contain toxic ingredients that might be hazardous if inhaled. In either case, you should wear a fitted respirator with a suitable filtration cartridge. If the paint is new and presents no toxicity hazard, a simple dust mask should suffice.

Recommendations

Choosing the right drill attachment for paint removal involves balancing speed against roughness, ease of use, and durability. If you're working on fine furniture, for example, you'll want an attachment that won't damage the wood; speed and durability become less important factors. On big jobs, where appearance isn't crucial, look for a tool that's fast, easy to use, and comfortable.

No drill attachment is likely to be very effective in removing paint or rust from complex surfaces; they just can't get into nooks and crannies without gouging the surface.

For large-scale jobs, you'd be better off using the services of a professional or renting the equipment you need. To scrape the old finish off a floor, you should use a large drum sander plus a smaller sander for finishing the edges.

If you have to strip old paint from a house, rent a pressure-water-spray machine, which uses a high-pressure stream of water to clear away chalking or peeling sections without harming firmly adhered paint.

Finally, for furniture and other easily transported items, you might consider a commercial paint stripper, listed in the *Yellow Pages* under Furniture Stripping.

Heaters and rotary strippers

Paint removal is dirty, tedious work, but it need not be dangerous. With most tools, the risk of injury is minimal. Two types of tools, however, create hazards that are hard to avoid.

A number of devices use heat to soften paint to the point where it can easily be scraped away. Some of these consist of an electric heating element, similar to that used in a number of appliances, plus a metal shield and a handle. There may also be quartz-halogen lamps, very much like a home movie light, or propane fueled heater.

All pose a fire hazard. It is all too easy to set fire to paint with any of these heaters.

Drill attachments that are called "rotary strippers" are also unsafe. They consist of stiff wires bristling from a hub. In use, some of the wires can break off and fly away at high speed, which might injure the user or someone standing nearby.

The companies warn you not to apply pressure when using these tools, but this caution is difficult to follow.

Personal care

Cleansing creams and lotions

No cream or lotion can work miracles. These products just clean, though they may also help to make your skin feel more comfortable.

Most cleansing creams and lotions are oil-based formulas that act as solvents on the oils and grease that bind makeup and dirt with them. Many products contain emulsifiers that, like soap, help break down the greasy binders so they can be washed off with water.

Some products can be wiped off, others rinsed off with water. Still others can be either wiped or rinsed.

The essential ingredients in most cleansing creams and lotions don't vary much. Most contain mineral oil. Borax is a cleansing agent common in many of the wipe-off cleaners. Detergents are often used in the rinse-off types. Ingredients such as paraffin, beeswax, and cellulose gum affect the consistency of a product so that it feels soft and is easy to spread on and remove.

Other chemicals, such as sorbitan sesquioleate and methylparaben, fill a variety of functions. They prevent oil and water from separating, for example, or they control mold and bacterial growth. Various oils, from avocado to lanolin to wheat germ, are also commonly added. They may supplement the mineral oil, but probably more important, from the manufacturer's point of view, they also lend the ingredients list a touch of wholesomeness; for example, avocado, safflower, sesame, sweet-almond, castor, and wheat germ oils.

Other ingredients in cleansing creams and lotions are also there primarily to enhance sales appeal. Often they're perfumes or dyes, for these products frequently come in flowery fragrances and sport pretty colors.

Most cleansing products contain water. If there's a lot of water, the product is usually a lotion. Less water makes what's called a nonliquefying cream. When there's no water, the product is a liquefying cream. A few products are liquefying creams that turn into oily liquids when rubbed on the skin. Nonliquefying creams appear to vanish into the skin.

Important properties of cleansing creams are easy application, a comfortable feel while applying, easy removal, comfortable skin feel after use, overall convenience, and of course scent. Feel of skin after use is probably the most important characteristic. A good product shouldn't feel greasy during use, or afterward, nor should a cleansing cream leave your skin too dry or taut. Most products will clean well enough, but you may have to use a lot of some brands or even two applications to get your face clean.

You may prefer a fragrance-free cream because the quality of the scent in preferred cleaners can be less than superior, or you may object to a medicinal scent.

Packaging and selling

Truth-in-advertising regulations perhaps have taken some of the romance out of cosmetics' sales pitches. In its place, there is some solid information in the ingredients labeling that can be particularly helpful to individuals with known allergies.

Cleansing cream marketers are cautious about making claims for calendar-defying changes in anyone's face. Some suggest they are deep cleaning. But, in fact, the dirt and makeup these products help remove are on the surface of the skin. Cleansing creams and lotions may appear to clean more thoroughly than soap and water because they can often do their job with less scrubbing, or simply because the user thinks the creams and lotions can do a more thorough job. Some products purport to soften skin. They may, but the effect is fleeting.

A scientific pitch sells some products. There may be, for example, a little in-store "computer" to determine which of a particular brand's products are appropriate for which skin types—dry, normal, or oily.

Some cleansing lotions and creams come in fairly simple, functional containers. Plastic is better than glass, because greasy hands and glass don't mix.

Some containers could easily lead you to believe that they contain more of the product than is indicated on the label, particularly the ones that come in a jar within a jar. These double walls of plastic—with ample air-space between the walls—create a generous appearance on the outside, but the inside has less to offer.

Recommendations

In the world of cosmetics, expensive, beautifully packaged products have a certain mystique of effectiveness and "magic" ingredients. But few, if any, live up to the billing.

If you are now using an expensive, high-fashion cleansing cream, it could pay off to try an inexpensive one the next time. The experiment could prove interesting.

Dental irrigators

According to the *Dentist's Desk Reference*, published by the American Dental Association, an irrigator is not a substitute for a toothbrush and dental floss. There is no evidence, the *Reference* says, that irrigators remove plaque from the teeth or affect the health of the gums.

On the other hand, the jet of water from an irrigator may help clean out food particles and bacterial irritants that brushing misses. And an irrigator may also be useful for cleaning the teeth around crowns, permanent bridgework, or braces.

If you're looking for an irrigator, you won't find much of a selection. Just a few years ago, nearly a dozen brands were on the market, but only a few brands of electric-powered irrigators remain.

Electrical safety

From the standpoint of electrical safety, the bathroom can be a very unsafe place, and not just because there's water in the sink, tub, and toilet. Bathrooms are humid, which heightens the risk of a shock from an appliance that leaks electricity, especially in case of an accident when an irrigator, perched on the edge of the sink, is knocked over and comes into contact with a basin full of water. A dental irrigator can leak dangerously high levels of current if the pump part is accidentally immersed while plugged in even if turned off. Like any appliance made for use in the bathroom (showers, hair driers, etc.), dental irrigators should be used with caution.

How they work

Irrigators share the same basic design: Water from a small reservoir is pumped through a hose and out of a jet tip. All are supplied with interchangeable tips, and all have a control that lets you vary the water pressure.

The American Dental Association recommends using the lowest water pressure that's effective for cleaning. A high-pressure jet of water can be painful and can damage tender tissue. It can even propel bacteria into the blood vessels in the mouth, causing or aggravating an infection. That's why the ADA advises against the use of an irrigator if you have an infection or an abscess, or if you have some condition that predisposes you to bacterial infections.

Just as important as water pressure is the control you exercise over the jet of water itself. You should keep the tip in constant motion, directing the jet of water from side to side. Moving the jet up and down tends to force bits of debris under the gum flaps. Your dentist should show you the proper irrigation technique before you try it yourself.

The controls for some units are on the base, which means you have to hold the jet tip in your mouth with one hand while you turn on the motor with the other. Another has an extra switch on the handle of the jet tip that lets you turn the water on and off, so you can use the irrigator with one hand, which is convenient. Changing jet tips requires a twist-and-push or twist-and-pull motion.

The controversial Keyes techniques for treating periodontal disease involves massaging a paste of baking soda and hydrogen peroxide into the crevice between the gums and the teeth. Those who practice this treatment have no choice but to buy a unit that can be used with a salt solution. Instructions with some irrigators advise against using a salt solution; it could damage the irrigator's pump.

Recommendations

An irrigator isn't a substitute for a toothbrush or dental floss. Before you spend money on a dental irrigator, check with your dentist to see if it's really necessary.

Try to obtain a wall bracket kit to mount the irrigator on the wall, for safety's sake.

Ratings of dental irrigators

Listed according to performance. All are supplied with four removable tips; additional tips are available. Prices are as published in a March 1984 report.

Acceptable

WATER PIK DELUX MODEL 300W, $45. 7½-inch vertical clearance required in use. Pressure control and on-off switch are on base. Only model tested that can be used with salt solution. Attaching tip to handle judged somewhat inconvenient. Reservoir relatively small. Water reservoir also serves as cover for handle, hose, and tips. Tip may be left in handle, and uncovered, when reservoir is inverted for storage. Wall bracket kit, about $4, mounts irrigator to wall.

WATER PIK STANDARD MODEL 200W, $35. 7½-inch vertical clearance required in use. Wall-bracket kit, about $4. This model, when immersed in water in CU's tests, leaked excessive amounts of electrical current. Pressure control and on-off switch are on base.

NORTHERN ORAL WATER JET MODEL 6270, $24. 8-inch vertical clearance required in use. Combination on-off switch and pressure control is on base; slide switch on handle turns water on and off. Water reservoir also serves as cover for handle, hose, and tips. This model, when immersed in water in CU's tests, leaked excessive amounts of electrical current.

Hand and bath soaps

Soap has been around a long time, and starting as far back as fifty years ago or more, differences in cleaning effectiveness among soaps have been slight, regardless of their perfume or fancy packaging. Soap is merely a cleanser that removes dirt, oil film, and bacteria from your skin.

The ads for soaps are pure soap opera. They always have been, for unfortunately soap doesn't possess any magical properties.

- A woman in a TV commercial says, "I could see an incredible difference in my face. My skin felt so soft, in just seven days."
- Suggestive ads claim that "the body bar with bath oil . . . gives you the soft you just can't get from soap."

Some commercials made in the "great outdoors" seem to suggest that the earthy, red-cheeked, healthful look of the actors will rub off on you.

This fanciful image making isn't surprising since it's not easy to sell something that performs about the same as its competitors. As one trade publication put it: "In mature product categories, especially where unique technologies are unavailable, real consumer product differentiation is difficult."

One real difference between soaps is price. An expensive bar may sell for nearly forty-five times the price of the cheapest. A related difference might be called "durability"—how quickly or slowly the soap disappears from the soap dish or container. That translates into how much the product costs in actual use. Lathering is another consideration, as is free fatty matter (one measure of "moisturizing" ability) and pH content (alkalinity). Fragrance is a quality that induces many people to pay a premium for certain soaps.

The real price

Comparison shopping for soap isn't easy. You'll find a multitude of prices, sizes, packages, even shapes. Unit pricing, which lets you compare price per ounce, is one helpful guide out of this maze. Even so, per-ounce prices may be misleading. A better measure of value is the number of hand washings a soap delivers.

How many hand washings you get from a soap depends on its dissolution rate, that is, how fast it disappears. Some bars of soap, like some rolls of toilet paper, seem to vanish overnight.

How many hand washings you get also depends on how you use the soap. Although it may sound peculiar, with bar soap you tend to use more of a brand that dissolves either very slowly or very quickly and less of a brand that has an average dissolution rate. The bars that have a very slow dissolution rate take more rubbings to get your hands clean, and hence deliver fewer washings; the fast dissolving soaps give fewer washings because they tend to dissolve under the faucet.

In general, liquid soaps are more expensive than bars. How fast liquid soap disappears depends largely on its container. Most have pump dispensers, which serve up varying amounts of soap. A few liquid soaps come in a squeeze container, letting you squeeze out as much as you like.

Lather

Some soaps lather more profusely than others, but lathering has little to do with a soap's cleaning ability. Lathering is actually a result of the water interacting with the soap and depends upon the chemical makeup of the soap. Soft water, which contains few minerals, makes soap lather easily. In hard water, soaps that contain detergent lather better than plain soap. Some people like a lot of bubbles, some just a little. In fact, most soaps lather copiously, except possibly plain soap in hard water.

Fat

Soap is irritating to the skin, not soothing to it. Soap removes dirt and natural oil, which is very drying. In an attempt to make soap less drying and therefore less irritating, some makers have added extra fats—such as lanolin, moisturizing cream, or cocoa butter—and have made much of their moisturizing formulas in their advertising. Most soaps have about the same amount of "free fatty matter"—less than 2 percent—and even a super-fatted soap does not moisturize well since its cleaning ingredients have a drying effect. A moisturizing lotion applied immediately after bathing works better.

Soap can irritate because it is alkaline. Most soaps are moderately alkaline, with a pH of about 10. Despite what ad copy may say about pH, it doesn't matter for most people. Normal skin quickly returns to its natural acidic level after encountering soap. Granted, some people may be sensitive to an alkaline soap. If you are one of those individuals you may want to consider an essentially neutral soap.

When TV and magazine ads aren't promoting "moisturizing" soap or neutral pH soap, they're often selling "deodorant" soap. These soaps contain antiseptics such as triclocarban or triclosan. The antiseptics reduce skin bacteria and thereby slow the development of odor, which may or may not help your social life. Unfortunately, deodorant soaps may do far more than mask B.O. They may cause a rash or other allergic reaction if you have sensitive skin. Furthermore, the antiseptics in a deodorant soap can be absorbed through the skin into the bloodstream. The amount absorbed is minimal, but no one knows whether these amounts present any danger in the long run. You may want to avoid regular use of deodorant soap. Bathing with plain old soap can be just as effective for most people.

Scent

Bars of soap perfume closets and drawers. Once in the soap dish, they waft their scent pleasantly through the bathroom. The fragrance may even add to the sensuousness of the bathing experience.

Perfume isn't new to soap. Since the beginning of soap making, it has been used to mask the unpleasant odors of other ingredients. Perfume is, of course, another way to get you to buy one brand over another. According to a paper delivered at a symposium of the American Society of Perfumers, scent influences consumers to perceive performance differences where none exist. The paper referred to a test in which "consumers perceived the product with the preferred perfume to be superior even when all attributes are equivalent."

Despite perceived differences or individual preferences, even the strongest soap fragrance won't last long on your skin after bathing. The nature of soap is such that it removes most of its own traces from your skin when you rinse. If you want to smell nice, use a perfume or cologne.

Various soap scents can be characterized as floral, woodsy, spicy, herbal, sweet, fruity, or coniferous. Most are floral, often with other aroma undertones as well.

Recommendations

When it comes to ordinary cleaning, all soaps are equal. Your choice of brands, then, should be determined by economy and by personal needs and preferences and not by the ads.

Healthy skin can handle just about any soap. Sensitive or dry skin may fare better with soaps that do not have added perfume or antiseptics. Many soaps have an ingredients list, so you may be able to avoid a brand that contains an ingredient to which you're sensitive. If you have oily skin it's more important to keep your skin clean—no matter how often that means washing—than to use any particular brand of soap.

Soap can cost you anywhere from $.18 to $8 per 100 hand washings. On average, bar soap is cheaper than liquid soap. A more expensive bar soap, however, costs about as much to use as most liquid soap.

You needn't feel guilty about choosing an expensive soap over a cheap soap because you prefer its aroma, but you should be aware of how much you're paying. Consider two bars that weigh the same and dissolve at the same rate. One sells for $2.58 a bar, ten times as much as a cheap personal-size bar. At fifteen bars a year, a preference for the scent of the more expensive soaps would cost you an additional $35 annually.

Whether you bargain shop for soap or treat yourself to the most expensive, you can make a bar of soap last by minimizing the time it spends in water. Use a raised soap dish and remove a bar from the bath water promptly. According to folklore, unwrapping a bar of soap and allowing it to "harden" will lengthen its life. That's just wishful thinking. The only benefit you'll reap from stockpiling unwrapped soap is that it may make your closet or bathroom smell nice.

Ratings of hand & bath soaps

Listed by types. Within types, listed in order of increasing cost of use based on test results and on average price paid for size given. Prices are as published in a January 1985 report. Except as noted, all have an ingredients list, all were low in free fatty materials, and all liquid soaps come in a pump dispenser.

More ◄──────► Less

Product	Cost per 100 hand washings	Price of bar or container	Size (oz. or fl. oz.)	Lather	Fragrance
Bar soaps					
P & Q Deodorant (A & P) [1]	$.18	$.27	5.00	●	Slight floral/spice
Generic Deodorant (Grand Union) [1]	.20	.27	4.50	●	Light floral/spice
Ivory Personal Size [1]	.20	.21	3.50	○	Soapy/spice

Product	Cost per 100 hand washings	Price of bar or container	Size (oz. or fl. oz.)	Lather	Fragrance
Cashmere Bouquet Bath [1]	.21	.30	4.75	◗	Floral/sweet
Scotch Buy White Complexion (Safeway) [1]	.21	.19	3.00	◗	Slight floral/citrus
Cost Cutter Deodorant W/Lanolin (Kroger)	.23	.33	4.75	◗	Fruity/floral
Generic Deodorant (Lucky) [1]	.23	.33	4.75	◗	Slight fruity
Lux [1]	.23	.33	4.75	◗	Floral/sweet
Cashmere Bouquet Regular [1]	.26	.25	3.25	◗	Floral
Jergens Lotion Bath [1]	.26	.38	4.75	○	Floral/fruity
No Frills Deodorant (Pathmark) [1]	.27	.27	5.00	◗	Light floral/spice
Palmolive Gold Deodorant	.27	.39	4.75	◗	Floral
Truly Fine Ocean Mist Deodorant (Safeway)	.29	.43	5.00	◗	Floral/spice/leafy
Palmolive Mild Bath [1]	.29	.41	4.75	◗	Floral
Irish Spring Double Deodorant Bath	.29	.44	5.00	◗	Floral/herbal
Dial Deodorant (Gold)	.31	.33	3.50	◗	Floral/sweet
Ivory Bath Size [1]	.32	.43	4.50	◒	Floral/spice
Fiesta Deodorant	.33	.48	4.75	◗	Floral/leafy
Gentle Touch Bath Bar With Baby Oil [2]	.35	.50	4.75	◗	Floral/spice
Safeguard Deodorant	.38	.57	5.00	○	Floral
Lifebuoy Deodorant	.41	.39	4.75	◗	Slight floral/spice
Zest Deodorant	.42	.69	5.50	◗	Floral/spice
Coast Deodorant	.46	.69	5.00	○	Citrus/herbal

(Continued)

Product	Cost per 100 hand washings	Price of bar or container	Size (oz. or fl. oz.)	Lather	Fragrance
Camay [1]	.47	.49	3.50	○	Light floral/sharp
Caress Body Bar With Bath Oil [6]	.48	.69	4.75	○	Floral/patchouli
Dove ¼ Moisturizing Cream [6]	.52	.55	3.50	○	Floral
Tone Glycerin And Cocoa Butter	.55	.52	4.75	◑	Floral/herbal
No Frills Glycerin (Pathmark) [1] [2]	.57	.40	3.50	◒	Fruity
Basis Superfatted [1]	.60	.60	3.30	◉	Floral
Yardley Cocoa Butter	.62	.79	4.25	◉	Slight floral/spice
Yardley English Lavender	.62	.79	4.25	◉	Strong floral
Yardley Oatmeal	.62	.79	4.25	◉	Floral
Shield Extra Strength Deodorant	.69	.69	5.00	◑	Fruity/mint
Nivea Cream [1]	1.64	1.48	3.00	◉	Floral
Johnson's Baby Bar [6]	1.66	1.49	3.00	○	Floral/spice
Pears Transparent [1]	1.78	1.39	2.60	◉	Slight spice/medicinal
Neutrogena Original Formula Unscented [1]	1.89	1.98	3.50	◒	Light floral/sweet
Neutrogena Original Formula [1]	1.90	1.99	3.50	◒	Slight woodsy/spice
CVS Glycerin [1]	2.07	1.09	3.50	◑	Fruity/woodsy
Roger & Gallet Savon Rose Thé [1]	2.46	2.58	3.50	◉	Floral/leafy
Myrurgia Jabon Maja [1]	2.47	2.00	2.88	◉	Floral
Jergens Medicated Clear Complexion Bar	4.17	2.03	3.25	◒	Fruity/medicinal

Product	Cost per 100 hand washings	Price of bar or container	Size (oz. or fl. oz.)	Lather	Fragrance
Clinique Facial Mild [1] [2]	4.72	8.50	6.00	◓	Slight floral
Estée Lauder Basic Cleansing Bar [3] [6]	6.00	8.50	5.00	○	Floral

Liquid soaps

Product	Cost per 100 hand washings	Price of bar or container	Size (oz. or fl. oz.)	Lather	Fragrance
Ivory Liquid Soap Refill [1]	1.00 [4]	1.59	18.00	◓	Floral/spice
Ivory Liquid Soap [1]	1.00	.99	9.00	◓	Strong floral/spice
Yardley English Lavender Liquid Soap [6]	1.00	1.99	17.50	◓	Strong woodsy/piney
Showermate Liquid Shower Soap [6]	2.00 [5]	1.99	12.00	◓	Slight fruity/leafy/ cocoa
Softsoap Original Formula Refill	3.00 [4]	1.79	15.00	◓	Herbal
Softsoap Liquid Soap [6]	3.00	1.19	7.50	◓	Slight fruity/herbal
Liqua 4 Skin Cleansing System [6]	3.00 [5]	.57	2.50	◉	Floral/herbal
Liquid Neutrogena	8.00	9.00	8.00	○	Slight floral/ medicated

[1] Lacks ingredients list or has incomplete list.
[2] High in free fatty materials.
[3] Very high in free fatty materials.
[4] Cost determined by dispensing from original pump dispenser.
[5] In squeeze bottle; amount dispensed is average for pumped soaps.
[6] Essentially neutral, neither acid nor alkaline.

Mouthwashes

Consumer fear of committing the "social offense" of unpleasant breath or halitosis, an occasional and normal human condition, has turned the mouthwash business into a $350-million-a-year industry.

Much of the mouthwash is sold merely to freshen the breath—a legitimate cosmetic use though hardly a vital hygienic function. Yet mouthwash manufacturers, true to their product's past as a patent medicine, often promise—or seem to promise—even greater potency.

Several companies make rather modest additional claims for their products. The most common is that the mouthwash is an aid in treating "minor sore throat irritation" or "minor mouth irritation." Warner-Lambert, the company that makes **Listerine**, has been more aggressive. **Listerine** has long carried the slogan "Kills germs by the millions on contact"—an impressive claim to anyone who isn't aware that the healthy mouth normally contains billions of bacteria, or "germs." Because of the possibility of misinterpretation, a panel advising the U.S. Food and Drug Administration on mouthwashes has recommended that such germicidal claims be banned.

For a long time, **Listerine** was promoted as being helpful in preventing colds and flu. After lengthy litigation with the Federal Trade Commission, Warner-Lambert was forced to run corrective ads saying that the mouthwash had no such effect.

Then Warner-Lambert advertised **Listerine** as useful in reducing the buildup of plaque on the teeth. Warner-Lambert may have been onto something with this claim.

Reducing plaque

Scientists and consumers alike tend to be skeptical about any claim made for a mouthwash, but some mouthwashes may have a useful role in dental hygiene. The buildup of plaque on teeth may be significantly reduced by the usual brushing and flossing, plus regular use of a mouthwash containing antimicrobial ingredients. Reducing plaque can keep your teeth looking better between professional cleanings and can also help prevent gingivitis, the first stage of periodontal disease.

Mouthwashes specially formulated to reduce plaque contain the chemical chlorhexidine, an effective plaque reducer, and have been undergoing tests. Many U.S. mouthwashes, however, contain other chemicals known to reduce plaque, including cetylpyridinium chloride and domiphen bromide. Studies commissioned by the maker of **Cepacol**, one such product, showed that regular use of **Cepacol** reduced plaque by an average of about 25 percent.

Warner-Lambert commissioned its own tests of **Listerine**. The tests, conducted by various university researchers, showed that **Listerine** also reduces plaque by about 25 to 50 percent, depending on how the reduction is measured.

Neither mouthwash, however, has been shown to reduce the incidence of gingivitis. Warner-Lambert's later ads were carefully worded to portray plaque reduction as a cosmetic benefit, not a medicinal one.

Old claims

What of the other benefits that have long been claimed for mouthwashes?

Do they reduce bad breath? Mouthwashes can't "cure" bad breath because bad breath is not a disease. Whether they can reduce it depends on its cause. Bad breath is sometimes a symptom of an infection in the throat or mouth. Mouthwashes can't cure such infections.

Nor can mouthwashes do much for bad breath that originates in the lungs. The aroma of garlic and onions, for instance, lingers on the breath because chemicals in those foods are absorbed into the bloodstream in the stomach and are eventually released from the blood into the lungs. Similarly, smoker's breath is a product of lung air rather than of anything in the mouth. Mouthwashes may mask such odors temporarily, but studies have found that the effect lasts no more than fifteen or twenty minutes.

Nevertheless, mouthwashes can affect one very common cause of bad breath—bacteria. Certain bacteria that live on the tongue and around the teeth act on leftover bits of food and cells shed from the mouth to produce odorous sulphur compounds. Such bacteria are most active at night, when sleep stills the tongue and slows the flow of saliva. The result is the unpleasant odor and taste of that common condition, "morning mouth."

Simply brushing your teeth (and your tongue), eating breakfast, or rinsing out your mouth with water can eliminate or reduce the odor, but a mouthwash can give a longer lasting effect. Some mouthwash ingredients (those that contain a zinc compound, for example) may react with the sulphur compounds and neutralize them. The antimicrobial ingredients found in many mouthwashes can reduce the mouth's population of bacteria, including those that produce odor, for as long as three or four hours. After that time, however, the bacterial population gradually returns to normal.

Can they treat a sore throat or mouth? Various mouthwash ingredients might make a sore throat or mouth feel better, but mouthwashes in no way cure such afflictions. Even if a mouthwash contains antimicrobial ingredients, the infections that cause sore throats or mouths lie much deeper than the chemicals in a mouthwash can reach.

There are several ways a mouthwash can make a sore throat or mouth feel better, at least for a time. Mouthwashes that contain menthol, phenol, or sodium phenolate can have a temporary anesthetic effect. Glycerin can spread a protective layer over irritated tissue, and an astringent such as zinc chloride encourages a protective coating to form over tissue. Simply getting rid of irritating mucous can make a sore throat feel better. For that, you don't need a bottle of mouthwash—gargling with salty water works fine.

Mouthwash labels

Some mouthwash ingredients are antimicrobial. Except for cetylpyridinium chloride and domiphen bromide, the ingredients may or may not have an effect on dental plaque.

Because many of the name-brand mouthwashes come in several variants, and because supermarket and discount brands tend to copy the successful products, most mouthwashes fall into three "color/flavor" groups:

Amber medicinal. **Listerine** is the archetypal amber medicinal mouthwash. There are a number of imitators sold under chain store and supermarket labels. Amber medicinal mouthwashes have a high alcohol content (from 22 to 30 percent), high enough so that the alcohol might actually be considered an active ingredient and not just a way of keeping the various other ingredients in solution.

The flavor and presumably much of the effectiveness of amber medicinal mouthwashes come from a combination of aromatic oils originally derived from plants: thymol (thyme), eucalyptol (eucalyptus), menthol (peppermint), and methyl salicylate (wintergreen). The products in this group also contain benzoic acid or sodium benzoate, antimicrobial chemicals.

Green minty. These products tend to have an alcohol content about two-thirds as high as the amber medicinal ones. **Scope**, a popular green/minty mouthwash, is the one the store brands usually imitate. **Scope** contains the plaque-reducers cetylpyridinium chloride and domiphen bromide. In addition, green minty products may contain a form of the antimicrobial chemical benzoic acid as well as boric acid, a once common mouthwash ingredient that has been designated as unsafe by the FDA's advisory panel on mouthwashes. It's not prudent to buy any mouthwash that lists boric acid on its label.

Some green minty mouthwashes don't contain any antimicrobial chemicals. Ingredients such as zinc chloride or sodium zinc citrate act as astringents or odor-neutralizers. Glycerin, another common ingredient in green minty mouthwashes, adds a sweet taste and serves as a soothing agent. Most mouthwashes of this type also contain saccharin as a sweetener.

Red spicy. This cinnamon-flavored variety generally has a low alcohol content (most are about 5 percent alcohol) and its main active ingredients are glycerin and a zinc compound.

Miscellaneous. Several mouthwashes on the market fall outside the three main color and flavor categories. They may come in a yellow medicinal version containing cetylpyridinium chloride. A greenish mixture may list the anesthetic phenol as its only active ingredient; yet another type contains phenol and glycerin. These mouthwashes claim to relieve some throat pain. A few products are concentrates, meant to be diluted before using as a mouthwash; undiluted, their alcohol content is high enough so that they would be useful as local antiseptics.

Recommendations

There's no harm in using a mouthwash if you are worried about committing a "social offense." Whether antimicrobial mouthwashes are indeed a worthwhile addition to a properly performed oral hygiene routine depends on the results of studies. Store brands cost considerably less than the name-brand mouthwashes they imitate. Many of them seem to be essentially similar to the products they copy.

Fluoridated mouthwashes

Mouthwashes that contain fluoride may look like mouthwashes—and may even freshen the breath like a mouthwash—but technically, they aren't mouthwashes. They're "anticavity dental rinses."

In one study, conducted in an area that lacked fluoridated water, schoolchildren who used a rinse containing 0.2 percent fluoride only once a week, under supervision, showed an average reduction in tooth decay of 35 percent. Daily use of a more diluted rinse (0.05 percent fluoride) showed similar results.

Even if your water supply is fluoridated and your children use a fluoride toothpaste, the fluoride in a rinse can give additional protection against cavities. Adults can also benefit from the use of fluoride, but not in as many ways.

Representative fluoridated mouthwashes contain 0.05 percent fluoride, and have been marketed primarily for use by children.

These products all contain about as much alcohol as beer does. Of course, none of the rinses should be swallowed, as the label on each warns. For that reason, children under the age of five probably shouldn't use these products, and the bottle should be kept out of their reach. Older children should be carefully instructed in the use of a fluoride rinse. If a child should occasionally swallow some fluoride rinse, there's no reason for panic. The amount of rinse recommended for daily use contains about 5 milligrams of sodium fluoride, higher than the recommended daily internal dose but still below harmful levels.

You may opt for a bottle with a built-in cup in its neck; when you squeeze the bottle, the cup fills with the correct dose. A child can then easily pour it into a glass without danger of pouring out too much or spilling the entire bottle.

Ratings of mouthwashes

Listed by types. Within types, listed in order of increasing cost per fluid ounce as published in a March 1984 report. Alcohol content determined by CU tests; other ingredients as stated on labels. In the columns, √ means yes, — means no.

Brand	Cost per fluid ounce	Alcohol content	Aromatic oils①	Benzoic acid or sodium benzoate	Cetylpyridinium chloride	Domiphen bromide	Glycerin	Zinc chloride or sodium zinc citrate	Others
Amber medicinal									
No Frills Amber (Pathmark)	3¢	22%	√	√	—	—	—	—	—
K Mart	4	30	√	√	—	—	—	—	—
Pathmark Amber	5	30	√	√	—	—	—	—	—
Safeway	6	28	√	√	—	—	—	—	—
CVS Amber	7	29	√	√	—	—	—	—	—
Listerine	10	29	√	√	—	—	—	—	—
Green minty									
Generic (Dublic Generics)	4	19	—	√	√	√	√	—	—
K Mart Mint	4	20	—	√	√	√	√	—	—
Cost Cutter Green (Kroger)	5	11	—	√	√	√	√	—	—
CVS Green	8	21	—	√	√	√	√	—	—
Signal	10	16	—	—	—	—	—	—	—

(Continued)

Brand	Cost per fluid ounce	Alcohol content	Aromatic oils[1]	Benzoic acid or sodium benzoate	Cetylpyridinium chloride	Domiphen bromide	Glycerin	Zinc chloride or sodium zinc citrate	Others
Lavoris Formula-Z Mint (concentrate)	11[2]	5[2]	–	–	–	–	✓	✓	–
Listermint	12	13	–	–	–	–	✓	✓	–
Scope	12	21	–	–	✓	✓	✓	–	–
Cepacol Mint	20	16	–	–	✓	–	✓	–	–

Red spicy

Brand	Cost per fluid ounce	Alcohol content	Aromatic oils[1]	Benzoic acid or sodium benzoate	Cetylpyridinium chloride	Domiphen bromide	Glycerin	Zinc chloride or sodium zinc citrate	Others
K Mart Cinnamon	4	5	–	–	–	–	✓	✓	–
Pathmark Red	5	5	–	–	–	–	–	✓	–
CVS Red	7	6	–	–	–	–	✓	✓	–
Lavoris Formula-Z Cinnamon (concentrate)	11[2]	5[2]	–	–	–	–	✓	✓	–
Lavoris	12	5	–	–	–	–	✓	✓	–
Listermint Cinnamon	12	15	–	–	–	–	✓	✓	–

Miscellaneous

Brand	Cost per fluid ounce	Alcohol content	Aromatic oils[1]	Benzoic acid or sodium benzoate	Cetylpyridinium chloride	Domiphen bromide	Glycerin	Zinc chloride or sodium zinc citrate	Others
Astring-O-Sol (concentrate)	4[2]	5[2]	–	–	–	–	–	✓	[3]
Dr. Tichenor's (concentrate)	4[2]	12[2]	–	–	–	–	–	–	–
Pathmark Oral Care	5	15	–	–	✓	–	✓	–	–
Cepacol	13	16	–	–	✓	–	✓	–	–
Cepastat	22	0	–	–	–	–	✓	–	Phenol
Green Mint Chlorophyll	25	15	–	✓	–	–	–	–	[4]
Chloraseptic	29	0	–	–	–	–	–	–	Phenol

[1] Thymol, eucalyptol, menthol, methyl salicylate.
[2] Calculated according to recommended dilution of concentrate.
[3] Methyl salicylate.
[4] Chlorophyll copper complex, urea, glycine.

Shampoos

Shampoo is basically detergent plus coloring agents, scents, and other ingredients that may or may not make a difference in the appearance of your hair. Dishwashing liquid is basically detergent, too. When the advertising and packaging are stripped away, it's reasonable to wonder how much of a difference exists between the two. If you think of shampoo as hair detergent, you might not be so willing to pay ten times more for it than you pay for liquid dishwashing detergent. To the extent that the difference between the two types of detergent is illusory, it's advertising that creates the illusion.

The shampoo merchants have to peddle dreams. How else can they get consumers to differentiate among the several hundred shampoos on the market? Years ago, things were simpler. People washed their hair with a bar of soap. Much later, recognizing that detergent has some advantages over soap, people used one or another of a reasonable number of shampoos.

Times have changed. Hair has grown in length and, especially among men, in cosmetic significance. Now, as you survey the dazzling array of shampoos on the shelves of a supermarket or drugstore, you may feel obliged to consider the options carefully. Is your hair oily, dry, or normal? Do you want a shampoo that claims to control dandruff? A shampoo meant for damaged hair? Do you want one that will give your hair "extra body"? One that will "repair" split ends? A shampoo with protein? With eggs? With lemon? Would you rather smell like a raspberry, a green apple, a peach, an apricot, an avocado, or a pine tree?

What is in all of those products on the shelf? Usually, just water (lots of it), detergent, foaming agents, some fragrance, and a variety of other component chemicals. Shampoos may not do all the marvelous things that ads claim they do, but they can be counted on to do a better job than just plain soap unless soap is used in very soft water. Plain soap used in hard water leaves a film on the hair. The detergents in shampoos operate without forming that film. Ordinary soap leaves hair clean, but a bit dull.

A good shampoo leaves it clean and shiny, just as the ads promise.

Another way to sell shampoo is to stress a certain ingredient, particularly a "natural" one. Fruit is out, botanicals are in: aloe vera, jojoba, henna, chamomile, ginseng, white nettle, and so forth. Food substances—especially milk, lemon, beer, and egg—have long been used in shampoos. "Keratin protein" and "essential fatty acids" seem to be fashionable.

Many shampoos are "conditioning" shampoos, using ingredients and claims once reserved for separate, post-shampoo conditioning rinses. Indeed, shampoo-brand successes were first successful as conditioner brands before they were introduced as shampoos.

Men and women disagree

A Consumers Union panel test revealed that far more women than men use such after-shampoo products as hair sprays, rinses, or conditioners. Not surprising, the female panelists wore their hair longer than the men. Perhaps because they have longer hair, women often consider their hair limp, while men are more likely to think of their hair as having "normal" body. Such differences would seem to indicate that men and women require very different things of a shampoo.

The chances are good that if you have strong preferences for a certain shampoo, they're based on something other than hair cleaning ability or how well the shampoo conditions your hair. It might be the smell of the shampoo, or even its color. It might be the kind of container it's in, or you may like a certain brand simply because using it makes you feel good. You may be tempted by a new brand simply because you hope that, as the ads promise, the product will work magic with your hair.

One measure of the importance of emotional appeal is the poor sales record of store-brand shampoos. Like other private label cosmetics, they have never been particularly successful. People don't want to trust their hair to a no-name brand.

Magic, therefore, is not a reasonable expectation of shampoo. What is? When you know a few facts about hair, you see that shampoo ads often contain bits of truth greatly adorned with innuendo and mystery.

About hair

Though many shampoo ingredients sound like—or indeed are—food substances, they can in no way "nourish" your hair. The only way you can do that is through your mouth. Hair is formed by special cells deep in the skin, in a pattern largely determined by your genes. A poor diet (or poor health) can also produce poor-looking hair.

By the time hair emerges from the scalp, where shampoo can reach it, hair is lifeless. Still, hair is a protein-keratin, the same substance that makes up fingernails, claws, beaks, and feathers. That fact opens up attractive possibilities for statements regarding "protein" and "keratin protein" in advertising copy.

Hair is more than a mere thread of hardened protein. The outermost layer of a strand, the cuticle, is a series of minute, overlapping scales or shingles, a product of cells deep in the skin. Sebaceous glands secrete sebum, which coats hair and helps give it shine by smoothing down the scales of the cuticles. "Dull" hair can be caused by dirt caught in the sebum or by light reflecting unevenly from ruffled scales of the cuticle. The cuticle protects the cortex, a strong, flexible structure that contains the pigment that gives hair color. If the cuticle wears away, the cortex can fray into split ends.

Shampoos can affect only the cuticle of a normal strand of hair; to reach the cortex, harsh, strong chemicals such as bleaches or waving solutions must be used. Compared with those chemicals, shampoos are quite mild. In fact, there's nothing wrong with washing your hair as often as you want.

Sebaceous glands in the scalp give hair a protective coat of oily sebum. Sebum gives hair shine and helps the scales of the cuticle lie flat. Too little sebum, and hair appears dry and "lifeless," as the ads would say. Too much sebum, and you've got "the greasies." Sebum also collects bacteria and dirt, making hair look dull instead of shiny.

What shampoo does

Shampoo's primary function is to remove dirt and excess sebum from hair. The ingredients that do the work are long molecules called surfactants. One end of these molecules is attracted to oil, the other to water. That allows them to grab sebum and whatever dirt it contains and rinse it out of your hair.

Soap, which used to be the main cleaning ingredient in shampoos, is one type of surfactant, but soap reacts with the minerals that make water hard, leaving a scummy film on hair. Such a film can be removed with an acidic rinse; that's why people started rinsing their hair with lemon juice or vinegar or even beer, which is mildly acidic.

Shampoo manufacturers have by and large turned to surfactants less troublesome than soaps. These ingredients are often called detergents, to differentiate them from soaps. Many are derived from the fatty acids of coconuts.

There are dozens of surfactants, each with its own properties. Some are much milder than the name "detergent" implies—they might remove dirt but little sebum, or they might not sting if they get into your eyes. Others are especially effective at penetrating and removing oil. Some clean but don't foam; others produce a rich lather. Some leave hair looking better than others.

A manufacturer usually uses several surfactants in a shampoo, one being the principal cleaning agent and the others there to modify its effect. The range of surfactants and their possible combinations provide lots of room for claims of "special" formulations. A manufacturer often alters the combination of surfactants to make its shampoos for dry, normal, and oily hair. A dry hair formulation also typically contains conditioners that an oily hair version lacks.

That's the theory. Whether you can truly perceive a difference in cleaning and conditioning ability between an oily formulation and a dry one is questionable. In fact, the degree of oiliness you attribute to your hair may have little connection with your shampoo preference.

If a shampoo stripped all the oil from hair—or failed to replace it with another oil such as a lanolin derivative, balsam, or even soybean or corn oil—the hair would be a mess. The scales of the cuticle would all be flared out, like a feather ruffled backward.

If the scales of the cuticle aren't lying flat, hair won't lie neatly or slide easily when combed. Ruffled scales don't reflect light evenly, so hair looks dull. Alkaline substances such as detergents tend to ruffle the scales. Acidic substances such as creme rinses or lemon juice tend to smooth them down. That's the origin of the fuss some companies make about having a "pH balanced" shampoo.

A product's "pH" is a means of expressing acidity or alkalinity. Something neutral (not acid, not alkaline) will have a pH of 7. Acids will have lower pH values, with orange juice, for example, having a pH of 3 or 4. Values above 7 indicate alkalinity. Hand soaps have a pH value of about 9. Human skin and hair are slightly on the acid side. Therefore, shampoo makers contend that a nonalkaline shampoo is gentler, less irritating to the skin, hair, and eyes.

Shampoo ingredients that don't affect pH values can still sting the eyes. Most shampoos these days are formulated to be, if not acidic, at least not very alkaline. That's typically done by adding citric acid.

The "healthiness" of your hair is directly related to the condition of the cuticle. As hair grows longer and older, the cuticle can wear away, allowing the cortex to fray into split ends. The harsh chemicals used to change hair's color or degree of waviness can also permanently damage the cuticle. Heat from hair dryers or curling irons, physical abuse such as incautious combing or excessive brushing, and overexposure to swimming pool chlorine or sunlight can do the same.

Many shampoos, even those not marketed as "conditioning" shampoos, contain substances that can help damaged hair look better. Some conditioners are oils, aiding or replacing sebum. Some are protein, commonly "hydrolized animal protein." Protein coats the hair shaft, making hair feel thicker and less limp. It also glues split ends together temporarily. There's no evidence that an exotic sounding protein—collagen, placenta, nucleic acid—works any better than a plain sounding protein. The only sure cure for split ends is to cut them off.

A third type of conditioner is a group of chemicals called

quaternaries. One thing they can do is neutralize the negative charge of static electricity that washing and combing impart to hair, thus calming down flyaway hair.

The conditioning effects of shampoo are necessarily at odds with shampoo's cleaning functions. Using a separate conditioner may make better sense, especially if your hair is badly damaged.

Some of the "natural" shampoo ingredients such as jojoba, henna, and aloe may also have conditioning effects, but such effects have not been well documented. Additionally, shampoos containing henna, chamomile, and other botanicals are often sold for their effect on hair color. Some of those ingredients have been so used for centuries. In a special coloring preparation, they may indeed change or highlight color but in a product such as shampoo, their effect, if any, is likely to be unnoticeable.

There are dozens of other ingredients used in shampoo, many of which have little to do with hair and a lot to do with the "esthetics" of the product. Fragrance is the most obvious such ingredient.

Nearly all shampoos also have added coloring, thickeners or thinners. They adjust the viscosity of the product, which can affect how easy it is to move the shampoo measured into your hand onto your hair. Sequestering agents help keep calcium and magnesium in hard water from leaving residues. Preservatives are usually added to keep ingredients such as protein from spoiling. Foam-enhancers are often used because people equate lots of lather with lots of cleaning power, although low-foaming surfactants can clean hair just as well as high-foaming ones.

Dandruff

Most people have dandruff, and for most people it's nothing to worry about. Despite what the dandruff shampoo ads imply, simple dandruff is usually easy to keep under control.

Human skin continually sloughs off bits of its dead outer layer. On the scalp, those bits are fairly large and tend to get trapped in the hair. There they combine with oily secretions from the seba-ceous glands and with dust and other debris to form what most people call dandruff (although many dermatologists believe the word shouldn't be applied to the mild normal condition).

Normal dandruff can be kept under control by frequent shampooing, which rids the hair of dead skin scales and normal, oily secretions. Any shampoo—or soap, in soft water—should do the job nicely. Daily brushing may also help control dandruff, although excessive brushing may damage the hair.

If you have flaking despite such measures, you may find that some dandruff shampoos will help control it. There are five safe and effective ingredients used in various dandruff shampoos: coaltar preparations, sulphur preparations, selenium sulfide, salicylic acid, and zinc pyrithione. Severe flaking, however, can be a sign of seborrheic dermatitis of the scalp. That condition requires attention by a doctor, who may prescribe special treatment beyond over-the-counter preparations.

Recommendations

There really is no "best" shampoo. If the brand you currently use makes you and your hair feel good, there's no reason to change. It's doubtful whether you'll find a shampoo that will turn plain hair into a glorious mane. If you do enjoy switching from shampoo to shampoo—sniffing, sudsing, and testing for shininess—no harm done.

You don't have to spend a lot of money on a "hair care system" in order to have clean, healthy hair. Relatively inexpensive shampoos contain perfectly adequate cleaning and conditioning ingredients. If you want to spend money on an expensive shampoo, do it knowing that you're indulging your psyche, not your hair.

Even among mass-marketed shampoos, there's a wide range in prices. Consider, however, that price differences can be wiped out by the amount of shampoo you use to clean your hair. A concentrate, for example, will usually go significantly further per ounce than a liquid.

If you are quite satisfied with the shampoo you use and don't want to hunt and sniff for a new brand, relax. Whether you shop around or sit tight, don't believe the ads. Just trust your own hair and your own instincts. Keep the following story in mind.

One Consumers Union staffer working on the shampoo project found himself fascinated by a blurb that stated that the shampoo left hair "smelling like the first day of spring in a Garden of

Earthly Delights." He took a sample home, shampooed his hair, and asked his wife how his hair smelled. She sniffed, thought a moment, and replied: "It smells like you just washed your hair."

A final thought: If all you want from a shampoo is economy and clean hair, you may want to try a dishwashing liquid, but be aware that some individuals may be sensitive to its ingredients.

Ratings of shampoos

Listed alphabetically. All preferences were judged slight. Men and women on CU's panel showed different preferences; the top ten and bottom ten for each sex are noted. Shampoo type is as claimed by manufacturer; fragrance is as characterized by CU. Prices are as published in a September 1984 report.

Most preferred ● ◐ ○ ◑ ● Least preferred

Brand	Type	Package Cost per oz.	Package Size (fl. oz.)	Package Price	Fragrance	Panelists' preferences Women	Panelists' preferences Men	Panelists' comments Women	Panelists' comments Men
Agree	Extra body	20¢	16	$3.17	Floral/citrus	○	○	—	—
Agree	Extra cleansing	18	16	2.89	Floral/citrus	○	◐	—	A,B,D,E
Agree	Regular	20	16	3.17	herbal/citrus	○	◐	B	D,F
Alberto VO5	Extra body	11	15	1.69	Woody/medicinal	○	○	—	—
Alberto VO5	Normal	11	15	1.67	Woody/medicinal	○	○	—	—
Avon Body Bonus	—	39	7	2.76	Sweet/spicy	○	○	—	P
Avon New Vitality	Normal/dry	43	7	2.99	Spicy/citrus	◑	◑	R	—
Body on Tap	Normal	24	11	2.68	Fruity	○	○	—	E
Breck	Dry	15	15	2.27	Floral/spicy	◐	○	D	—
Breck	Normal	15	5	2.21	Floral/spicy	○	○	—	—
Breck	Oily	16	15	2.35	Floral/spicy	○	○	—	A
Clairol Condition	Dry	16	16	2.60	Spicy	○	◑	—	—

(Continued)

Brand	Type	Package Cost per oz.	Package Size (fl. oz.)	Package Price	Fragrance	Panelists' preferences Women	Panelists' preferences Men	Panelists' comments Women	Panelists' comments Men
Clairol Condition	Oily	12	16	1.95	Spicy	○	○	D	D
Clairol Condition	Normal	16	16	2.60	Spicy	◐	○	–	–
Clairol Herbal Essence	Normal	14	15	2.12	Leafy/herbal	○	◐	–	A,D
Clairol Herbal Essence	Oily	15	15	2.22	Leafy/herbal	◐	○	–	–
Colgate's Octagon Liquid Detergent	–	3	48	1.50	Spicy/medicinal	◐	◐	–	–
CVS Balsam & Protein Treatment	Normal/dry	10	16	1.57	Woody/spicy	○	○	–	–
CVS Concentrate	–	31	7	2.19	Spicy/anise	◐	○	C	–
Dimension	–	20	15	2.99	Floral/citrus	◐	◐	–	K,N,O
Enhance	Normal	20	16	3.19	Herbal/spicy	○	○	–	–
Fabergé Brut 33	–	13	15	1.96	Floral/spicy	○	○	P,S	–
Fabergé Organics	Normal	10	15	1.56	Herbal/spicy	○	○	–	–
Fabergé Organics	Extra body	11	15	1.68	Herbal/leafy	◐	◐	–	K
Finesse	Extra body	27	11	2.96	Herbal/pine	○	○	–	–
Finesse	Regular	27	11	2.96	Herbal/pine	○	○	J	J
For Oily Hair Only	–	25	11	2.74	Herbal/spicy	◐	◐	A	B
Gee, Your Hair Smells Terrific	Normal/dry	29	6	1.75	Floral/spicy	○	○	–	–

Most preferred ● ◐ ○ ◑ ● Least preferred

Product	Type				Scent				
Head & Shoulders (tube)	—	44	7	3.09	Floral/spicy	○	○	L	—
Head & Shoulders	Conditioning	27	15	4.05	Floral/spicy	○	○	—	—
Jheri Redding Milk'N Honee	Extra body	16	16	2.52	Fruity/floral	○	○	—	—
Jheri Redding Milk'N Honee	Normal	17	16	2.64	Fruity/floral	◐	—	—	C,E
Jhirmack E.F.A.	Dry	31	12	3.76	Citrus	●	◐	—	—
Jhirmack Gelave	Normal	31	12	3.67	Herbal	◐	—	—	H,I
Jhirmack Gelave	Oily	31	12	3.76	Herbal	○	○	—	I
Jhirmack Nutri-Body	Extra body	29	12	3.42	Fruity	○	◐	—	E,L
Johnson's Baby Shampoo	—	21	16	3.41	Floral/citrus	◐	◐	—	I,K
Kroger Family Pride Extra Balsam & Protein	Normal/dry	6	16	.92	Spicy	○	—	—	—
L'oreal Ultra Rich	Normal	15	16	2.47	Floral	◐	—	—	—
Natural's	Normal	15	16	2.39	Citrus/herbal	◐	○	H,I,K,N,O,T,U	I,K,N,T,U
Pert	Dry	20	15	2.99	Herbal/leafy	○	—	—	G,M
Pert	Normal	20	15	2.95	Herbal/leafy	○	—	—	—
Pert	Oily	20	15	2.95	Herbal/leafy	○	—	—	—
Prell	Normal/dry	19	16	3.05	Herbal	◐	●	—	F
Prell	Normal/oily	19	16	3.08	Herbal	◐	●	—	—
Prell Concentrate	Normal/dry	44	7	3.07	Herbal	○	—	—	—
Prell Concentrate	Normal/oily	41	7	2.87	Herbal	○	—	—	Q
Revlon Flex	Extra body	15	15	2.19	Woody/spicy	●	◐	—	—
Revlon Flex	Normal/dry	17	15	2.48	Woody/spicy	○	—	—	—
Revlon Flex	Oily	14	15	2.07	Woody/spicy	●	◐	—	—
Revlon Milk Plus 6	Normal	27	8	2.17	Herbal/spicy	○	—	G	—
Silkience	Regular	20	15	3.06	Floral/soapy	○	—	K	—

(Continued)

Preference key	
●	Most preferred
◐	
○	
◑	
●	Least preferred

Brand	Type	Package Cost per oz.	Size (fl. oz.)	Price	Fragrance	Preferences Women	Preferences Men	Comments Women	Comments Men
Suave Balsam & Protein	Extra body	9	16	1.42	Spicy	◑	○	E	—
Suave Balsam & Protein	Normal/dry	9	16	1.49	Spicy	◑	○	E	—
Suave Balsam & Protein	Oily	9	16	1.39	Spicy	◑	○	—	—
Suave Full Body	Normal/dry	10	16	1.53	Herbal	○	○	—	—
Truly Fine (Safeway)	Normal/dry	15	16	2.42	Herbal/leafy	○	○	—	—
Vidal Sassoon	—	28	12	3.34	Sweet/almond	○	○	—	—
Wella Balsam	Normal	16	16	2.63	Herbal/pine	○	◑	A	—
Wella Balsam	Dry	13	16	2.11	Herbal/pine	○	○	A	—
Wella Balsam	Extra body	17	24	3.99	Herbal/pine	◑	◑	A	—
Wella Balsam	Oily	17	16	2.72	Herbal/pine	○	○	—	—

KEY TO PANELISTS' COMMENTS

A-Easier to apply than most.
B-Produced more lather than most.
C-Left hair looking better than most.
D-Cleaned better than most.
E-Left hair more manageable than most.
F-Smelled better than most.
G-Controlled dandruff better than most.
H-Harder to apply than most.
I-Produced less lather than most.
J-Irritated eyes less than most.
K-Left hair looking worse than most.
L-Irritated eyes more than most.
M-Prevented itching better than most.
N-Cleaned worse than most.
O-Left hair less manageable than most.
P-Smelled worse than most.
Q-Milder than most.
R-Controlled dandruff worse than most.
S-Harsher than most.
T-Harder to lather than most.
U-Harder to rinse than most.

Facial tissues

When you buy tissues, you face a lot of choices. You can choose by color: a blue print for the master bath, solid yellow for the kitchen. You can choose tissues by the container they come in: big box for the family room, a little cube for a nightstand, a shallow box to fit in a drawer. Maybe there's a "decorator" box for the den.

It could happen that all the varieties you buy are made by one manufacturer. Kimberly-Clark, the company responsible for **Kleenex** (a name that's practically synonymous with tissues), offers the widest selection of package designs and sizes, but it's far from being the only company that attempts to glamorize cleansing tissues. Selling tissues is a highly competitive business.

Many manufacturers put a great deal of effort—and money—into creating shelf appeal for their products.

If design doesn't capture your fancy, price may. The price per 100 tissues can have a range of five or six to one from one brand to another, with store brands and the so-called branded generics at the low end. Branded generics are plainly packaged tissues with a brand name that's unique to the store. The branded generics are usually a few cents cheaper than the store brands.

Do you sacrifice quality when you buy a cheap tissue? Does a higher price buy more than fancy colors and premium packaging? Claims abound. One brand is softer; another one can stand up to a sneeze. This one is bigger; that one thicker. This one is scented; that one is lanolin treated.

Generally you do get what you pay for, be it raspberry tissues in a burgundy floral box (which is fine, if that's important to you) or extra softness or strength.

Nose comfort

For an occasional discreet nose blow, almost any tissue will do. The persistently runny, sneezy nose of a cold or allergy is a sensitive thing. No tissue can be really soft enough for the sore, reddened beak.

You can't comfort a sensitive nose with a cheap tissue. Lower priced store brands and branded generics aren't likely to be any better than fair in softness, but paying more is no guarantee of superior quality.

If tissue lint strikes you as messy or makes you sneeze, relatively soft tissues also tend to be the lintiest. If lint doesn't bother your nose, how about perfume? Somehow, a scented tissue seems the last thing someone with an irritated nose would want.

Tissue strength

Softness might not be a virtue if a tissue dissolves while catching a sneeze or when removing makeup. Probably differences in dry strength are not enough to matter in actual use. Any tissue should do for wiping off makeup. Differences in wet strength are greater, however. A strong tissue should do best at such chores as removing a face full of cold cream or blowing a nose.

Some tissues are interfolded in their boxes so pulling out one tissue makes the next tissue pop up. That's convenient if you want only one tissue. If you want a handful, you can pop the tissues out one at a time or scrape your knuckles on the narrow opening of the box to grab a bunch. You will probably like a box with a large opening that provides access to the stack of tissues from the top of the box and part-way down the side. This design makes it easy to take a single tissue or to grab a bunch.

Recommendations

Certainly there's nothing wrong with paying a premium price for tissues in a pleasing color or an attractive package, if that's important to you. Tissues are, after all, a relatively inexpensive purchase. If performance and economy are also important to you, you might want to buy different tissues for different uses. In order to find the best combination for you and your household, experiment with a number of brands until you find the combination that fits your needs best.

Ratings of tissues

Listed by groups in order of estimated overall quality, based primarily on tests for sneeze resistance and softness. Within groups, listed in order of increasing cost per 100. Except as noted, all are unscented and two ply and come in a rectangular box that lacks a pop-up design. All were judged adequate in dry strength and water absorption. Prices are as published in a February 1983 report.

● ◑ ○ ◐ ●
Excellent ◄────────► Poor

Brand and model	Tissues per box	Price	Cost per 100	Sneeze-resistance	Softness	Wet-strength	Comments
Scotties	200	$.87	$.44	◉	○	◉	A
Puffs	200	.93	.47	◉	◉	◑	B,J
Kleenex Casuals	100	.68	.68	◑	◑	○	H,I,K
Posh Puffs Florals	100	.84	.84	◑	◉	◑	H,I,J,K
Kleenex Man Size	60	.96	1.60	◉	○	◉	F,G,K
Kleenex Vogue	60	1.01	1.68	◉	◑	◑	F,G,K
Truly Fine (Safeway)	200	.59	.30	◉	◐	◑	—
Nice 'n Soft	200	.83	.42	◉	◐	◉	—
Chiffon	200	.94	.47	◉	◐	◉	—
Vanity Fair	134	.74	.55	◑	○	◐	F
Lady Lee	200	.57	.29	◑	◐	◐	M
Zayre	200	.79	.40	◑	◐	◐	M
Hudson Showcase	200	.82	.41	◑	◑	◐	—
Kleenex	200	.82	.41	○	◑	○	C,I,K,L
Coronet Delta	150	.66	.44	◑	◐	◐	J
Delta by Coronet	150	.67	.45	◑	◐	◐	J,M
Kleenex Softique	175	.91	.52	◐	◉	○	D,J,K
Kleenex Boutique	125	.89	.71	○	◑	○	H,I,K

(Continued)

Brand and model	Tissues per box	Price	Cost per 100	Sneeze-resistance	Softness	Wet-strength	Comments
No Frills (Pathmark)	200	.46	.23	○	◐	◐	I
P&Q (A&P)	200	.45	.23	○	◐		—
Cost Cutter (Kroger)	200	.48	.24	○	◐		—
Basics (Grand Union)	200	.49	.25	◐	◐		—
Pathmark (Pathmark Stores)	200	.52	.26	○	◐		—
Ann Page (A&P)	200	.56	.28	◐	◐		—
Grand Union (Grand Union Stores)	200	.56	.28	◐	◐		—
ECO	150	.44	.30	○	◐	◐	I,L
K Mart (K Mart Stores)	200	.63	.32	◐	◐	◐	—
Swansoft (Kroger)	200	.64	.32	◐	◐	◐	—
Marcal Fluff Out	200	.65	.33	○	◐	◐	E,I
Marcal Fluff-In	200	.65	.33	○	◐		—
Northern	175	.81	.46	○	◐	○	L,M
Woolco (Woolworth)	150	.53	.35	●	◐		—

KEY TO COMMENTS

A-In 300-tissue box, avg. cost 40¢ per 100.
B-In 280-tissue box, avg. cost 38¢ per 100.
C-In 100-tissue box, avg. cost 70¢ per 100; In 280-tissue box, avg. cost 38¢ per 100.
D-In 100-tissue, cube-shaped box with pop-up feature, avg. cost 87¢ per 100.
E-In 280-tissue box, avg. cost 31¢ per 100.
F-3-ply.
G-Larger than most; 11.9 × 11 in.
H-Cube-shaped box.
I-Pop-up design.
J-Scented.
K-Produced more lint than most.
L-Sneeze-resistance varied.
M-Wet strength varied.

Toilet paper

Some people resent spending any more than they have to for something that gets flushed down the toilet. Others put comfort and presumed quality above all else, including price. The marketplace provides for both needs, as well as for a middle ground of quality and value, traditionally inhabited by supermarket brands and regional brands.

Superficially, the distinctions between these categories of toilet paper are clear. The premium brands sell at the highest price; the medium brands, at a moderate price; the cheapest brands, at the cheapest price of the three categories. The premium brands are assumed to be the "best," because people expect that of a more expensive product. That's not necessarily the case.

What's best?

In addition to judging a brand of toilet paper by how much it costs, you might use other clues to quality: How heavy is the package? How densely is it packaged? Is the paper one ply or two? Do the words on the package or in the brand's name connote softness? In fact, a heavy, dense package of two-ply toilet paper is apt to be of a better overall quality than a light, squishy package of one-ply paper.

Claims of softness are another matter; a "soft" brand can be relatively scratchy. As for absorbency, some papers lap a few drops of water in less than a second; the drops will remain on other brands for a minute or more. In the important characteristic of wet strength, there are large differences among the brands. Most brands tear cleanly at the perforations, but some are imperfectly perforated, leading to annoying ragged tears. Most brands do well with respect to the paper holding together in use without shredding, falling apart, or pilling up.

As for softness, if you have traveled abroad you appreciate the softness of any American toilet paper. Among American brands, there's still a wide range of softness, from very soft to scratchy. That's because it's expensive to make soft yet strong paper. To make a soft toilet paper that won't disintegrate when you don't want it to, a company has to use either more paper or additional paper-making processes.

At first, soft toilet paper had to be made up of two plies—the only way to compensate for the inherent weakness of the paper was to double it up. Since two-ply paper costs more to produce than one-ply paper, a company that could make a soft yet strong one-ply paper could reduce its production costs and that could help improve a company's profit picture.

In the early 1960s, a new paper-making process involved air drying the fibers, which fluffed the paper and provided single-ply softness without an unacceptable loss of strength. Later, other techniques were used. Adding hardwood fibers makes a softer paper than using pulpwood alone. To give soft paper strength it otherwise wouldn't have, a pattern can be impressed that helps hold the paper together. A binding substance can be printed onto the paper to do the same thing. A single-ply tissue can be built up as a sandwich, with a strong layer in the middle and soft layers on the outside.

Any of these processes, of course, add to the expense of paper making, costs that are passed along. You can't find a soft toilet paper among the cheapest brands. Despite the advances in paper making, most of the softest brands are still two-ply papers. Soft papers also tend to be more absorbent than scratchy papers and most soft papers are strong and durable.

A brand of toilet paper bought in one part of the country sometimes performs very differently from the same brand bought elsewhere. Presumably, different plants make the papers; that's a common practice in the industry, since paper is bulky, and therefore paper products are costly to ship.

Value

Toilet paper is priced to fall into certain price ranges, and often an apparently cheap (or expensive) brand is indeed cheaper (or more expensive) than others.

Making reliable cost comparisons in the supermarket is increasingly difficult, however. Toilet paper manufacturers have long disguised price rises in their products by paring the products' size. Once, a typical sheet of toilet paper was 4 1/2 by 5 inches. Now, sheets 4 1/2 inches square are the generous ones. Furthermore, some companies have trimmed an additional tenth of an inch from each sheet of their products.

The number of sheets in a roll has also been declining. Once, 400 sheets per roll was the norm. If it seems you're using up toilet paper faster than you used to, you may be using one of several brands that have fewer sheets in a roll.

The number of rolls in a package also varies, from one to eight. As a consequence of all this juggling, the square feet per package, noted on all the labels, varies drastically. That makes in-store price comparisons difficult, unless your supermarket figures its unit prices on the basis of square footage.

Recommendations

To a large degree, you do have to pay more to get good toilet paper. Actually, buying the cheap brands may turn out to be a false economy. Depending on how you measure out the amount of toilet paper to use, you could use twice as much of these one-ply papers as you would of a more expensive two-ply paper.

You don't have to buy the best quality, however. Two-ply supermarket brands can be quite good, and have moderate prices.

Several brands are scented, which you may or may not find attractive.

Ratings of toilet paper

Listed in order of estimated overall quality. Products judged equal are bracketed, listed alphabetically. Differences between closely ranked products were slight. Prices are as published in an August 1984 report.

Better ◀ ● ◑ ○ ◐ ● ▶ Worse

Product	Cost per 100 sheets	Package price	Rolls in package	Sheets in roll	Plies	Softness	Absorbency	Wet strength	Durability	Ease of tearing
Northern (Western version)	7¢	$0.99	4	350	2	○	●	●	●	●
Vanity Fair	8	1.75	6	375	2	○	●	●	●	●
Cottonelle	8	1.29	4	400	1	○	●	◐	●	●
Truly Fine (Safeway)	6	0.99	4	400	2	○	●	●	●	●
White Cloud	9	1.13	4	300	2	●	◑	○	◑	●
Pathmark (2-ply)	6	0.89	4	400	2	○	●	◑	◑	●
Skaggs Alpha Beta (2-ply)	6	0.97	4	400	2	◐	●	●	●	●
Coronet	8	1.89	8	300	2	◐	●	◑	◑	●
Delsey	8	0.99	4	330	2	○	●	○	◑	●
Banner	6[1]	0.99	4	400	1	◑	●	○	◑	○
Marina	7	0.99	4	350	2	○	●	◑	●	●
Nice 'n Soft	6	0.99	4	400	1	◐	●	◑	◑	●
Northern (Eastern version)	9	1.29	4	350	2	◑	●	○	●	◑
Skaggs Alpha Beta (1-ply)	6	0.95	4	400	1	◐	●	○	◑	●
Acme	6	0.99	4	375	2	○	●	◑	◑	◑
Marcal Sofpac	6	0.79	4	330	2	●	●	◑	●	●
Delta	7	1.59	6	400	1	◐	◑	◐	●	●
Arrow	6	0.99	4	400	2	◐	●	○	◑	◑
Basics (Grand Union)	5	0.79	4	400	1	●	○	○	●	●
Lady Lee (Lucky)	6	0.89	4	400	1	●	◑	◐	●	●
Scottissue	5	0.49	1	1000	1	◐	◑	○	◑	○

(Continued)

Brand and model	Cost per 100 sheets	Package price	Rolls in package	Sheets in roll	Plies	Softness	Absorbency	Wet strength	Durability	Ease of tearing
Charmin	7	1.13	4	400	1	◉	○	◓	◓	◒
No Frills (Pathmark)	5	0.79	4	400	1	○	◉	◓	○	○
Econobuy (Acme)	4	0.67	4	400	1	●	◒	○	○	◉
Lilac	5	0.79	4	400	1	●	◒	◓	◒	◉
Soft Weve	10	0.79	2	400	1	●	◒	◓	◑	◉
Waldorf	7	1.19	4	400	1	◒	○	○	○	◉
Econobuy (Skaggs Alpha Beta)	5	0.85	4	400	1	●	○	◓	◒	◉
Generic (First National)	4	0.69	4	400	1	●	○	◓	◒	◉
Hi-Dri	6	0.99	4	400	1	●	◓	◓	◉	◉
Hudson Mr. Big	7	1.93	6	480	1	◒	○	◓	◑	○
Scotch Buy (Safeway)	5	0.79	4	400	1	●	◒	○	◒	◉
Pathmark (1-ply)	4	0.35	1	1000	1	◒	○	◓	◒	◒
Generic (Dublin)	5	0.73	4	400	1	◒	○	◓	◓	◉
Marcal	4	0.39	1	1000	1	●	●	○	◒	◒
P&Q (A&P)	5	0.79	4	400	1	●	○	○	◒	◉
Cost Cutter (Kroger)	5	0.77	4	400	1	◒	◒	◓	●	◉

[1] But note that sheets were smallest of any tested.

Toothpaste

More than half the U.S. population lives in places where the local water supply contains significant amounts of fluoride, either from natural sources or because fluoride has been added. Residents in those communities have enjoyed a better than 50 percent drop in tooth decay over the past thirty years. The consequence has been a focus on gum disease, a precursor of tooth loss and other dental problems.

In their pitches for bigger shares of the $1 billion worth of toothpaste Americans squeeze onto toothbrushes every year, toothpaste manufacturers have rediscovered gum disease. Procter & Gamble toothpaste marketers have turned to what might be called the tartar tactic, with new products being promoted as plaque fighters.

The new selling strategy has come about because the toothpaste market has matured in two ways. First, demand for the product has leveled off. After all, the 98 percent of Americans who brush their teeth can use only so much toothpaste each day. More important, consumers themselves have matured. The generation of baby boomers is approaching its forties, the age at which worry about gums replaces worry about tooth decay.

In addition to those changes, fluoride, whose presence in a toothpaste was once a potent selling tool, ceased to be remarkable as more and more products included it. All in all, the time was ripe for some new ways to sell toothpaste.

Plaque

Plaque is a soft, sticky film that coats teeth. It's made of living and dead bacteria—"flora" naturally found in the mouth—and various bacterial by-products, some of which are irritating toxins. If sufficient plaque accumulates on teeth and grows down into the crevices between teeth and gums, gingivitis, a mild form of gum disease, may result: Gums become swollen and inflamed, and they bleed easily. If gums are neglected, periodontitis develops. Plaque continues to grow below the gums, destroying the fibers that connect teeth to gums and causing pockets where more plaque collects. Eventually, as periodontal disease progresses, an increasing amount of bone and tissue supporting the teeth is destroyed, and teeth may be lost.

If plaque isn't brushed away, it can combine with minerals in saliva to form tartar—the calcified plaque that dentists call calculus. Tartar is rock-hard, a white or yellowish deposit that can only be "scaled" from teeth and from under gums during professional cleaning.

For all the discomfort such scaling might cause, tartar isn't the main culprit in gum disease—plaque is. Tartar itself is largely inert, at least on the crowns of teeth. Controlling tartar there is a cosmetic concern, not a health concern. Below the gum line, however, tartar may accelerate the progress of periodontal disease.

Regular and thorough brushing and flossing can remove almost all plaque, and most people can also keep tartar off, too. (Tartar collects mainly on those tooth surfaces most exposed to saliva, so extra brushing near the salivary glands—the tongue side of the lower front teeth and the cheek side of the upper back teeth—can prevent much of the buildup of tartar.)

Plaque and tartar control is, however, a never-ending process. As soon as plaque is cleared away, new deposits start forming. That's why dentists recommend brushing at least daily.

Can a specially formulated toothpaste help? As far as plaque is concerned, the mechanical action of flossing and brushing is even more important than the brand of toothpaste you use. Brushing with any toothpaste will do. That really makes all toothpastes genuine "plaque attackers."

Colgate's **Dentagard**, for example, has no special ingredient to fight plaque; indeed, its ingredients are similar to those of ordinary toothpaste.

The only antiplaque ingredient in **Dentagard** products and some of the other self-styled plaque-fighting toothpastes is plain elbow grease. Any brand of toothpaste could make such claims. So could any manufacturer of toothbrushes, since a toothbrush used with plain water can remove plaque (but not stains)—indeed, you can find plaque-fighting claims on toothbrush packages. (Chemical means to fight plaque formation as explained on page 185.)

Toothpastes that make antitartar claims, however, do contain effective antitartar ingredients. They contain chemicals clinically proven to stop tartar from accumulating on teeth, but one has to note carefully just what their claims are. Unfortunately, the new products won't do anything to dissolve tartar that's already on your teeth—only the dentist or hygienist can remove that. Further, the products inhibit tartar buildup only above the gum line; they're helpless to head off tartar that forms where toothbrushes cannot reach. Therefore, the benefits are strictly cosmetic, since tartar above the gum line doesn't cause gum disease.

In sum, despite studies showing that tartar-inhibiting toothpastes might reduce the accumulation of new tartar by one-third or more, these new products have no consequence for dental health.

Harshness

To help remove plaque and stains, toothpastes all contain abrasives such as hydrated silica or phosphate salts. Some products, in fact, contain up to 50 percent of such substances, but more isn't necessarily better.

Tooth enamel—the nonliving material that forms the visible crown of a tooth—is the hardest substance in the human body. As such, it's virtually impervious to any wear that brushing or dentifrices may cause. When gums recede with age or disease, however, softer dental tissues become exposed. Those tissues include dentin (cellular material below the enamel that forms the bulk of each tooth) and cementum (a bonelike material that helps anchor the tooth in place). Either can be damaged by a toothpaste that's too abrasive.

No general-purpose dentifrice is likely to be totally nonabrasive to dentin, but some are quite good in that respect: A general-purpose toothpaste will probably be within an acceptable range of abrasion.

Dentifrices that claim special effectiveness against tobacco stains will almost certainly be considerably more abrasive than a general-purpose product.

Price and containers

You would expect to pay more for toothpaste in a pump than in a tube. A pump, after all, is a more complicated container. The premium, if any, is trivial—13 cents per month per person, at most. Some pumps actually work out to be cheaper than their tube counterpart because they deliver a thinner ribbon of toothpaste. Pumps also promote economical use because they're easier to empty completely. Pumps can add to domestic tranquility, too, if your family fights over the proper way to squeeze and roll up the toothpaste tube.

There are basically two kinds of pump design. The **Colgate-Palmolive** type works on the "pole climber" principle, with an internal piston climbing a central threaded rod after each use. That design is easy enough to use, except when it comes to telling how much toothpaste is left. A solid panel across the bottom makes that difficult.

Other pumps use vacuum pressure to pump out the paste. They are also easy to work. With that design, the pump's bottom moves up after each use.

Fluoride

It's been known for more than forty years that fluoride can reduce the incidence of cavities. Fluoride is most effective when included in proper amounts in the diet of growing children. Hence, it's added to many community water supplies. Fluoride incorporates itself into the crystalline structure of tooth enamel, rendering the enamel substantially less vulnerable to decay.

In older children and adults, fluoride inhibits decay somewhat differently. Fluoride in a toothpaste helps teeth overcome mineral loss from acid-producing bacteria in the mouth, which is the first stage in tooth decay. The fluoride also slows further acid production. People of any age can get both these benefits from fluoride in toothpaste. That's why so many toothpastes now include fluoride. If people's drinking water is fluoridated as well, the benefits are even greater.

Fluoride has also proved to have some good effect if merely applied directly to the teeth by a dentist or hygienist—or even by a youngster using a fluoridated toothpaste. In fact, the evidence indicates that the benefits are additive: A child is best protected from cavities with fluoride in the diet, periodic applications of fluoride by a dentist, and the use of a fluoridated toothpaste.

Will any added fluoride work? Not necessarily. There may not be enough fluoride added, or some other ingredient in the toothpaste could render the fluoride useless. Because of that uncertainty, the American Dental Association (ADA) has set up procedures to evaluate fluoride toothpastes (see page 187).

To get the ADA's "seal of acceptance" as "an effective decay-preventive dentrifice," manufacturers have to present compelling evidence that their products do indeed prevent decay.

Special products

Some kinds of products may appeal to particular groups of people:

People with sensitive teeth. Some folks cringe at the idea of biting into hot or cold foods. They may want to consider a desensitizing toothpaste (see page 186).

Smokers. A few products are formulated specifically for smokers. At least their advertising is aimed at smokers. Abrasiveness is the main weapon these toothpastes use to combat tobacco stains. Although the abrasiveness of these "smokers' toothpastes" is on a par with that of some regular toothpastes, their prices are typically twice that of a regular toothpaste.

Flavor. Taste is important to everyone, young or old. In a Consumers Union survey, flavor was named as one of the most important factors in choosing a brand of toothpaste, second only to a toothpaste's ability to fight plaque.

Recommendations

To protect yourself against tooth decay and gum disease, brush your teeth and floss regularly and thoroughly. That's not quite as easy as it sounds, considering that a full set of teeth has 148 surfaces to clean, but your dentist will be glad to show you how. Ask your dentist the next time you visit. Ask too about toothbrushes. Many dentists suggest brushing with soft, rounded bristles; they're kindest on teeth and gums.

Just what should you put on that toothbrush? Use the least abrasive toothpaste that gets your teeth clean, especially if your gums have begun to recede. People with heavily stained teeth may require a more abrasive toothpaste, at least occasionally.

Another important factor in choosing a toothpaste is fluoride. A fluoride formula that has been shown to be effective can give everyone, regardless of age, added protection against cavities. Try to choose a product that has earned the ADA's seal. Other important factors include taste (personal preference) and cost (store specials and coupons can lead to good buys). Factors *not* to consider include antiplaque and antitartar claims. Every toothpaste removes plaque whenever you brush and most people probably do not need a special tartar-inhibiting toothpaste. Dentifrices that position themselves as "plaque attackers" are only telling half-truths. The one person in ten who develops tartar unusually quickly is an exception to the rule. Typically, very little tartar accumulates on teeth between dental cleanings, and controlling this is largely a cosmetic concern anyway.

Chemical warfare on plaque

The main way currently available to fight plaque is mechanical—you brush it off teeth. Plaque fighters of the future, however, are likely to be chemical. Chemicals that kill plaque-forming bacteria will be formulated into toothpaste or mouthwash.

Listerine has been advertising itself as a plaque fighter for a couple of years. Studies have shown that when **Listerine** is used in conjunction with regular brushing, plaque is reduced more than by brushing alone. Its combination of "essential oils" is apparently what fights plaque.

Chlorhexidine is another plaque-fighting chemical already in use in Europe in both toothpastes and mouth rinses. Chlorhexidine is the most widely studied and effective antibacterial agent in dentistry, but it has important drawbacks. It tastes bad, and it may stain teeth, either by itself or in combination with coffee, tea, and other foods. Further, for some people the chemical may irritate the soft tissues of the mouth.

If chlorhexidine does find its way into an American toothpaste or mouthwash, the product is likely to be available only by prescription, at least at first, so dentists can supervise patients' use of the chemical and monitor their reactions to it. Chlorhexidine and other antiplaque agents are more likely to be incorporated in mouthwashes than in toothpastes, since other toothpaste ingredients may interfere with the agents' plaque-fighting ability.

New antiplaque products could show up soon—and there

will be a seal of acceptance for them from the American Dental Association. In December 1985, the ADA completed guidelines it would use to evaluate such products.

Products containing another plaque-inhibiting ingredient are already on the market, although the ingredient isn't labeled as such. (Making an explicit "therapeutic" claim about an ingredient usually obligates a manufacturer to seek clearance from the U.S. Food and Drug Administration before marketing the product; by not making such claims or not tying them to specific ingredients, companies can avoid the FDA altogether.) The chemical is a botanical—sanguinaria extract—derived from the bloodroot plant. For many years used as an ingredient in cough syrup, sanguinaria has been put into mouthwash and a toothpaste sold under the **Viadent** name by a small Colorado company. Sanguinaria has been found to curb plaque formation.

Toothpaste for sensitive teeth

If you feel a twinge of pain when something hot, cold, or sour touches a tooth, the tooth is hypersensitive. A number of dentifrices on the market claim to relieve such sensitivity.

Most frequently, a tooth becomes sensitive as a result of exposed dentin, a relatively soft material usually protected above the gum line by hard enamel and, below the gum line, by cementum, a bonelike material. As gums recede with age, the cementum is exposed. The wear and tear of chewing and brushing can gradually erode or abrade the cementum until the dentin is exposed, resulting in sensitivity in an otherwise normal tooth.

Teeth may also become hypersensitive as a result of decay, microscopic cracks in the enamel, inflammation of a tooth's nerve, or recently placed dental restorations. Poorly aligned teeth may also bring on hypersensitivity, since they can damage supporting structures as you chew. Such problems won't be relieved by desensitizing agents.

Dental hypersensitivity is a condition that calls for a dentist's attention. Unless your dentist recommends a desensitizer, these toothpastes should be considered first-aid items, not dentifrices for normal use.

Since exposed dentin is relatively soft and therefore subject to damage by abrasion, it follows that any toothpaste sold expressly to relieve sensitivity should be relatively nonabrasive.

A do-it-yourself toothpaste

A mixture of hydrogen peroxide, baking soda, and salt is used by some people for routine oral hygiene, as a substitute for commercial dentifrices. Hydrogen peroxide, baking soda, and salt can all kill some plaque bacteria under some circumstances, but what you use as a dentifrice is probably less important than how conscientiously and thoroughly you use it. If you use the so-called Keyes paste, a hydrogen peroxide–baking soda mixture, you give up the value of the fluoride in fluoridated toothpastes.

The standard recipe for the Keyes paste is $1/2$ capful of standard 3 percent hydrogen peroxide mixed with 1 tablespoon of baking soda. The paste sometimes causes gum irritation, probably because of the hydrogen peroxide, so daily use is not recommended. Diluting with water may help. If you try the paste, use it only as a dentifrice, not to treat gum disease. Some press reports imply that with a little peroxide and baking soda people can quite literally take the treatment of periodontal disease into their own hands. Don't try it: Your dentist's contribution is critical.

There are commercial dentifrices that contain some of the same ingredients as the Keyes paste. They may be better tasting, less irritating, and more convenient than the Keyes paste, but no evidence has shown them to offer any special benefits.

ADA approval

"**Crest** has been shown to be an effective decay-preventive dentifrice that can be of significant value when used in a conscientiously applied program of oral hygiene and regular professional care."

When the ADA, the 127-year-old dentists' professional organization, awarded those words to **Crest** more than a quarter of a century ago, the brand doubled its share of the toothpaste market. Several other toothpaste manufacturers have since obtained that statement and the accompanying seal from the ADA's Council on

Dental Therapeutics, a process that involves submitting rigorous research data on the products and their ingredients. That seal is the only way you can be certain the fluoride in a toothpaste actually works in preventing tooth decay.

More recently, however, the antiplaque and antitartar claims that some ADA-accepted toothpastes have been making in ads and on packages have confused the issue. When you pick up a tube of one of the new products you might well wonder whether its official seal pertained to fighting cavities, fighting plaque, fighting gingivitis, or fighting tartar.

In fact, the ADA statement on **Aim, Aqua-Fresh, Crest Tartar Control Formula**, and **Dentagard** mention *only* decay prevention, an ADA official noted. Those words first seen on **Crest** packages long ago are indeed mum on questions of plaque, tartar, or gum disease. Still, when the seal is used independently of the statement, it's easy for the seal's credibility to rub off onto the other claims made on packages or in ads.

The ADA, perhaps in recognition of that fact, continues to monitor the product, its advertising, and package claims from the time a seal is granted, even though the seal may have originally applied only to the efficacy of the product's fluoride formula. If a manufacturer makes new claims about anything, it must provide new data backing up the claims; likewise, if it modifies the formula, it must satisfy the ADA's Council that the toothpaste is still safe and still effective in preventing decay. Failure to satisfy the ADA on either count can lead to a seal's revocation, though that's never happened to a fluoride toothpaste.

The ADA readily acknowledges that the new toothpaste claims could be misleading, but also stands firmly behind everything those products claim to do; their makers have had to submit research data. If you were to ask the ADA whether the plaque-fighting promises made by various makers might be just a bit exaggerated—any toothpaste, after all, can honestly say it fights plaque since the mere act of toothbrushing removes the sticky film mechanically—the answer could be, "That's what marketing is, isn't it?"

Other dentists contend that new products and ad campaigns, no matter how contrived, can only do good by raising everyone's awareness of gum disease and the need for good oral hygiene.

Ratings of toothpastes

Listed by types; within types, listed in order of increasing abrasiveness. Differences between closely ranked products are small. Prices are as published in a March 1986 report.

Milder ← → Harsher

Product	Package type (tube or pump)	Price/size, oz.	Cost per month[1]	Abrasiveness	Fluoride[2]
General-purpose products					
Peak[3]	T	$2.19/6.3	$.81	◉	—
Colgate Regular	T	1.87/7.0	.59	◉	A
Colgate Regular	P	1.49/4.5	.48	◉	A
Dentagard	T	1.76/6.4	.48	◉	A
Dentagard	P	1.86/4.5	.55	◉	A
Colgate Winterfresh Gel	T	1.87/6.4	.59	◉	A
Colgate Winterfresh Gel	P	1.49/4.5	.49	◉	A
Ultra Brite[3]	T	1.99/6.0	.71	◗	B
Aqua-Fresh for Kids	P	1.67/4.6	.47	◗	A
Macleans Mildmint[3]	T	2.65/7.0	.81	◗	A
Crest Regular	T	1.87/6.4	.50	◗	A
Crest Regular	P	1.64/4.6	.59	◗	A
Aim Mint	T	1.89/6.4	.41	◗	A
Aim Mint	P	1.59/4.5	.37	◗	A
Check-Up	T	2.66/6.4	.56	◗	B
Check-Up	P	2.42/4.1	.62	◗	B
Aim Regular	T	1.71/6.4	.39	◗	A
Aim Regular	P	1.86/4.5	.52	◗	A
Aqua-Fresh	T	1.66/6.4	.54	◗	A
Aqua-Fresh	P	1.63/4.6	.53	◗	A
Check-Up Gel	T	2.43/6.4	.52	◗	B

(Continued)

Product	Package type (tube or pump)	Price/size, oz.	Cost per month[1]	Abrasiveness	Fluoride[2]
Check-Up Gel	P	2.42/4.1	.56	◖	B
Macleans Peppermint[3]	T	2.69/7.0	.86	○	A
Close-Up Fresh Mint[3]	T	1.89/6.4	.65	○	B

Tartar-inhibiting products

Prevent Anti-Tartar	T	2.22/2.7	1.27	◖	B
Crest Tartar Control Formula	T	1.79/6.4	.48	◖	A
Crest Tartar Control Formula	P	1.64/4.6	.54	○	A

Smokers' products

Pearl Drops Smoker's Gel	T	3.28/3.0	1.70	◖	B
Topol Mint[3]	T	5.99/7.0	1.89	○	—
Topol Smoker's Gel[4]	T	4.92/6.4	1.34	○	B

Desensitizing products[5]

Denquel[3][6]	T	2.55/3.0	1.63	●	—
Thermodent[3]	T	3.25/4.0	1.21	○	—
Sensodyne[3][6]	T	2.99/4.0	1.21	○	—

[1] Based on roughly ½ inch of toothpaste used twice daily.
[2] A—Contains ADA-accepted fluoride formula. B—Contains fluoride, but not ADA-accepted for decay-prevention.
[3] Test results are from Consumer Reports, March 1984; price is current.
[4] Contains FD&C Yellow No. 5, to which some aspirin-sensitive people may also be sensitive.

Stains and spots

Stains and spots on fabrics

The best time to remove a spot or a stain from fabric is right away. Many stains can "set" as they age and become much harder to remove.

Before you try any stain-removal method, make sure that removing the spot won't leave the fabric permanently marked. Silks, satins, velvets, taffetas, crepes, rayon moires, and gabardines may be spoiled by efforts to remove spots. Check a garment's care label. If the instructions say "professionally dry-clean only" (as it should with the fabrics named above), don't attempt to remove a stain yourself. Take the garment to the cleaners and tell them what caused the stain. If the label indicates the garment should not be dry-cleaned, avoid using spot removers; their solvents may damage the fibers.

Before you use a spot remover, take a moment to test your spot-removal method, if possible, on some inconspicuous part of the article—on a seam allowance, hem, pocket, or shirt tail. Manipulate the fabric in the test as you would in cleaning a real spot. Even though the fibers may be undamaged, the appearance of a fabric can be spoiled by rings, running dyes, or a marred fabric finish caused by the spot remover, the manipulation, or a combination of both.

What to do right away

Before you do anything, read the care label (if there is one) and observe any precautions. When a staining accident occurs, it is always safe to absorb excess liquid with a clean cloth, a white paper towel or tissue, a sponge, or absorbent cotton. Barely touch the drop of liquid with the tip of the absorbent material to avoid forcing the staining material further into the fabric. Do not apply any pressure to the stained area.

If the stain is not greasy, you may be able to remove some of the liquid that has soaked into the fabric by adding a little water to it. Water may cause spotting on some fabrics. It is safe to use water if the care label says the article is washable. If the garment is not washable or there is no care label, test the fabric first in an out-of-the-way place.

Place clean, dry, white absorbent material (paper towels or cotton cloths) under the stained area. Sprinkle a few drops of cool water on the stain and blot immediately with more clean, dry absorbent material. Repeat until no more stain appears on the absorbent material. Use a clean, dry piece or section of the absorbent material above and below the stain each time water is added.

Sponge oily stains as soon as possible with dry-cleaning solvent. If the stain is on a garment being worn, be careful not to let dry-cleaning solvent come in contact with skin. Dry-cleaning solvent can cause skin irritation and be absorbed into the body. Use only a very small amount and place absorbent material between the garment and skin. Do not allow areas of clothing sponged with dry-cleaning solvent to touch skin until all the solvent has evaporated.

Dry-cleaning solvents and other stain-removal materials are hazardous. You should follow the instructions and precautions starting on page 218, Stain- and Spot-removal Supplies, as well as any precautions on product labels.

If the staining material has the consistency of a paste, remove the excess with a dull knife or spoon, taking care not to force the stain further into the fabric.

Treating stains

Here are some ways to use stain removers along with the procedures mentioned in the Stain Removal Guide starting on page 197.

Testing stain removers. Before you use any stain remover, including water, test it to be sure that it will not harm the fabric or dye. Test each stain remover and each method of treatment on an unexposed portion of the article—a seam allowance, hem, inside of pocket, or tail of shirt or blouse.

Some stain removers or treatments damage certain fibers. They may also cause fading or bleeding of dyes, loss of luster, shrinkage, or stretching. They may remove nonpermanent finishes, designs, or pigment prints. Loosely woven fabrics and fabrics woven from low-twist yarns are likely to suffer yarn slippage if brushed or rubbed while wet.

If the substance needed to remove a stain will damage the fabric, take the article to a dry cleaner as soon as possible. Unfortunately, even a dry cleaner cannot correct damage caused by some stains. Liquids that contain a high percentage of alcohol bleed some dyes, making it impossible to restore the color. Some fingernail polishes and polish removers cause permanent damage to acetate fabrics.

Working surface. The working surface for stain removal should be a hard surface of a material that will not be affected by any of the chemicals used.

A heavy glass pie pan, turned upside down, makes a good working surface. Other glass surfaces may also be used. A table or countertop should be protected from spilled or dripping chemicals with aluminum foil. Chemicals used for removing stains can damage the finish of a table or countertop and then transfer a new stain to the fabric on which you are working.

Sponging. When directions call for sponging, use the following procedure.

Place the stained area, stained side down, over a pad of absorbent material. Dampen another piece of absorbent material with the stain remover you have been directed to use. Sponge the stain lightly from the center toward the edge. The stain is less likely to form rings if you work from the center to the edge.

Keep the wet area around the stain as small as possible. Sponge the stain irregularly around the edges so there will be no definite line when the fabric dries.

Change the sponging pad and the absorbent material under the stain as soon as you can see that any stain has been transferred to them. They should be changed frequently so that the released staining material will not be returned to the fabric.

If a fabric tends to form rings when sponged with a stain remover, use special care in sponging the stain. Apply only enough stain remover to the sponging pad to barely dampen it. Touch the pad to the stain very lightly so that the fabric will absorb the stain remover slowly. Try not to let the wet area spread.

Before you dry the article, place the sponged area between dry absorbent material to remove excess moisture. Dry as rapidly as possible, but do not use heat on fabric treated with anything besides water.

When trying to remove hardened stains, such as old paint or tar, place an absorbent pad under the stain and a pad dampened with the recommended stain remover on top of the stain. Allow the article to soak until the stain has softened. This may take from a half hour to several hours. Keep the stain damp by adding more stain remover as needed.

Flushing. Flushing the stain is necessary to remove released staining material and to remove stain-removal chemicals.

When the directions call for flushing, place clean absorbent material under the stain, then add the proper stain remover in small amounts.

Do not add stain remover faster than the absorbent material can soak it up. Keep the treated area as small as possible. Change the absorbent material several times as you flush the stain.

Flushing is one of the more important steps in stain removal. If a stain-removal chemical remains in the fabric, it may later damage the fabric or cause another stain.

When you flush with water, and you are working on a washable article, it is all right to use a bowl of water for rinsing. Dip the stained area up and down repeatedly in a bowl of warm water. Change the water at least twice.

Tamping. Tamping the stain with a soft, dense-bristled brush can be effective in removing stains. When tamping, place the stained area directly on the working surface without any absorbent material under the stain.

The tamping action is similar to driving a tack with a small hammer. Raise the brush 2 or 3 inches above the fabric and place it down squarely. Use a light action. Never use so much pressure that the bristles bend.

Fabric damage is much more likely to occur if the edge of the brush strikes the fabric squarely. Striking with the edge is also less efficient in removing stains.

Use the least amount of tamping that will remove the stain and never tamp enough to damage the fabric. Too much tamping can chafe the yarn or cause yarn slippage.

The amount of tamping a fabric can take without damage depends on the weave and yarn. A closely woven fabric of high-twist yarn will not be damaged as easily as a loosely woven fabric or yarn with a slight or moderate twist.

Textile fiber classes

The following table shows many of the classes of textile fibers that are used on labels of fiber content, including some not now in production.

Natural Fibers

Cellulose (plant):
    cotton
    jute
    linen
    minor fibers:
        abaca
        banana
        cattail, cisalpha
        hemp
        hennequen
        kapok
        pina
        raime, grass linen
        sisal

Protein (animal):
    silk
    wool
    minor (specialty) fibers:
        alpaca
        angora
        camel hair
        cashmere

Man-made Fibers

Cellulose-based:
    acetate and triacetate
    rayon

Protein-based:
    Azlon

Mineral-based:
    glass
    metallic

True synthetics:
    acrylic
    Anidex
    Aramid
    modacrylic
    Novoloid
    nylon
    Nytril
    olefin
    polyester
    rubber and Lastrile
    Saran

Natural Fibers	**Man-made Fibers**
Protein (animal):	*True synthetics:*
fur fibers	Spandex
horsehair	vinyl
llama	Vinyon
mohair	
vicuna	

Suede, leather, and vinyl

It is safest not to attempt any major stain removal from suede and leather garments. These articles are impregnated with oils and finishes that are readily affected by dry-cleaning solvents. An attempt to remove a grease or oil stain with dry-cleaning solvent usually disturbs the finish and produces a light-colored area. The most that should be done is to very lightly sponge the surface with a cloth barely dampened with solvent.

Most dyes on suedes, especially the darker colors, are easily bled by stain removers containing water. Before trying any removal method, test the color of the article by very lightly sponging an unexposed seam allowance with a damp cloth. If no color is transferred to the damp cloth, try very lightly sponging small stained areas with a cloth that is barely damp with water only. Do not use detergent or other stain-removal agents.

When a suede or leather article becomes damp from water, whether from rain or stain removal, dry it in room temperature air. Do not apply heat in any way.

Some vinyl articles are resistant to dry-cleaning solvents, but many are likely to be damaged by solvents. Dry-cleaning solvents can remove the plasticizers used to soften vinyl, causing stiffening and greatly reducing garment life. If removal of an oil or grease stain is attempted, the procedure should consist of very lightly sponging the surface of the vinyl with a cloth barely dampened with dry-cleaning solvent. Do not make more than a few strokes of the sponging cloth. Repeated rubbing will remove the plasticizer and may change the appearance of the vinyl surface.

Stain removal procedures using water and hand dishwashing liquid with vinegar and ammonia are usually safe on vinyl. Test a hidden seam allowance before trying to remove the stain. A blotting action is the safest method for treating stains on vinyl. Do not use a rubbing or tamping action, because this may change the surface appearance.

Stain-removal guide

To use this guide, look up the stain you want to remove in the Fabric Stain Index at the end of this section. The index will direct you to a stain-removal procedure. Most stains in this guide are classified into nine groups.

Before treating a stain, read the preceding section on Treating Stains. Follow the safety precautions given in the Stain- and Spot-removal Supplies section on page 218 and on fabric care labels.

Use extra care in treating nonwashable fabrics. Keep the treated area as small as possible and do not wash the fabric. Nonwashable fabrics are more likely to be damaged by a tamping brush.

It may not be necessary to go through all the steps to remove the stain. When all the stain is gone, or when you have finished all the steps, wash the article if it is washable. If the stained article is not washable, be sure that all chemicals are thoroughly flushed out using the appropriate procedure in the instructions.

Work carefully and patiently. Often the results depend as much on how you do the job as on the remover used.

Group 1 stains

(For stains preceded by an asterisk, see step 10 following this list.)

Adhesive tape	*Eye liner
Automobile wax	*Eye shadow
Calamine lotion	Face powder
Crayon, wax or grease	*Felt-tip marker ink
*Eyebrow pencil	*Floor wax

*Furniture polish
Furniture wax
Grease
Hair spray
Hand lotion
India ink
Insecticides
Lard
Lubricating oil
Makeup, liquid or
  pancake
Margarine
*Mascara

Nose drops
Ointment or salve
Paint, solvent base or
  water emulsion
Putty
Rouge
*Shoe dye, black
*Shoe polish, all colors
  except white
*Smoke
Soot
Tar
Typewriter ribbon ink

Washable and nonwashable fabrics

1. Sponge with dry-cleaning solvent.

2. For delicate fabrics, apply dry spotter to stain and cover with a pad of absorbent material dampened with dry spotter. Let stand as long as any stain is being removed. Change pad as it picks up stain. Keep stain and pad moist with dry spotter.

For stronger fabrics, apply dry spotter and tamp. Keep stain moist with dry spotter and blot occasionally with absorbent material. Continue as long as any stain is being removed.

3. Flush with dry-cleaning solvent.

4. Repeat steps 2 and 3 until no more stain is removed.

5. Allow to dry completely.

6. Sponge with water.

7. For delicate fabrics, apply wet spotter and a few drops of ammonia. Cover with a pad of absorbent material dampened with wet spotter and let stand as long as any stain is being removed. Change pad as it picks up stain. Keep stain and pad moist with wet spotter and ammonia.

For stronger fabrics, apply wet spotter and a few drops of ammonia, then tamp. Keep stain moist with wet spotter and ammonia and blot occasionally with absorbent material. Continue as long as any stain is being removed.

8. Flush with water.

9. Repeat steps 7 and 8 until no more stain is removed.

10. Chlorine bleach may remove the final traces of stains marked by an asterisk. Chlorine bleach should not be used on certain fabrics (see the section on Stain- and Spot-removal Supplies.) *Test colors to be sure they will not be changed.* Use a solution of 1 teaspoon bleach to 1 tablespoon water. Apply with a dropper. *Don't allow this solution to remain on the fabric more than two minutes.* When the stain is removed, or after two minutes, flush with water onto clean absorbent material. Apply 1 teaspoon white vinegar and again flush with water. Be sure that all bleach is removed.

Group 2 stains

(For stains preceded by an asterisk, see step 10 for washable fabrics following this list.)

*Cake frosting	Cream, dairy	Pudding
*Catsup	Egg yolk	Salad dressing
*Cheese	Gravy	Sauces
*Cheese sauce	Ice cream	Soups containing
*Chili sauce	Mayonnaise	vegetables
*Chocolate	Meat juice	*Steak sauce
Cocoa	Milk	

Washable fabrics

1. Sponge with dry-cleaning solvent.
2. For delicate fabrics, apply dry spotter to stain and cover with a pad of absorbent material dampened with dry spotter. Let stand as long as any stain is being removed. Change pad as it picks up stain. Keep stain and pad moist with dry spotter.

For stronger fabrics, apply dry spotter and tamp. Keep stain moist with dry spotter and blot occasionally with absorbent material. Continue as long as any stain is being removed.
3. Flush with dry-cleaning solvent.
4. Repeat steps 2 and 3 until no more stain is removed.
5. Allow to dry completely.
6. Sponge with water.

7. For delicate fabrics, apply a few drops of hand dishwashing liquid and a few drops of ammonia. Cover with a pad of absorbent material dampened with water and let stand as long as any stain is being removed. Change pad as it picks up stain. Keep stain and pad moist with detergent and ammonia.

For stronger fabrics, apply a few drops of hand dishwashing liquid and a few drops of ammonia, then tamp. Keep stain moist and blot occasionally with absorbent material.

8. Flush with water. It is important to remove all ammonia.

9. Soak in a solution of 1 quart warm water and 1 tablespoon enzyme product for thirty minutes. Rinse with water.

10. Bleaching may remove the final traces of stains marked by an asterisk. For chocolate stains, proceed to step 11. For other stains marked by the asterisk, use chlorine bleach as for Group 1 stains.

11. For chocolate stains, bleach with hydrogen peroxide. Wet the stain with hydrogen peroxide and add a drop or two of ammonia. Add more hydrogen peroxide and a drop of ammonia as needed to keep stain moist. Do not bleach longer than fifteen minutes. Rinse with water.

Nonwashable fabrics

1. Follow steps 1 to 8 for washable fabrics.

2. Moisten the stain with a solution of 1/2 teaspoon enzyme product and 1/2 cup warm water. Cover with a clean pad that has been dipped in the warm enzyme solution and squeezed nearly dry. Let stand thirty minutes. Add more warm enzyme solution if needed to keep the area warm and moist, but do not let the wet area spread.

3. Flush with water.

4. Bleaching may remove the final traces of stains marked by an asterisk. For chocolate stains, proceed to step 5. For other stains marked by an asterisk, use chlorine bleach as for Group 1 stains.

5. For chocolate stains, use hydrogen peroxide as directed in preceding step 11 for washable fabrics.

Group 3 stains

Aftershave lotion
Bath oil
Blood
Body discharge
Egg white

Eye drops
Fish glue
Fish slime
Hide glue
Mouthwash

Mucus
Sherbet
Soups containing
  meat
Starch
Vomit

Washable fabrics

1. Soak in a solution of 1 quart warm water, ½ teaspoon liquid hand dishwashing detergent, and 1 tablespoon ammonia for fifteen minutes.

2. If the fabric is strong enough, tamp. Blot occasionally with absorbent material. Continue as long as any stain is being removed.

3. Soak another fifteen minutes in the solution used in step 1.

4. Rinse with water. It is important to remove all ammonia.

5. Soak in a solution of 1 quart warm water and 1 tablespoon enzyme product for thirty minutes.

6. Wash.

7. For all stains except blood, repeat step 5, then wash again.

8. For a blood stain that is not completely removed, wet the stain with hydrogen peroxide and add a drop of ammonia. Do not bleach longer than fifteen minutes. Rinse with water.

Nonwashable fabrics

1. Sponge with water.

2. For delicate fabrics, apply wet spotter and a few drops of ammonia. Cover with a pad of absorbent material dampened with wet spotter and let stand as long as any stain is being removed. Change pad as it picks up stain. Keep stain and pad moist with wet spotter and ammonia.

For stronger fabrics, apply wet spotter and a few drops of ammonia, then tamp. Keep stain moist with wet spotter and ammonia and blot occasionally with absorbent material. Continue as long as any stain is being removed.

3. Flush with water. It is important to remove all ammonia.

4. Moisten the stain with a solution of ¹/₂ teaspoon enzyme product and ¹/₂ cup warm water. Cover with a clean pad that has been dipped in the warm enzyme solution and squeezed nearly dry. Let stand thirty minutes. Add more enzyme solution if needed to keep stain warm and moist, but do not let the wet area spread.

5. Flush with water.

6. If any stain is left, except a blood stain, repeat steps 2 to 5, then dry.

7. For a blood stain that is not completely removed, wet the stain with hydrogen peroxide and add a drop of ammonia. Do not bleach longer than fifteen minutes. Flush thoroughly with water.

Group 4 stains

(For stains preceded by an asterisk, see step 7 following this list.)

Airplane glue	Household cement
Carbon paper	Lacquer
*Carbon typewriter ribbon	*Mimeograph correction fluid
Contact cement	*Mimeograph ink
Corn remover	Mucilage
Cuticle oil	Plastic
Cuticle remover	Plastic glue
Fingernail hardener	Solder, liquid
Fingernail polish	Varnish

Washable and nonwashable fabrics

1. Sponge with dry-cleaning solvent.

2. For delicate fabrics, apply dry spotter to stain and cover with a pad of absorbent material dampened with dry spotter. Let stand as long as any stain is being removed. Change pad as it picks up stain. Keep stain and pad moist with dry spotter.

For stronger fabrics, apply dry spotter and tamp. Keep stain moist with dry spotter and blot occasionally with absorbent material. Continue as long as any stain is being removed.

3. Flush with dry-cleaning solvent.

4. Repeat steps 2 and 3 until no more stain is removed. Allow to dry completely.

5. Apply amyl acetate to stain and cover with a pad of absorbent material dampened with amyl acetate. Keep moist for fifteen minutes, blotting occasionally with absorbent material. When not working on the stain, keep it covered with an inverted bowl to minimize evaporation.

6. Flush with dry-cleaning solvent.

7. Bleaching may remove the final traces of stains marked by an asterisk. Use chlorine bleach as for Group 1 stains.

Group 5 stains

(For stains preceded by a asterisk, see step 7 following this list.)

Beer	*Fruit preserves	*Suntan lotion
Berries	Home permanent	*Tea
*Caramelized sugar	*Jam	*Tobacco
Casein glue	*Jelly	Tomato juice
*Coffee	Maple syrup	Toothpaste
Cordials	*Mixed drinks	Vegetable juice
Corn syrup	Molasses	*Vegetables
Cough syrup	*Mud	*Vinegar, colored
Fruit	Shaving cream	*Whiskey
*Fruit juice	*Soft drinks	*Wine

Washable fabrics

1. Soak in a solution of 1 quart warm water, ½ teaspoon hand dishwashing liquid, and 1 tablespoon vinegar for fifteen minutes.

2. Rinse with water.

3. Sponge with alcohol.

4. Wash.

5. Soak in a solution of 1 quart warm water and 1 tablespoon enzyme product for thirty minutes.

6. Wash.

7. Bleaching may remove the final traces of stains marked by an asterisk. Use chlorine bleach as for Group 1 stains.

8. Wash the fabric.

Nonwashable fabrics

1. Sponge with water.

2. For delicate fabrics, apply wet spotter and a few drops of vinegar. Cover with a pad of absorbent material dampened with wet spotter and let stand as long as any stain is being removed. Change pad as it picks up stain. Keep stain and pad moist with wet spotter and vinegar.

For stronger fabrics, apply wet spotter and a few drops of vinegar, then tamp. Keep stain moist with wet spotter and vinegar. Blot occasionally with clean absorbent material. Continue as long as any stain is being removed.

3. Flush with water.

4. Apply alcohol to stain and cover with a pad of absorbent material dampened with alcohol. Let stand as long as any stain is being removed. Change pad as it picks up stain. Keep stain and pad moist with alcohol.

5. If any stain is left, moisten the stain with a solution of ½ teaspoon enzyme product and ½ cup warm water. Cover with a pad that has been dipped in the warm enzyme solution and squeezed nearly dry. Let stand thirty minutes. Add more warm enzyme solution if needed to keep stain warm and moist, but do not let the wet area spread.

6. Flush with water.

7. Bleaching may remove the final traces of stains marked by an asterisk. Use chlorine bleach as for Group 1 stains.

Group 6 stains

(For stains preceded by an asterisk, see step 7 following this list.)

Antiperspirant
*Candy (for chocolate candy, see Group 2 stains)
Deodorant
*Fabric dye, red
*Food coloring, red
*Hair coloring, red
*Mercurochrome
*Merthiolate
*Perspiration
*Stamp pad ink, red
*Urine
*Watercolor paint, red
 Writing ink, red

Washable fabrics

1. Soak in a solution of 1 quart warm water, ½ teaspoon hand dishwashing liquid, and 1 tablespoon ammonia for thirty minutes.
2. Rinse with water.
3. Soak in a solution of 1 quart warm water and 1 tablespoon vinegar for one hour.
4. Rinse with water. Dry.
5. For delicate fabrics, apply alcohol and cover with a pad dampened with alcohol. Let stand as long as any stain is being removed. Change pad as it picks up stain. Keep stain and pad moist with alcohol.

For stronger fabrics, apply alcohol and tamp. Keep stain moist with alcohol and blot occasionally with clean absorbent material. Continue as long as any stain is being removed.
6. Rinse with water.
7. Bleaching may remove the final traces of stains marked by an asterisk. Use chlorine bleach as for Group 1 stains.

Nonwashable fabrics

1. Sponge with water.
2. Apply wet spotter and a few drops of ammonia. Let stand as long as any stain is being removed. Press stain every five minutes with clean absorbent material. Keep moist with wet spotter and ammonia.
3. Flush with water.
4. Apply wet spotter and a few drops of vinegar. Let stand as long as any stain is being removed. Press stain every five minutes with clean absorbent material. Keep moist with wet spotter and vinegar.
5. Flush with water.
6. Apply alcohol to stain and cover with a pad of absorbent material dampened with alcohol. Let stand as long as any stain is being removed. Change pad as it picks up stain. Press pad hard onto the stain each time you check it. Keep stain and pad moist with alcohol.
7. Flush with water.

8. Bleaching may remove the final traces of stains marked with an asterisk. Use chlorine bleach as for Group 1 stains.

Group 7 stains

Bluing
Fabric dye, all colors except red and yellow
Food coloring, all colors except red and yellow
Gentian violet
Hair dye, black or brown
Ink, black, blue, green, or violet
Shoe dye, brown
Stamp pad ink, all colors except red and yellow
Watercolor paint, all colors except red and yellow

Washable fabrics

1. Soak in a solution of 1 quart warm water, $1/2$ teaspoon hand dishwashing liquid, and 1 tablespoon vinegar for thirty minutes. Agitate occasionally.
2. Rinse with water. Dry.
3. Apply alcohol to stain and cover with a pad of absorbent material dampened with alcohol. Let stand as long as any stain is being removed. Change pad as it picks up stain. Press pad hard onto the stain each time you check it. Keep stain and pad moist with alcohol.
4. Flush with alcohol. Allow to dry.
5. Soak in a solution of 1 quart warm water, $1/2$ teaspoon hand dishwashing liquid, and 1 tablespoon ammonia for thirty minutes.
6. Rinse with water.
7. If any stain is left, use chlorine bleach as for Group 1 stains.

Nonwashable fabrics

1. Sponge with water.
2. Apply wet spotter and a few drops of vinegar. Let stand thirty minutes or more. Blot every five minutes with clean absorbent material. Add wet spotter and vinegar as needed to keep stain moist.
3. Flush with water. Dry.

4. Apply alcohol to stain and cover with a pad of absorbent material dampened with alcohol. Let stand as long as any stain is being removed. Change pad as it picks up stain. Press pad hard onto the stain each time you check it.

5. Flush with alcohol. Allow to dry.

6. Sponge with water.

7. Apply wet spotter and a few drops of ammonia. Let stand at least thirty minutes. Blot with clean absorbent material every five minutes. Add wet spotter and ammonia as needed to keep stain moist.

8. Flush with water. Dry.

9. If any stain is left, use chlorine bleach as for Group 1 stains.

Group 8 stains

Asphalt	Cod liver oil	Rubber cement
Butter	Corn oil	Safflower oil
Castor oil	Linseed oil	Vegetable oil
Chewing gum	Olive oil	
Coconut oil	Peanut oil	

Washable and nonwashable fabrics

1. Place clean absorbent material under the stain. Apply dry-cleaning solvent and cover stain with a pad of absorbent material dampened with dry-cleaning solvent. Change the absorbent material as it picks up stain. Keep stain and pad moist with solvent.

2. Apply dry spotter. Cover stain with a pad dampened with dry spotter. If the fabric is strong enough, remove pad every five minutes and tamp. Continue the alternate soaking and tamping until all stain has been removed.

3. Flush with dry-cleaning solvent. Allow to dry.

Group 9 miscellaneous stains

Acids

1. Sponge with water and ammonia.
2. Flush with water.
3. Add more water and ammonia and flush with water again.

Note: Strong acids may cause permanent damage.

Alkalies

1. Sponge with water and white vinegar.
2. Flush with water.
3. Add vinegar and flush with water again.

Note: Strong alkalies may cause permanent damage.

Ballpoint pen ink

1. Try dabbing liberally with alcohol, using an absorbent underlayer of paper towels—and quickly sponge off. Then, if necessary, apply lukewarm glycerin. If fabric is strong enough, tamp. Blot frequently by pressing hard on the stain with absorbent material. It is important to remove loosened stain immediately. Keep stain moist with glycerin. Continue as long as any stain is being removed.
2. Flush with water.
3. Apply wet spotter.
4. For fabrics that will not be damaged, tamp gently with a brush.
5. Add several drops of ammonia and continue to tamp.
6. Flush with water.
7. Repeat steps 3 to 6 until no more stain is being removed.
8. Flush with water.
9. If any stain is left, use chlorine bleach as for Group 1 stains.

Candle wax

1. Place stain between blotting papers or folded paper towels. Iron at low temperature. Replace papers and iron again. Continue changing papers and ironing until no more wax melts.

2. Sponge with dry-cleaning solvent until all wax has been removed.

3. If any stain is left, use chlorine bleach as for Group 1 stains, step 10 (see page 199).

4. If any stain is left, apply wet spotter and a few drops of ammonia. If the fabric is strong enough, tamp.

5. Flush with water.

6. Repeat steps 4 and 5 until no more stain is removed.

Chlorine

1. Mix ¼ teaspoon color remover with ½ cup cool water. Sponge stain with this solution.

2. Flush with water.

Epoxy cement

This stain cannot be removed.

Grass

1. Sponge with dry-cleaning solvent as long as any stain is being removed.

2. Allow to dry.

3. Apply amyl acetate and rub stain gently with a pad of absorbent material dampened with amyl acetate.

4. Flush with dry-cleaning solvent. Allow to dry.

5. Sponge with water. If fabric is strong enough, tamp.

6. Add a small amount of wet spotter and several drops of vinegar. Continue tamping as long as any stain is being removed.

7. Flush with water. Allow to dry.

8. Sponge with alcohol and rub gently with a pad dampened with alcohol.

Lipstick

1. Apply dry-cleaning solvent and dry spotter and blot immediately with absorbent material.

2. Repeat step 1 until no more stain is removed. If stain begins to spread, flush immediately with dry-cleaning solvent. Then continue to repeat step 1.

3. Let all dry-cleaning solvent evaporate.

4. Sponge with water.

5. Apply wet spotter and a few drops of vinegar. If fabric is strong enough, tamp. Blot frequently with absorbent material.

6. Flush with water.

7. Apply wet spotter and a few drops of vinegar. If fabric is strong enough, tamp. Blot frequently with absorbent material.

8. Flush with water. Allow to dry.

9. Sponge with alcohol. Allow to dry.

10. If any stain is left, use chlorine bleach as for Group 1 stains.

Metal

Take to dry cleaner.

Mildew

1. Gently brush off excess stain.

2. Flush with dry-cleaning solvent.

3. Apply dry spotter and amyl acetate. Pat stain with a pad of absorbent material dampened with dry spotter. Work cautiously, because mildew weakens fibers.

4. Flush with dry-cleaning solvent. Allow to dry.

5. Sponge with water.

6. Apply wet spotter and vinegar. Pat stain with a pad of absorbent material.

7. Flush with water. Allow to dry.

8. Apply alcohol and pat stain with a pad dampened with alcohol.

9. Flush with alcohol.

10. Repeat steps 8 and 9 until no more stain is removed.

11. Allow to dry.

12. If any stain is left, use chlorine bleach as for Group 1 stains.

Mustard

1. Place stain on a smooth surface and brush or carefully scrape off excess mustard.

2. Flush with dry-cleaning solvent.

3. If the fabric is strong enough, tamp.

4. Flush with dry-cleaning solvent. Allow to dry.

5. Sponge with water.

6. Apply wet spotter and vinegar. If the fabric is strong enough, tamp.

7. Flush with water.

8. Repeat steps 6 and 7 until no more stain is removed.

9. If any stain is left, wet the stain with hydrogen peroxide and add a drop of ammonia. Do not bleach longer than fifteen minutes.

10. Flush with water.

Pencil

1. Erase excess stain with a soft eraser. Be careful not to distort the weave.

2. Flush with dry-cleaning solvent.

3. Apply dry spotter and rub gently with a pad of absorbent material dampened with dry spotter.

4. Cover stain with a pad dampened with dry spotter. Let stand thirty minutes.

5. Flush with dry-cleaning solvent. Allow to dry.

6. Sponge with water.

7. Apply wet spotter and a few drops of ammonia. If fabric is strong enough, tamp.

8. Flush with water.

9. Allow to dry.

10. If any stain is left, repeat steps 6 to 8 until no more stain is removed.

Perfume

Washable fabrics

1. Sponge with water.
2. Apply wet spotter.
3. If the fabric is strong enough, tamp.
4. Flush with water.
5. Apply alcohol and cover with a pad of absorbent material dampened with alcohol. Let stand as long as any stain is being removed. Change pad as it picks up stain. Keep stain and pad moist with alcohol.
6. Flush with water.

Nonwashable fabrics

1. Sponge with water.
2. Flush with water.
3. Apply alcohol and cover with a pad of absorbent material dampened with alcohol. Let stand as long as any stain is being removed. Change pad as it picks up stain. Keep stain and pad moist with alcohol.
4. Flush with water.

Rust

Take to dry cleaner.

Scorch

Note: Scorched fabrics may be weakened. Stain removal treatment may further damage the fabric.

1. Wet the stain with hydrogen peroxide and add a drop of ammonia. Let stand for at least several minutes. Full bleaching action may take up to an hour. Keep area moist with hydrogen peroxide and ammonia.
2. Flush with water.

Shellac

1. Sponge with dry-cleaning solvent.
2. Apply dry spotter. If the fabric is strong enough, tamp.
3. Flush with dry-cleaning solvent.
4. Apply alcohol. If the fabric is strong enough, tamp.
5. Flush with alcohol.

White shoe polish

1. Sponge with dry-cleaning solvent.
2. Apply dry spotter. If the fabric is strong enough, tamp.
3. Flush with dry-cleaning solvent.
4. Repeat steps 1 to 3 until no more stain is removed.
5. Sponge with amyl acetate. If the fabric is strong enough, tamp.
6. Flush with dry-cleaning solvent. Allow to dry.
7. Sponge with water.
8. Add a few drops of vinegar. If the fabric is strong enough, tamp.
9. Flush with water.
10. Repeat steps 7 to 9 until no more stain is removed.

Unknown stains

1. Sponge with dry-cleaning solvent.
2. Apply dry spotter. If the fabric is strong enough, tamp.
3. Flush with dry-cleaning solvent.
4. Repeat steps 1 to 3 until no more stain is removed.
5. Apply amyl acetate. If the fabric is strong enough, tamp.
6. Flush with dry-cleaning solvent. Allow to dry.
7. Sponge with water. Add wet spotter and a few drops of vinegar. If the fabric is strong enough, tamp.
8. Apply wet spotter and a few drops of ammonia. If the fabric is strong enough, tamp.
9. Allow to dry.
10. Sponge with alcohol and pat with a pad of absorbent material dampened with alcohol.

11. Allow to dry.

12. If any stain is left, use chlorine bleach as for Group 1 stains, step 10.

Fabric stain index

floor	1	Writing ink	
furniture	1	red	6
Wax crayon	1	yellow (*see* Unknown	
Whiskey	5	stains)	
Wine	5	other colors	7

Stain- and spot-removal supplies

Most of the following items are ordinary household supplies. Substitutes are suggested for a few materials that may be difficult to obtain.

Follow carefully all precautions for the storage and use of hazardous chemicals.

Absorbent materials

You will need an ample supply of clean absorbent materials, such as absorbent cotton, white paper towels, white facial tissues, and soft white cloths. Sponges are also useful, but test them with stain removers to make sure they will not be damaged.

Alcohol

Use rubbing alcohol or denatured alcohol (70 percent or 90 percent concentration) or, in an emergency, try vodka. Do not use alcohol with added color or fragrances.

Alcohol fades some dyes, so test the fabric for color fastness before using alcohol on a stain.

For use on acetate, dilute alcohol with two parts water to one part alcohol.

Caution: Poisonous and flammable. Observe all precautions on the label.

Ammonia

Use household ammonia. Do not use ammonia with added color or fragrances.

Ammonia changes the color of some dyes. To restore the color, rinse the color-changed areas thoroughly with water and apply a few drops of white vinegar. Rinse well with water again.

For use on wool and silk, dilute ammonia with an equal amount of water.

Caution: Poisonous. Avoid inhaling ammonia fumes. Ammonia will cause burns or irritation if it comes in contact with the skin or eyes. Observe all precautions on the label.

Amyl acetate

Amyl acetate (banana oil) is sold in drug stores. Ask for "chemically pure amyl acetate."

If you cannot obtain amyl acetate, you may substitute fingernail polish remover. Do not use oily-type nail polish remover.

Caution: Amyl acetate is poisonous and flammable. Do not breathe the vapors. Avoid contact with the skin.

Amyl acetate is a strong solvent for plastics. Do not allow it to come in contact with plastics or furniture finishes.

Brushes

Brushes are used for a stain removal procedure called tamping. The most suitable brush is the type used for applying shoe polish, usually sold in a package of two.

Brushes used for stain removal should be new and should not be used for any other purpose. It is best to have two brushes, so that one can be used for stain removers that contain water and the other for dry-cleaning solvent and amyl acetate.

The brushes should have nylon bristles, because hair bristles become soft when wet with water. The bristles should be cut square, with all the bristles the same length.

If the brushes have plastic handles, test the handles with stain removal chemicals, especially amyl acetate, to make sure that chemicals will not damage the handles. This could cause additional stains.

Chlorine bleach

Chlorine bleach is used to remove many kinds of stains. Check the label of bleach to be sure that it contains chlorine (usually in the form of sodium hypochlorite).

Chlorine bleach damages some fibers, dyes, and finishes. Check the care label for cautions regarding the use of bleach and read the label on the bleach container. Test the fabric in an inconspicuous place before you use bleach on the stain. Do not use chlorine bleach on fabric with a fire-retardant finish unless the care label states that chlorine bleach is safe.

The resin in some special finishes absorbs and retains chlorine, which weakens and yellows the fabric. Some fabrics do not show evidence of damage until they are ironed; then they may be severely weakened or discolored. To remove chlorine from such fabrics, mix 1/4 teaspoon color remover with 1/2 cup cool water. Sponge the stain with this solution. Then flush with water (page 194). Chlorine stains on silk, wool, or Spandex fibers cannot be removed.

Do not use bleach in metal containers or with metal objects, because metal may speed up the action of the bleach enough to cause fiber damage. Also, metal in contact with bleach may tarnish and cause additional stains on fabrics. Avoid spilling or spattering bleach on garments and nearby surfaces.

Caution: Poisonous. Chlorine bleach will cause burns or irritation if it comes in contact with the skin or eyes. Observe all precautions on the label.

Coconut oil

Coconut oil is sold in drug stores and health food stores and other food stores. It is used in the dry spotter solution (see below), which is used to remove many kinds of stains. If you cannot obtain coconut oil substitute mineral oil (sold in drug stores), which is almost as effective.

Color remover

Color remover is sold in drug stores, grocery stores, and variety stores, usually in the display of home dyes and tints.

Color remover is safe for most fibers, but fades or removes many dyes. If color remover causes a distinct color change rather than fading, you may be able to restore the original color by rinsing the area with water immediately. Hang the article to dry.

If color remover causes fading, the original color cannot be restored.

Do not use or store color remover in metal containers or use it with metal objects.

Caution: Poisonous. Avoid prolonged contact with skin. Observe all precautions on the label.

Detergent

Use hand dishwashing liquid detergent. Detergents for automatic dishwashers, heavy-duty household detergents, and laundry detergents may contain chemicals that could set some stains.

Dry-cleaning solvent

Dry-cleaning solvent is sold in drug stores, grocery stores, variety stores, hardware stores, and automobile service stations.

Caution: Poisonous; may be flammable. Store dry-cleaning solvent in tightly capped unbreakable containers. Store it out of the reach of children and where it cannot be ignited by flames or sparks.

Dry-cleaning solvent gives off poisonous fumes and can be poisonous on contact with the skin. When using dry-cleaning solvent, work outside or in a well-ventilated room, and arrange work so that fumes are blown away from you. Do not lean close to your work. Use only a small quantity at a time. Do not pour solvent into a bowl. Do not allow children or pets into the room.

If you spill dry-cleaning solvent on your skin, wash it off immediately. If you spill it on your clothes, change immediately and hang garments outdoors until all solvent has evaporated.

Neither flammable nor nonflammable solvent should be used in a room with an open flame or gas pilot light, or where there is a chance of electric sparks from refrigerators, fans, vacuum cleaners, or static from a rug. Do not smoke. Although nonflammable solvents do not ignite in contact with a flame or spark, they decompose and produce extremely toxic vapors.

Never use dry-cleaning solvent in a washing machine. Do not put articles that are damp with solvent in a dryer.

Observe all precautions on the label.

Dry spotter

To prepare dry spotter, mix one part coconut oil and eight parts dry-cleaning solvent. This solution is used to remove many kinds of stains.

Dry spotter keeps well if the container is tightly capped to prevent evaporation of the dry-cleaning solvent.

If you cannot obtain coconut oil, use mineral oil in the same amount as coconut oil.

Caution: Dry-cleaning solvent is poisonous and may be flammable. Follow all precautions given above for dry-cleaning solvent.

Enzyme product

You should use either an enzyme presoak or an enzyme-containing laundry detergent. These products may be stored as purchased, but become inactive if stored after they have been made into a solution.

Glycerin

Glycerin is sold in drug stores. It is used to prepare "wet spotter," which is used to remove many kinds of stains. It is also used to remove ballpoint ink stains after you have first tried alcohol.

Hydrogen peroxide

Use the 3 percent solution sold as a mild antiseptic. Do not use the stronger solution sold in cosmetic departments for bleaching hair.

Hydrogen peroxide is safe for all fibers, but dyed fabrics should be tested for color fastness.

Store in a cool, dark place. Hydrogen peroxide loses strength when stored for extended periods of time.

Bleach that contains sodium perborate or "oxygen-type" bleach may be substituted for hydrogen peroxide, although it is slower acting. Very thorough rinsing is needed to remove this type of bleach from fabric.

Do not use or store hydrogen peroxide or oxygen-type bleach in metal containers or use it with metal objects. Metal may speed up action of the bleach enough to cause fiber damage. Also, metal in contact with hydrogen peroxide or bleach may tarnish and cause additional stains on fabrics.

Vinegar

Use white vinegar; colored vinegar can leave a stain. Vinegar is safe for all fibers but changes the color of some dyes. If a dye changes color after vinegar has been used, rinse the color-changed area thoroughly with water and add a few drops of ammonia. Then rinse well with water again.

Wet spotter

Prepare wet spotter by mixing one part glycerin, one part hand dishwashing liquid, and eight parts water. Shake well before each use. This mixture is used to remove many kinds of stains.

Wet spotter may be conveniently stored in a plastic squeeze bottle with a small cap.

Tips on how to clean practically anything

Acetate fabric. Although laundering instructions may be present on the care label, dry cleaning is safest. If laundered, avoid wringing or twisting. Drape over a line for drying.

Air conditioner (window type). Change the filter once a season to keep the machine's efficiency as high as possible. Some filters are washable in soap and water after vacuum cleaning the loose dirt. When cleaning or changing the filter, vacuum clean the cooling coils (be careful not to cut yourself; there may be sharp edges). The outside condenser coils require cleaning too, but the unit may have to be removed from the window to do the job. In very sooty areas, or if the air conditioner is in a window overlooking a heavily trafficked street, professional steam cleaning may be needed.

Aluminum. Soapy steel wool is the cleaner of choice for pots and pans, and may work better than special chemical cleaners for other aluminum articles as well.

Appliance exterior. Most large kitchen and laundry appliances have painted (baked enamel) finishes. Unlike glass-hard porcelain enamel, commonly used on cooking ranges and sometimes washing machine tops and other hard-wear surfaces, baked enamel scratches quite easily. It needs gentle cleaning care. Never use abrasive cleaners. If soap and water don't do the job, specially formulated products sold for the purpose can do nicely for combined cleaning and waxing.

Asphalt tile. Damp mop for day-to-day cleaning. Avoid solvent-based wax; it can soften flooring. Also see "Linoleum."

Attic ventilation. Vacuum clean or brush insect screening in attic openings at least once a season to keep air flow at its peak rate.

Automobile finish. Wash regularly with clear, cool water and a mild detergent. Wipe with the softest possible cloth. Occasional waxing helps maintain the paint's sheen and wards off the finish's tendency to attract dirt.

Automobile interior. A battery-powered minivacuum cleaner won't help much with gravel, adherent pet hair, dried grass, or sand. You will do better with a full-sized canister machine; it has the necessary high suction for such chores.

Barbecue grill. An abrasive, powdered cleanser or an oven cleaner can help remove baked-on dirt.

Bare floors. For everyday use, a lightweight upright vacuum cleaner should do the job on loose dirt. For stains and adherent soil, however, you will obviously need a sponge mop or equivalent.

Brass and copper. Soapy steel wool works, but copper and brass are relatively soft metals, and steel wool's tiny scratch tracks will show up. Try a special polish after steel wooling. Even better, use just the polish (instead of steel wool) if the layer of corrosion isn't too thick.

Butcher block. See Wood work surface.

Carpets. Daily vacuuming removes dirt from heavy traffic areas; a lightweight upright can do this job handily. Vacuum thoroughly once a week with a full-sized cleaner in order to remove the embedded dirt. Wipe up spills before they have a chance to soak through to the backing. For the most effective cleaning, use a machine with a motorized, rotating nozzle brush. See also Rug shampoo.

China ware. If the pattern on dishes has sections that are less glossy than the surrounding area and are slightly raised, the sections may be overglaze decorations. Be wary of machine dishwashing; the detergent may damage the pattern.

Chromium plate. This commonplace metal finish is extremely thin and easily worn away. Try to make do with the mildest possible cleansers, avoiding abrasive cleaners altogether. Protect chrome plate on automobiles with a heavy coating of wax.

Clothes dryer. A machine's lint screen becomes partially clogged with just about every load. Keep the screen clean to maintain dryer efficiency and to avoid excessive heat buildup. Every once in a while, vacuum clean any obvious lint accumulations from inside the machine (just the parts you can see; leave any disassembly for a service technician).

Coffee maker. The residue from brewing a pot of coffee can give the next batch an off taste if the coffee-brewing container and associated parts are not scrupulously clean. Wash the coffee maker carefully after each use, paying particular attention to the insides of tubes and spouts. Coffee-maker cleaners, sold in supermarkets and hardware stores, can help. Follow the label instructions explicitly.

Continuous clean oven. The porous surface finish absorbs dirt up to a point. Once the surface material's absorbency capacity has been used up, there's not much to be done. A practical course is to protect the surface from becoming soiled in the first place. Use aluminum foil on the oven bottom, but be careful to avoid blocking any vents in a gas oven, or short-circuiting an electric oven's element.

Cooktop (gas or electric). Keep a spare set of drip pans or reflectors handy for making the cooktop presentable on a moment's notice. Clean drip pans and reflector bowls with the least abrasive cleanser that will keep them looking up to par.

Copper. See Brass and copper.

Cotton. A highly absorbent fabric. Stains easily but launders well. Chlorine bleach is effective. Cotton/polyester blends are often used for permanent-press fabrics, which require a warm or cold wash and rinse to retain their noncreasing properties.

Countertop. Laminated plastic work surfaces are quite soft and therefore intolerant of abrasive cleaners. Clean these surfaces with the gentlest possible products. Never use an abrasive powder. Hot utensils can cause hard-to-remove marks, or even loosen the bond between the finished surface and the base material.

Crystal glassware. Hand washing is probably best; there's a chance of chipping and breakage if you wash delicate glassware in a machine.

Curtains. Thin fabrics can be vacuum cleaned, but with reduced suction. Your vacuum cleaner may have a suction reducer for such applications, in the form of a ring, slide, knob, or lever that lets you bleed air into the hose to cut suction down to the point where thin fabric will not be drawn into the cleaning nozzle.

Dish sanitation. Even a dishwasher that "sanitizes" isn't of much help in promoting family health. Once clean dishes are stacked away, they pick up household microbes, the ones present everywhere else in the house.

Dishwasher. Check the inside from time to time for dried-on bits of food or detergent specks. Wipe them away with a wet sponge. Check the drain as well and remove any scraps of food that may have become lodged there. If the detergent isn't doing as good a job as in the past, the powder may have gone "stale." Dishwasher detergents should be bought in small containers unless you use them up quite rapidly. Open detergent boxes allow moisture to permeate the powder and can affect its ability to dissolve in water.

Disinfecting. It isn't realistic to prevent the spread of germs in the house by using a disinfectant. In medical situations that require using a germicide, seek a doctor's advice—and follow it.

Drains. Chemical drain cleaners are for stopped-up or sluggish drains. It's better to keep drains open in the first place by keeping hair and lint out of them as much as possible, and by flushing drains with boiling, soapy water at least once a week.

Dryer. See Clothes dryer.

Dusting. Use a spray polish as a one-cloth duster. A little bit of polish makes the cloth tacky enough to pick up dust.

Electric appliances. See specific appliance.

Electric blanket. Usually washable, but follow manufacturer's instructions carefully in order not to displace or break the thin heating wires that are sewed into channels within the blanket.

Fans. Dirt often accumulates on blades. Seasonal cleaning can make the appliance look better as well as help maintain optimum efficiency. If the fan's blades are made of metal, clean them cautiously to avoid bending and thereby creating an imbalance and vibration when the fan is turned on. Clean louvers and screens of whole-house fans at least once a season.

Floor coverings. Surfaces that don't need waxing (at least not when they are still new) nevertheless require cleaning. Products intended for application to such floors are often called "self-cleaning," and include a polishing agent of one kind or another. They pick up dirt and leave some polish behind. Damp mopping will keep the floor looking presentable. Vinyl asbestos, asphalt tile, and linoleum floor surfaces tend to be rougher than "no-wax" flooring materials. Regular cleaning and waxing seals the rough surface, keeping the floor cleaner and shinier than just cleaning alone. Also see Linoleum.

Floor waxing. Spread liquid or paste wax with an applicator intended for the purpose. Use a machine only for polishing and buffing.

Freezers. Use a plastic auto-windshield ice scraper to remove loose frost accumulations. Be very careful not to damage plastic or metal surfaces. When defrosting completely, wash and dry freezer surfaces, using a cleaning solution of water and bicarbonate of soda (baking soda). Keep frozen food wrapped in newspapers while the defrosting process is going on. Also see Refrigerator/freezer.

Furniture wood. Polish provides luster and protects wood's finish, but only to a degree. The furniture's original oil or lacquer finish offers the best protection. Clean up spills quickly, before they have a chance to attack the finish. Always use the softest possible cloth for dusting. Polishing every time you dust can result in excessive wax buildup, with consequent loss of wood's natural beauty, not to mention difficulty in attaining the kind of luster you really want. Avoid wiping against the grain. Use pads under hot, heavy, or sharp objects or containers. For dents or burns, try steam (from a steam iron) applied through several thicknesses of heavy, colorfast fabric, preferably wool. You can use a dry iron too, with thicknesses of dampened wrapping paper. Several applications can act to swell the wood enough to bring it up to the surrounding level. Then refinish as necessary.

Glass fiber fabric. Hand launder only. Tends to shed fine particles. Dirt resistant and decorative, but very fragile.

Glass windows and mirrors. Use as little cleaner as possible that will do the job. Any residue can be wiped off with a damp paper towel. Plain water streaks the least. Keep glass cleaners away from white painted surfaces; they can become stained. Other painted surfaces may soften on contact with a glass cleaner. Apart from plain water, the best cleaner of all could be your own mix of half a cup of sudsy ammonia, a pint of rubbing alcohol, a teaspoon of liquid dishwashing detergent, and enough water to make up a gallon of solution.

Heater. Many electric space heaters depend on a shiny, reflecting surface for their effectiveness. Use a vacuum cleaner to blow dust away from that surface (first unplug the heater). Clean the surface directly once a season, but only if the manufacturer's instructions advise such cleaning.

Heating pad. Always use with a fabric cover. Wash the cover as necessary. Throw away any pad that has frayed wiring or a hole in the waterproof pad cover.

Heating system. Radiators or radiation fins should be vacuum cleaned regularly. Warm air system filters should be changed or cleaned from time to time during the heating season, or periodically the year round if the air ducts also serve as part of a central air conditioning system. Clean filters help keep the system's efficiency up to par.

Humidifier. You can reduce the risk of spreading bacteria and airborne molds by cleaning a large humidifier once a week with a liquid chlorine bleach solution (about a tablespoon of bleach per pint of water). The newer ultrasonic humidifiers pose a much lower risk of spreading molds and bacteria. Steam vaporizers are best of all; the steam kills microbes.

Iron. Dry, steam, or steam/spray irons can accumulate debris on their soleplates, particularly metal that doesn't have a nonstick finish. Clean with soap and water, or with a fine metal polish. Avoid abrasives that cause scratching. When clean, run the soleplate over a piece of ordinary waxed paper, with the iron at a low setting. Use distilled or deionized water to minimize accumulations of residue from water, particularly if the water in your area is at all hard. If the iron's steam vents do become clogged, follow the manufacturer's instructions for cleaning.

Jeweler's rouge. Try a stick of this material for polishing heavily tarnished silver. Apply the rouge to a flannel cloth—and then rub.

Laminated plastic. See Countertop.

Linen. Durable fabric. Appearance and "feel" improve with laundering. If linen has been chemically treated for wrinkle resistance, the fabric may not be able to withstand hot water washing.

Linoleum. Damp mop for day-to-day cleaning, but keep water away from seams and edges to prevent loosening of the linoleum or wetting of the floor under the covering. This applies to sheet vinyl as well and, in general, to any floor covering with seams.

Lint removal. A washing machine's lint filter helps. A clothes dryer helps even more. Line drying saves wear and tear on delicate items, but can leave them linty.

Microwave oven. If not kept scrupulously clean, the inside of a microwave oven can become quite smelly. That's because the oven never gets hot. Wipe up spills and remove stains promptly, using a damp, not wet, sponge. Most importantly, keep the door seal and surrounding areas clean to maintain the oven's ability to keep hazardous microwave radiation inside the oven.

Mildew. A common household mold with a characteristically unpleasant odor and appearance. Mold grows profusely on just about any surface, and thrives in dark, damp, poorly ventilated places. Once established, mildew is hard to eliminate. Chlorine bleach (diluted four parts water to one part bleach) is a good mildewcide. The chemicals in moth flakes and pellets can keep mildew under control. Keep a 40-watt bulb burning continuously in a closet during humid, summer weather to reduce mildew growth. (For a large closet use a 60-watt bulb; a smaller bulb should do in a smaller size enclosure. Be certain that the bulb is well away from any stored articles.) The electricity cost is low; about $2.25 per month at national average rates, plus the price of a bulb once a month, assuming a bulb life of 750 hours.

Nylon. Wash white nylon separately because it can pick up color from other things in the same laundry load. Oily substances may adhere to nylon. Treat oily stains quickly, before they have a chance to set.

Oven. See Continuous clean oven and Self-cleaning oven.

Oven cleaner. A chemical cleaner can do a good job on porcelain enamel and glass surfaces. Use these strong chemicals very cautiously. Don't let them splatter on floors or adjacent surfaces—or on your skin. If possible, use a noncorrosive cleaner (see page 77).

Painted surfaces. All-purpose cleaners (page 60) can do very well, but try on an inconspicuous area first. Cleaners containing pine oil can damage paint rapidly.

Paper towel. Keep two rolls of towels handy. Use a high-quality towel for washing windows, a cheaper towel for wiping up spills and drying hands.

Polyester. Oily substances and polyester have a close affinity. Treat oily stains as soon as possible after you notice them. Even quick attention may not be enough to remove oily stains completely.

Porcelain enamel. This glass-hard, heat-resistant material is used as a finish on kitchen ranges, particularly range tops (as well as for the tops and other hard-wear areas of other appliances). You can tell whether a surface is porcelain enamel or paint (baked enamel) by trying to make a tiny scratch in an inconspicuous spot. Porcelain enamel will not scratch easily. Baked enamel will. Therefore, porcelain enamel is far more tolerant of cleaning than the baked variety.

Porcelain fixture. Bathtubs, sinks, and other plumbing fixtures are typically made of metal with a heavy outside layer of glasslike porcelain. You can scrub porcelain with abrasive cleansing powders without fear of rubbing off the porcelain, but you will gradually destroy the porcelain's shiny finish and thereby make successive cleanings more difficult. Stick to nonabrasive cleansers on new or nearly new fixtures in order to keep them in tip-top condition.

Protein stain. For blood, egg, and milk stains (and analogous materials), a laundry booster can help remove the stains when laundering. Using a booster is more effective than laundry detergent alone.

Pump spray. Cleaners in pump-spray containers often make control over quantity of substance dispensed and the area covered easier than possible with an aerosol can. In addition, you don't pay for aerosol propellant when you buy a cleaning substance in a pump-spray container.

Refrigerator/freezer. Vacuum clean any accessible smooth or finned tubing once a month. Areas behind the grille at the bottom of the appliance are particularly vulnerable to dust accumulation. Follow manufacturer's instructions carefully. (The drip pan is one area where odors can develop quickly.) Some areas may not be accessible with an ordinary vacuum cleaner attachment: You may have to blow the dirt out by connecting the vacuum cleaner hose so that the cleaner blows rather than sucks. Cleaning inside a refrigerator/freezer is best done with the mildest possible detergent—or with just a damp sponge. The object is to avoid scratching soft plastic surfaces. A solution of bicarbonate of soda (baking soda) and water is often enough to do the job. Wash glass shelves. Metal shelves can be soaked in a dishpan or sink if they are very soiled. Be especially aware of the need to keep the door gasket (seal) clean. Buildups of dirt quickly impair the gasket's ability to keep cold air in and warm air out, thereby increasing the appliance's running cost.

Rug shampoo. Always try a chemical or a machine on a small, inconspicuous area. Check for damage to the surface, for color change, and for whether the sample area came out as clean as you would like. Shampoos and powders that don't go below a rug's surface can make the surface look quite good after you vacuum up the dried, powdery residue along with the dirt the chemical has picked up. However, this type of cleaning is no substitute for the deep cleaning that is occasionally necessary to remove embedded dirt that causes carpet wear by damaging the fibers at the carpet's base structure.

Scented cleaner. Lemon doesn't help clean floors, dishes, or furniture. Scented cleaners may be appealing to children, however, and should be kept out of their reach.

Scratches on furniture. Some may disappear if you apply a polish containing color that darkens the wood. Careful use of appropriate-colored crayons can also be helpful in making scratches less obvious.

Self-cleaning oven. Use this valuable feature as often as necessary. Energy cost at national average rates is about the same per cleaning as an application of a chemical cleaner in an oven without the self-cleaning feature.

Shaver. Men's electric shavers need blowing out after each use, and a full cleaning once a week to keep the precision parts moving in a way that ensures maximum effectiveness. Follow the manufacturer's cleaning instructions explicitly. If a shaver's head breaks or suddenly loses its shaving ability, buy a replacement head; don't junk the entire shaver unless there's a reason to do so.

Silk. Play it safe and dry clean. Water and silk are not at all compatible.

Silver cleaner. The electrolytic process can be effective. All you need is a clean aluminum pot, water, and a little bit of baking soda and table salt (see page 120).

Silver polish. Dip cleaners can damage nonuniform antique finishes by making them uniform. They are effective for uniform satin or other low-luster finishes. Keep silver polish away from the stainless steel portion of utensils with silver handles. Wear protective gloves when working with acidic dip-type cleaners.

Sink (porcelain). You may have to resort to a scouring cleanser for pot scrapes on the porcelain surface. Otherwise, see Porcelain fixture.

Smoke detector. Vacuum clean periodically to ensure that air can flow freely through the smoke "sniffer" circuitry.

Stainless steel. Ordinary cooking soil should surrender to soap and water. Heat stains need a special stainless steel polish/cleanser. However, these polishes—or soapy steel wool for that matter—won't sustain the mirror finish on highly polished stainless steel.

Stain on fabric. See chapter on Stains and Spots.

Stain (wood). Chlorine bleach may be effective, applied slightly diluted. Rinse with clear water. Oxalic acid (one teaspoon of powder or two teaspoons of crystals in a cup of hot water) can also be useful. *Oxalic acid is a poison and should be treated accordingly.* Wipe entire surface with bleach to avoid light spots. A tablespoon of ammonia in a quart of water helps stop the chemical action. Do not use ammonia after using bleach!

Steam iron. See Iron.

Steam vaporizer. See Vaporizer (steam type).

Television set. The screen surface tends to accumulate a lot of dust and grime, partly because of static electricity's "magnetic" effect on dust particles in the air and partly because of finger smudges. A damp sponge followed by paper towel wiping should take care of the problem. For stubborn smudges, use a window cleaning liquid, applied sparingly.

Toaster and toaster oven. A clean crumb tray helps prevent smoldering of leftover particles, thereby helping to protect the sensitive thermostat and mechanical door-opening mechanisms, as well as keeping the appliance looking presentable.

Toilet bowl. Forget about in-tank cleaners since they only color the water and disguise soil. If the bowl needs cleaning you need to use a liquid household cleaner or a specialized bowl cleaner. Use bowl cleaners carefully. Their acid content may be high enough to injure eyes and skin and damage clothing. Follow the label instructions to the letter.

Upholstery. For routine cleaning use a vacuum cleaner's upholstery nozzle. Try any chemical cleaner on an inconspicuous patch and check for color or texture change—and evident shrinkage. Use as little cleaner as possible, and be gentle. It is far better to use two light applications than one heavy one. For a flat-surfaced fabric, use a terry cloth towel rather than a brush. However, a brush is all right or even necessary (to restore the nap) after the fabric has dried. Powdery cleaners can be messy and are best used outdoors.

Vacuum cleaner. Blobs of dust sometimes clog a vacuum cleaner's hose. These can usually be dislodged with a mop or broom handle inserted into the hose, or else by a straightened hanger used very carefully to prevent puncturing the hose's plastic cover. Change the paper bag as soon as the cleaner's suction drops noticeably, even if the bag doesn't seem full.

Vaporizer (steam type). Rust accumulations are harmless, but should be cleaned out from time to time nevertheless, before storing the vaporizer.

Vinyl and vinyl asbestos floor. Damp mop for day-to-day cleaning. "Self-polishing" water-based wax is best for providing luster (depending on whether the floor has a "permanent" glossy finish or not). Also see Linoleum.

Washing machine. Clean the lint filter after each load. Clean under the agitator, following the manufacturer's instructions. Soap or detergent accumulations should be sponged from around the top of the machine. Use the "hot" setting only for very dirty laundry loads. Warm or cold water should do well for most clothes loads and saves energy (hot water) as well as maintaining the permanent press finish on a host of fabrics. Slow agitation and spin speeds also help to minimize wrinkling, and are musts for delicate items.

Water heater. Drain some water from the heater (perhaps a bucketful) periodically to get rid of accumulated solids. That can help keep the unit's efficiency at a peak level. Be sure the flue of a gas water heater is operating. Check with a candle flame. If the flue is not "drawing," your home's chimney may need cleaning. Have it done—for safety's sake.

Water spotting on glassware. A water conditioner agent added to the special dispenser in your dishwasher can help, particularly if you live in a hard water area.

Wood floor. Don't use water on a wood floor except for removing old wax or when refinishing—or if the wood has been thoroughly sealed with a urethane finish. Water can damage wood by raising the grain. For polishing, use a solvent-based wax rather than the "self-polishing" water-based type. The wax acts as a cleaner as well as a finish. Stains from friction between footwear and the floor can be removed by rubbing lightly with a cloth barely dampened with turpentine or paint thinner.

Wood work surface. Cutting boards and butcher blocks need cleaning after each use to minimize bacterial growth. When the surface is new, seal it with linseed oil.

Wool. Can be laundered, but only in cool or cold water, carefully, with minimum agitation and spinning to prevent shrinking and matting. Don't use bleach. Dry cleaning is safest, unless the garment is specifically designated as being machine washable.

Index